# BEAUTIFUL AFFAIR

# MIKE HANRAHAN

# BEAUTIFUL AFFAIR

## A JOURNEY IN MUSIC, FOOD AND FRIENDSHIP

HarperCollins*Publishers*

HarperCollins*Publishers*
1 London Bridge Street
London SE1 9GF

www.harpercollins.co.uk

First published by HarperCollins*Publishers* 2019

10 9 8 7 6 5 4 3 2 1

A catalogue record of this book is available from the British Library

ISBN 978-0-00-833300-3

Printed and bound by GPS

**MIX**
Paper from
responsible sources
**FSC™ C007454**

FSC
www.fsc.org

This book is produced from independently certified FSC™ paper
to ensure responsible forest management.

For more information visit: www.harpercollins.co.uk/green

*To Donna*

Sammy, Liza & Frank
Stockton's Wing
STOCKTONS WING
CELEBRATION
NYON FOLK FESTIVAL 1980
STOCKTONS WING
STOCKTONS WING
STOCKTONS WING
Revival
THE FIELD
POST PREMIERE SUPPER PARTY
THE FIELD
WORLD FILM
Aer Lingus
Beyond The North Wind
Frank, Liza & Sammy
THE ULTIMATE EVENT
I.R.F.U. STADIUM, LANSDOWNE ROAD
STAGE AREA PASS
VALID – SUNDAY
Weekend Ticket
93 ARTIST STOCKTON
German Tour
Tourpass

# CONTENTS

CHAPTER 1
FIREFIGHTER
8

CHAPTER 2
DOOLIN
42

CHAPTER 3
MAURA O'CONNELL
58

CHAPTER 4
TAKE A CHANCE ON ME
78

CHAPTER 5
BAND OF BROTHERS
106

CHAPTER 6
FINBAR FUREY
126

CHAPTER 7
RONNIE, I HARDLY KNEW YA . . .
144

CHAPTER 8
LEGENDS
164

CHAPTER 9
VAGABONDS
176

CHAPTER 10
BALLYMALOE COOKERY SCHOOL
192

CHAPTER 11
LEARNING CURVE
216

CHAPTER 12
PAT SHORTT'S BAR
230

CHAPTER 13
ELEANOR SHANLEY
260

CHAPTER 14
ARTISAN PARLOUR & GROCER
274

CHAPTER 15
ENCORE
300

ACKNOWLEDGEMENTS 304

# CHAPTER 1

# FIREFIGHTER

*Farmer John, plough your fields, bring the seed to grain,*
*Feed the hungry, fill the belly of the traveller as he sails,*
*A weary heart, a tired soul will try come what may,*
*Farmer John, plough those fields, help him on his way.*
            – 'Firefighter', *What You Know* (2002)

# THE CROSSING

My parents grew up in the neighbouring farming communities of
Barntick and Ballyea in County Clare. As a young couple they chose
to start their new life in the burgeoning outskirts of Ennis, which offered
opportunities for work and a new rented home in which to raise their young
family. In 1957 they moved to the just-built St Michael's Villas on the edge
of Ennis, and there they raised eight children, six boys and two girls: Gerard,
Joseph, Kieran, myself, Gabriella, Adrian, John and Jean. I was in the middle;
the youngest two were twins. Dad provided and Mother nurtured.

When we were young, our summers were spent secluded on my
grandparents' farm, a few miles from civilisation. We walked to and from the
village of Ballyea every Sunday morning, dressed in our finest to attend Mass
at the parish church. The farm was our domain, where our friends were the
animals and our sustenance came from the very land we roamed.

Come September, we returned to the bustling terraces of Ennis, playing
games on the green with the O'Loughlins, the Howards, the Hahessys,
the McMahons and the Dinans. By contrast with the farm, it was a noisy
playground where you fought to shout your name.

Even as children, our 'country' mentality jostled for position on the
streets and in our schools, while the country folk saw us only as townies.
We were somewhere in the middle, criss-crossing – in language, expression,
attitude and mind.

But home life had surety, unity and a purpose, constantly nourished with
wonderful music and beautiful food. Music and food have kept me on track
at every crossing.

# DAN JOE

My grandfather, Daniel Joseph Kelleher, was born in 1898 at No. 2 Victoria Villas, Victoria Cross in Cork City, and was sent to live with his aunt Mary, who lived with her husband Patrick Nagle in Ballyea in County Clare. It was not unusual in those days for large families to send some of their children to live with their aunts or uncles to help alleviate the pressure on food and board at home. Dan Joe grew up in Ballyea and married a local girl, Margaret McTigue. They settled down to raise their family of four boys and one girl, my beautiful mother, Mary Kelleher.

Dan Joe was a gentle man who worked for the local government and spent the rest of his time working the farm with Margaret, raising cattle, pigs, sheep, geese and hens. He wore a dark grey fedora that only left his head when he sat down to eat or attend Sunday Mass. We spent our entire summer school holidays on their farm, a playground of vast open acres of grazing fields, stables, hen houses, tackle room, straw-bedded sheds and a monstrous metal-framed hay barn that would fill to capacity during our stay. At the rear of the milking parlour was a slurry pit which fed the land and gave off the most noxious of smells in the July heat. Manual farm machinery speckled the yard, along with milk churns, water barrels, a couple of dogs and the ever-present Charlie, the wonder horse, our absolute best friend in the whole wide world.

Beyond his work on the farm, Dan Joe loved hurling and Irish music. He stood proud at the back of the Ballyea or the Clarecastle village halls whenever we performed at the variety concerts and always cheered our successes. He loved the sound of the accordion so much he gifted one to my brother Joe, who played it for a few years.

He was quite ill towards the end, and in his final days, a hush surrounded the visit of a local healer, who was called to administer the sap from the bark of a birch tree which was boiled in milk along with a few other secret ingredients. In rural parts of Ireland, doctors were expensive, so most people looked to the local healers and their folk medicine for help. The practitioners were dedicated, and believed in the virtue of their treatments, with very little money exchanging hands, if any at all. Some local communities continue to believe in the power of these natural remedies.

Alas, it was all too late for poor Dan Joe. I was almost twelve, and his was my first funeral, an event that left an indelible mark on my memory.

# THE WAKE

I still see that never-ending procession of black suits and shawls as they shuffled their way through the front door into the crowded parlour, passing the mirrored oak sideboard with its fresh flowers and photographs of happier days. Onwards they moved, in around to a smoke-filled kitchen with its glowing fire, down under the narrow staircase to a darkened room that smelled of church candles and lilies and echoed a constant hum of prayer and sorrow. Circling the bed, they blessed themselves as they passed by a very peaceful-looking Dan Joe, dressed in a crisp white shirt and a grey paisley tie. He lay motionless and cold, but free of all the pain that had etched his face in the recent days. Ushered on by my uncle Tom, the latest batch of mourners offered their condolences before rejoining the mêlée, talking, laughing, crying, whispering, drinking and eating from plates of sandwiches and cakes brought in by neighbours and distributed eagerly by all the grandchildren.

Later, as the crowd dwindled, I sat nervously staring at his figure, wondering how it was possible that I would never hear his voice again, never see that smile or feel the warmth of his arms around my shoulders, and my thoughts drifted to poor Charlie and I wondered how he would cope now that his master was silent. He would surely miss him in the morning and every other morning after that, the click of his voice, the gentle tug of the reins and all their little chats during the daily rituals of tacking and farming.

'How is all this possible?' I thought. Maybe in the morning he might come back to take us all down to the L-field to gather the cows. But the following morning was spent in a crowded church of whispered prayer followed by the short procession to an adjacent graveside where men lowered his coffin deep into the ground. A raw, sudden swell of tears and sadness filled the autumn air as the pebbles hit the wood to finally signal his end.

*On an old country lane where the wilderness still reigns*
*An old man takes a flower in his hand.*
*How I've watched you bloom and fade*
*and all the beauty you create*
*I'll take with me that pleasure as we part.*
— 'We Had It All', *Someone Like You* (1994)

# NANA KELLEHER

Dan Joe's wife, Margaret McTigue, came from a reasonably well-to-do local family, but her marriage to Dan Joe was not well regarded and her dowry reflected the disappointment in her choice to marry down. As a young woman she was sent to agricultural college in Tipperary, where, in addition to general agricultural studies, she specialised in butter- and cheese-making. I only learned of her cheese-making ability recently, and it may explain my own fascination with the craft. While a student at Ballymaloe Cookery School, I was hooked from our first cheese demo. The pleasure of working with the curd is sensational and I found it very therapeutic; little did I know then that

my Nana Kelleher may have passed on her cheese gene to me. She spent her days churning her butter, making cheese, feeding geese and hens, tending to the livestock and forever cooking or baking in Bastible ovens over a large open fire, which was constantly aglow.

Every autumn, neighbours came to the house to help with the curing of the pig. It was customary to gift the help with cuts of meat as they departed. The wonderful saying, 'We weren't all one when you killed the pig,' was often used and still is in some areas to remind certain houses of an oversight in such times of plenty.

The Feast of St Martin, or Martinmas, is celebrated on 11 November each year and was generally regarded as the date that all pigs be butchered and prepared for the winter. This date is also linked with ancient sacrificial geese and all sorts of darkness. My legend has it that St Martin invented the pig from a piece of beef fat. He gave it to a young girl, telling her to put it under a tub and turn it upside down and await further instruction. Being selfish, the girl split it in two and hid her own piece under a basin. The following day, a sow and twelve piglets appeared where Martin's morsel had been placed, but as punishment, the girl's sliver produced mice and rats, which ran off around the house and into the yard. St Martin then created the cat from a mitten, and sent it off to chase the vermin; to this very day cats continue to do his bidding – or so the story goes!

Every ounce of meat from the pig was used. The head was boiled to produce brawn, also known as head cheese, a terrine set in aspic. Sometimes the cheeks and jowls were removed, boiled and eaten as delicacies. Those traditions live on; for my own fiftieth birthday party, I cooked a pig on a spit and my friend and champion Tipperary hurler Nicky English phoned in a frenzy, saying he was delayed in town. 'Mike, has anyone touched the jowls yet? If not, put my name on them! Make sure no one goes near them, I'm on my way!' Sure enough, as soon as he arrived, he made a beeline for the pig's head. He was a very happy camper as he sat back on his chair with a beer and a jowl. Maybe there's something in them there jowls that's good for the hurling.

Nana used both a wet and a dry cure. After a few days' hanging, the pig was jointed and cured with salt; the following day, the moisture extracted by the salt was washed away and another coat of salt applied. This dry-cure process might take three to four days. A wet cure was a simple solution of salt and water in a barrel, left for days. The loin, shoulders, legs and belly were then hung from the rafters and used as required for rashers, bacon and

Bastible roasts. Some were placed in the chimney breast for smoking.

The cured bacon hung from the hooks in the main room, protected by two or three strips of flypaper. That paper gave off a very distinctive sweet odour, and its colourful package always conjured up images of America for some reason. Perhaps they were part of a parcel received from rich cousins across the Atlantic.

Nana cooked everything from chickens, stews, bacon and cabbage to vegetables, to breads and cakes on an open fire in a selection of cast-iron Bastible pots that hung from a metal crane. She fried pork chops, homemade puddings and eggs on griddle pans which sat among the burning sods of turf. Hanging from the crane was a great big giant black cast-iron kettle, always full of water, constantly on simmer ready for the tae or the washing-up. Bastible cooking required great skill and experience. There was no thermometer to monitor the heat, and certainly no alarm clocks to signal the end of cooking – it was sheer skill. Her breads and sweet cakes were placed in the ovens, with hot turf spread on to the lid to ensure even heat distribution. There is a beautiful saying – 'Never let the hearth go cold' – so at bedtime, a sodden piece of turf was laid, burning slowly through the night to keep the embers warm. In the morning flames returned with the help of a poker and some kindling.

Most of the milk from their herd was transported by horse and cart three mornings a week to the local creamery. Nana always kept one bucket at home, covered with a tea towel. The separated cream became butter, and the rest we drank liberally. As far as we were concerned, the butter was our Nana's only culinary weak spot. It was salt-free, and we all hated it with a vengeance. What was worse, we weren't just subjected to it over our summer holidays on the farm; during winter months she would send four pounds of the stuff weekly to our home, and the sight of it on the table brought many sighs and moans, much to my mother's chagrin.

Nana Kelleher was firm, very strict and fearless around animals. We often saw her chase away foxes or stray cats, but the best was her battles with the tiny field mice who were regular visitors to the cottage, searching for warmth and food. On one occasion a mouse hid in the scullery behind pots and pans. Nana stood there with her hawthorn stick, carefully removing the pots and basins one by one, until finally the mouse was exposed and made a dash for the opened door and his chance at freedom. As he sped past her, the swish of her stick sent him staggering across the farmyard, Nana in hot pursuit. Off he raced across the muddied track and to our delight reached the farmyard wall, where he disappeared into a crevice and off out into the safety of the L-field. Later that night during our bedroom whispers it was agreed that he would now be so scared of Nana he would never return. We all hoped he got home safe to warn his family and other mouse friends to stay well clear of the angry woman with the very big stick.

# ANIMAL FARM

The excitement of our first morning of summer holidays at the farm each year is etched in my memory. The sun beaming through the window, the farm already in full flow with the jangle of tackle as Granddad prepared Charlie for the creamery run, Nana swooshing the geese over to the sandpit, hens clucking to the sound of cock-crow and the little calves bellowing at the distant trough.

After a quick wash in the light blue ironstone basin with its pitcher of freezing cold water we moved from the parlour into the heat of the warming fire, to eat a bowl of porridge and some homemade bread with that loathsome butter, thankfully offset by Nana's beautiful homemade gooseberry jam. We then set off on the first of our many daily adventures. This vast open country playground was ours for the taking, and out there on the L-field, so named for its shape, we were anything our imagination conjured up: hurlers, soldiers, swashbucklers, farmers, truck drivers, Olympic runners, show jumpers, tennis players, Pelé or Pat Taaffe on Arkle chasing down Mill House for the Gold Cup.

Underneath the rows and rows of Scots pines that separated the cottage from the working farmyard was our very own battleground where we separated into little army corps, erected barricades and went to war with bundles of fallen pine cones. Occasionally a stone might be inadvertently introduced, and then the battle turned nasty; all bets were off when the first screams drew Nana from her busy day to scatter us away from the theatre of war, to hide in the hay shed and dream up our next escapade.

Charlie the horse, our best friend ever, was patient, passive, intelligent, hardworking and without doubt the most loved animal in the world. Whether he was resting or cooling in the shade, his ear perked at our calls, drawing him out of the haggard to amble his way to the top gate for a feed of apples and nuts with plenty tender loving care.

In the early morning we gathered the cows for milking. Some of the cows had pet names given to them by Nana and Granddad and each one had a personality of her own. Some were gentle to milk and others just lacerated you with their swishing tails. I am still convinced their massive eyes were laughing at each successful flick of the nape. The young calves were treated to nuts, and petted by all the children, unlike the poor geese who were taunted and riled into a frenzy until they lost their cool, dipped their necks and lunged after us in attack, hissing angrily as we ran screaming back into the safety of the hay shed.

Most of the farm chores were OK, but every now and then you pulled the short straw and had to clean out the filthy henhouses, or shovel the dung from the slurry pit into a wheelbarrow to be spread across a field at the back of the main yard. The worst job was clearing the 'yellow weeds', as Granddad called them. Rag weed or Ragwort was, and still is, a scourge on farms and regarded as dangerous to livestock, so every summer it had to be cleared. Fields were cordoned off and a concerted effort was made by the chosen ones to get every last stalk from the ground. A yellow weed day was long and extremely torturous.

# THE MEITHEAL: THE GATHERING

The animals lived well on the farm, with a diet supplemented by the hay that we saved during the long summer months and stored in the barn which stood beyond the pine-tree battle line. The meadow was located a few miles away in an area called 'the Slob', which was, to all intents and purposes, a very large allotment shared by many local farmers. In early summer the community gathered with their scythes and methodically made their way through the meadows, cutting the tall grass. At intervals during those long working days, tools were downed and the 'tae' was served, with sandwiches, scones, tarts and 'curnie' cakes, or spotted dick as it was also called. My mother used to add a pinch of ginger, nutmeg or allspice to her cakes, which gave the bread a great colour and a sharper taste. Each house had its own version.

The bottle of tea was wrapped in old newspapers or tea towels to retain the heat. On occasion, a different, magic bottle that no one ever seemed to mention was passed around among some of the elders.

Weeks later when the grass was dry, a team again assembled to rake the hay into little bundles, and then into small cocks, or 'trams' as we used to call them. They stood about eight feet high and were secured by a hemp rope also known as a *sugán*, which was weighted down on either side with large rocks. Sometimes a sheet of plastic was secured at the top of the tram to prevent the rain seeping through. The hay was then slowly transported by horse and float back to the barn. The float, an exceptionally well-designed piece of farmyard machinery, was a flat rectangular platform trailer with two front-mounted rope winches controlled by three-foot wooden levers. The float tilted to the ground, ropes were tied around the tram, and winched from the field on to the platform. The weight of the hay then levelled the float, and once secured, off we went to deliver to the waiting crew at the hay shed. Along the road we might stop and chat to the neighbours, including the likes of 'Great Weather', who always greeted us with 'Great weather, Dan Joe!' come rain or shine, or 'Winkers Kelly', who never failed to hurl abuse: 'Ya useless townies, ya!' – always answered with 'Go wan, ya big four eyes!'

The final trip of each week included a stop at Curry's pub, where Granddad drank his bottle of stout and treated his lucky little helpers to fizzy orange and crisps. On the odd occasion we might stop at our cousin's at McTigue's post office, which meant a pack of Stevie Silvermints or a bar of chocolate. Those of us left behind in the haggard had to listen to the gloating and wait another day.

One morning the quiet of the farm was interrupted by the distant sound of an engine that grew louder and louder with each second. 'That's Pa Joe McMahon and his buck rake,' my dad announced. 'It's over at Spellissy's now, I'd say. Won't be too long.'

Within a minute the roar of the tractor engine arrived, carrying a tram of hay on six large, pointed steel prongs. It dropped the load and was gone up the dirt road and out of sight in no time. 'I suppose this will speed up the gather,' Dad said with a hint of sadness in his voice. What had been weeks of drawing hay now took a matter of days. I remember a definite sense of sadness, though. The halcyon days were gone: no more trips to the meadow, no more float, no Winkers Kelly, or chewing the dry blade of grass as the world passed, and no more Stevie Silvermints after a long week's work. It was progress for sure, but the buck rake also delivered the end of a certain magic that morning.

## MICKY HANRAHAN

My other grandfather, Micky Hanrahan, was a jovial man. His family came from Fedamore in West Limerick and moved to Barntick in Clarecastle, a few miles from Ennis. He married Aggie from Labasheeda in West Clare, and they lived in a beautiful cottage on the top of the hill by New Hall Lake. The small farm was built on the edge of a rocky cliff with little growth, but it was a haven for their goats, sheep and a few head of cattle that roamed freely to forage the hazel or berry bushes. I always saw him as a reluctant farmer, as I somehow never really associated him with the land. He worked at the local pipe factory and left much of the farming to Aggie and his young family. Oddly enough I never really saw my own dad as a farmer either, although I have a vivid memory of looking on in dread and fear as he stood on top of a large reek of hay catching fork-loads from down below. Goats wandered freely around their farm amid the constant cackle of turkeys, and at the back of the cottage was an old West Clare Railway carriage which housed lots of chickens.

Once a week they travelled to Ennis to shop at Mick O'Dea's grocery and pub. From the street you entered a shop stocked with everything from the humble spud to packs of washing powder and everything in between. A door then led you to a small bar with a high counter usually housing a row of creamy pints. It was the most beautiful bar in the world, not for its decor, which was very retro, but for its clientele, its history and most of all the friendly atmosphere. Micky usually had a few in there while Aggie filled the messages box with the help of the shopkeepers in their brown coats, who later delivered to the cottage.

The O'Deas are practically cousins to us, such was the closeness of the two clans. I went to school with young Mick O'Dea, who followed his passion for art and is now a member of the Royal Hibernian Academy and has served as its president for a number of years. His work is exhibited internationally and he is regarded as one of our greatest portrait painters. Some of his work adorned the walls of the pub when his older brother John ran it after their dad retired. Sadly, John also retired, and with him went much of the pub's character and charm. Christmas week at O'Dea's was particularly wonderful, as the townies returned from all over the world to reconnect for the festive season. A small transistor radio sat on the shelf in between various trinkets and was only switched on for news or late-night specialist roots music shows. In the adjacent room, once the family sitting room, the TV transmitted sports and *The Late Late Show* to a select club of locals seated in front of a constant burning fire.

The grocery business was very important to my grandfather's generation. All the essentials were there: tea, butter, biscuits, cornflakes, cleaning supplies, all packed into large apple boxes and delivered on the day of purchase. O'Dea's supplied many families with their weekly shop, but it was also a place of social gathering. There was a bond of trust and friendship within its community. As the years passed supermarkets forced many of these beautiful quaint shops to close, but in the case of O'Dea's groceries, it was another harbinger of modernity, the health and safety officer, who finally closed the door for ever. A rarely used meat slicer on the counter drew her attention, and she instructed John that if he was to be selling fresh food, he'd have to add structural changes, which included a sink with hot and cold running water. John explained that he sold very little food, and was simply looking after a few of his older customers who had been coming for years; it wouldn't be worth his while putting the extra money in for such a small return. When she insisted, John sighed and said, 'Mam, there's a terrible siege going on over there in Sarajevo, and I hear there's hardly any food getting in at all. Yet I bet you the price of the sink that they sell more cold meat in downtown Sarajevo of a Saturday morning than I would here in a month of Sundays.' Unfortunately, his pleas fell on deaf ears and within weeks the few groceries were replaced with bottles and cans of beer as the pub engulfed what was left of the grocer's counter. Years of public service came to an abrupt end. Five generations of my family frequented O'Dea's pub, either sipping porter, drinking orange or buying supplies, while others preferred their mugs of tea with a little chat upstairs in Mrs O'Dea's kitchen.

## AGGIE HANRAHAN

My father's mother, Aggie, was formidable, the matriarch who ruled the house. In fairness, someone had to, as Micky was very easy-going and prone to stray onto the missing list. She ran the household with absolute authority, and cooked and baked the most delicious breads, cakes and scones. I still smell the griddle cake as she lifted it from the oven onto the table next to the butter dish and a pot of her homemade jam.

Aggie baked with sour milk purchased from a neighbour down the road. These days sour milk is not recommended and has been replaced with the conventional commercial product buttermilk. Since pasteurisation, souring your own milk is now a thing of the past. My mother usually left the bottle of milk out in the air to sour naturally before baking.

# Aggie's griddle bread
Makes one loaf

A little butter or oil, for greasing
350g plain white flour
A pinch of salt
1 tsp baking powder
1½ tbsp sugar
1 egg, beaten with 2 tbsp melted cooled butter
1½ tbsp melted butter
300ml buttermilk (you may not use it all)
Butter and homemade jam, to serve

1. Grease a griddle pan or heavy frying pan with a little butter or oil.
2. Sieve the flour, salt and baking powder into a bowl. Add the sugar. Whisk the ingredients further to add more air.
3. Add the egg, butter and most of the buttermilk. Gently bring together. If it's too dry, add more milk, but we don't want a very wet dough. Do not knead, as that will take the air from the mix. Shape to the size of the griddle pan, and ensure the dough is about 5cm thick.
4. Cook on a medium heat for 10 minutes.
5. Flip and cook for another 10 minutes.
6. Cut into wedges, and serve with butter and homemade raspberry jam.

Nana kept between fourteen and twenty goats in an old outhouse shed. Once a year they were herded west along the road to meet their puck, then returned to the farm and were encouraged to roam freely throughout the crag, where they feasted on nuts and roughage. They were never allowed too much time on grass, as it added far too much fat to their bodies. Kid meat was regular Easter fare in Clare, long before we turned to lamb, and the preparation of the feast varied from house to house. The meat certainly needed slow cooking, and some added juicy seasonal berries in with the roast for extra flavour, constantly basting. Others braised the meat in a broth of vegetables. The family drank the goat's milk, and my uncle Chris says that excess goat's milk might inadvertently find its way into the churn of cow's milk before it was sent to the creamery. No waste was allowed, and no one said a word. Some families made yogurt, or their own version of soft cheese. One of Ireland's best goat's cheeses, St Tola, is made on a family farm in Inagh in County Clare run by Siobhán Ni Ghairbhith and her team, who produce a variety of stunning hard and soft cheeses.

Aggie reared her goats for the Easter celebrations, but her pride and joy were the Bronze turkeys, with each member of the family receiving one every Christmas. Some did better out of it than others, though – once she posted a turkey over to her son Tony in Birmingham, but somewhere along the line the parcel was held up and arrived two weeks after the Christmas celebrations. By all accounts the scene when it was opened was not for the faint-hearted, and left an indelible mark on the poor children present.

Aggie's kitchen was the hub of Hanrahan life. The half door was constantly open for all to call and say hello. She always sat by the range while Micky sat at the table with his tiny transistor radio waiting for the latest result from Leopardstown. It was a great room for chat, food, music and gossip, and over the years a lot went on in that small confined space around the kitchen table with its ever-present pot of hot tea.

# MOTHER

*She's an angel, my angel, she moves me, she sees the child in me*
*Won't abandon me, my angel*
– 'Angel', Someone Like You (1994)

My mother was taken from school in her very early teens and sent to work at Fawl's on O'Connell Street in Ennis. Fawl's was a pub, shop and tea importer also known as the Railway Bar. Large tea chests arrived from Dublin and the tea was bagged for sale. When we were babies our playpen was one of those tea chests. Dad fixed a bicycle tyre round the top for safety and all was going well for a couple of years until my brother Kieran worked out a way to topple the chest and crawl to freedom. In the evenings after the long journey home, my mother helped with household chores and tended to the needs of her four brothers. I have difficulty understanding why her parents chose that path for her, cutting short her education at such a young age, but she never discussed it much with any of us, and explained it away as being a different time. She never really spoke much at all about her childhood, but her photographs always show a smiling, beautiful young girl. She met my father when they were both young, fell in love and spent the rest of their lives falling deeper and deeper into that love.

My mother and I share a great passion for food and for many years we exchanged various tips over the phone or on my short visits home. I never left home without a plate of her luscious scrambled eggs and toast to set me on my early-morning journey back to Dublin. She was a brilliant cook and baker. After years of trying, I finally managed to record some of her baking recipes.

'Right, Mum, are you ready to give up those recipes?'

'I suppose so.'

'So, Mother, your bread recipe – that brown one we all loved so much . . .' I switched on the Dictaphone. She eyed it suspiciously.

'I'm not talking into that yoke, Mike.' I quickly found a pen and opened my copy book. I was very excited; my mother was about to give up the family's secret recipes.

'Well, for the brown, I get a fist or two of plain flour; a fist of the brown flour; a fist of bran; pinch of salt; a good pinch of baking soda – not too much, because that sometimes turns it a bit yellow although it never stopped ye all from eating it. I suppose it's all really down to practice. After a while you get to know the ingredients and the feel of the mix, y'know. Oh yes –

I sometimes add a little bit of sugar. Sometimes I might add raisins, or currants, although I never liked using the currants for some reason . . . I preferred using the larger raisins. And sometimes a pinch of ginger, or allspice. And sure, it really came down to what I had in the cupboard. That's it.'

'What was wrong with the currants?'

She dipped her head, grimaced and eyed me over her spectacle rims, 'Sure I was eating most of them, Mike.' She continued.

'Well, then you need to mix them all with margarine or butter, half a pound or thereabouts, but I preferred the margarine, and then add an egg. Maybe not a full egg, it's hard to know, Mike, you just have to judge it. After that I added some sour milk to bring it all together – not too wet, but it can't be dry either.'

'What happened if you had no sour milk?'

'Well . . . if I had no sour milk, I would add a drop of vinegar to the good milk and that would sour it over about ten minutes. Did I mention not to use a full egg?'

'Why did you bake the bread in a frying pan?'

'Well, it was an old frying pan, and your father knocked off the handle for me as I thought it would make a good baking tray. It did – I used the same one for years and years. I'd butter the pan, put the paper at the bottom, pour the bread mix in and draw a sign of the cross on top with the knife and into the oven for about an hour or thereabouts. I'd turn the bread out then and leave it on top of the range, covered with a damp towel until we were ready to eat it. And that's it, Mike. Very simple. And shur, ye loved it. Or at least that's what ye told me, anyway.'

It was beautiful – not so sure about the simplicity of the recipe, though.

She went on to talk about her stews, casseroles, her mother's cheese and that horrible homemade butter – she admonished me once again for my description of the butter. I had a beautiful afternoon with Mum, even though the baking lesson lasted minutes, but it was good to talk food with her. I could not wait to get back to my own kitchen to try out the recipes for myself and translate those fists into grams . . .

# MY MUM'S RECIPES

After much trial and error, I managed to translate Mum's measurements. I'm thinking a fist of flour is about 150g. So, we can take it from there.

# Mum's brown bread mix

Makes one loaf

300g coarse wholemeal flour
300g plain white flour
2 tsp bicarbonate of soda
1 tsp salt
2 tsp brown sugar
100g soft margarine or butter
1 egg
450ml buttermilk
Butter, to grease

1. Preheat the oven to 200°C/180°C fan/gas 6.
2. Sieve the white flour, bicarbonate of soda, salt and sugar into a bowl containing the brown flour, and mix gently.
3. Rub in the margarine or butter with your thumb and forefinger to crumb stage.
4. Beat the egg into the milk. Make a well in the dry mixture and pour in the milk. Bring it all together. It should be a wet mixture.
5. Butter an old frying pan (if you have one) or a 1lb loaf tin and pour in the mix.
6. With a knife cut across and down the centre of the loaf, and bake in the oven for 1 hour.
7. Remove the bread from the oven, turn it in the pan, then cover with a damp tea towel for one hour before serving.

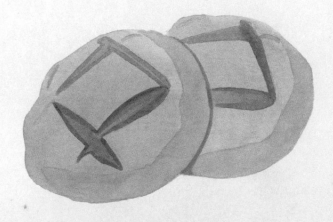

# My mother's spot of dick
Makes one loaf

Mum sometimes omitted the treacle and used a mix of brown and white flour. She preferred the large golden raisins. This recipe is open to any fruit, but the harder dried fruits will benefit from a little soaking before use.

Butter, to grease
500g plain white flour
2 tsp baking powder
A pinch of nutmeg
1 tsp salt
200g coarse brown flour
100g soft margarine
1 tbsp treacle (optional)
1 egg, beaten
400ml buttermilk
150g raisins or sultanas

1. Preheat the oven to 160°C/140°C fan/gas 3.
2. Butter a heavy oven-safe skillet or loaf tin and line it with baking parchment.
3. Sieve the white flour, baking powder, nutmeg and salt into a bowl. Add the brown flour and mix gently.
4. Rub in the soft margarine to crumb stage.
5. Add the treacle, if using, and mix with a spatula or wooden spoon.
6. Add the egg, buttermilk and dried fruit. Mix gently and transfer to the prepared skillet or tin.
7. Bake for 1 hour, then remove from the tin, turn it upside down on a wire rack and cover with a damp cloth.

## MUM AND HER ORANGE BIRTHDAY CAKE

January is when the Seville oranges come in, with many households creating their own distinct marmalades. My aunt Peggy's won hands down in our family, and she often added some lime to her marmalade. For many years my mum celebrated her birthday on 5 January, until the year she got her first passport for a once-in-a-lifetime trip to America to celebrate my brother Kieran's marriage to Mayo woman Pat Baines. Up to that point she had never needed her birth certificate, so when it arrived in the post, she was shocked to discover that she was in fact born on

6 January. I think we had two celebrations that year, and we're all still a little confused when the date comes around.

For one of her birthdays, I made a three-tier orange cake, complete with orange butter icing and strips of sweetened orange zest scattered over the top. I insisted on icing it at home in Dublin before a three-hour journey to Clare. I placed the cake in a tall, sturdy-looking box, wedged into the back seat of the car with my bag and a denim jacket. When I arrived in Ennis I glanced over my shoulder to see the cake box keeled over, and melted icing drifting slowly like lava onto the seat and all over my lovely denim jacket. Mercifully, my sister Jean arrived with the repair kit and we somehow managed to rebuild and camouflage the damage just in time.

# Flourless orange cake

Makes one 26cm cake

200g caster sugar
100g brown sugar
6 medium free-range eggs
2 oranges, boiled for 1 hour until soft (save the cooking water, quarter and remove pips, do not peel!)
250g ground almonds
1½ tsp baking powder

### For the syrup:
150g caster sugar
Reserved cooking water (see above)

1. Preheat the oven to 170°C/150°C fan/gas 3.
2. Put the sugars and eggs into a food processor, or use a bowl with a hand-held blender, and slowly blitz to a smooth paste.
3. Add the orange pieces and blitz.
4. Add the almonds and baking powder, and blitz again.
5. Pour into a 26cm cake tin lined with baking parchment and bake for 1 hour and 20 minutes. Check with a skewer to ensure it's cooked in the middle (the skewer will come out clean).
6. Meanwhile make the syrup. Stir to dissolve the caster sugar in the cooking water and boil for approximately 20 minutes.
7. Pour the syrup over the cooling cake while still in the tin. Allow to soak in and cool before turning it out onto a plate.

*For a cake with more moisture:*
*Zest and juice a third orange and add to the cooking water with the 150g of sugar. Boil for 20 minutes or so, until you have a syrup, and drizzle this on top sparingly (save some of the boiled zest for decoration). Simply dry the zest on kitchen paper and sprinkle on top once the cake has cooled.*

# THE SCULLERY AND THE STAGE

Our kitchen, the scullery, was a tiny room barely ten by eight feet that housed a sink, table top and stock cupboards. All hot food was cooked on the range in the living room. After a few years Mum somehow added a hob into that tiny spot. Historically, the scullery was a room in the depths of the great mansions that was used for washing dishes and the landlord's dirty clothes. My mum somehow managed to feed a small nation from that room. A curtain divided the scullery from a living room, the hub of many Hanrahan activities. There we drank early-morning milky egg whips, and ate breakfast, lunch and tea around a large adjustable table. Saturday dining was flexible but Sunday was the full show, a roast followed by a dessert of homemade jelly with ripple ice cream or Mum's delicious trifle.

In the evenings after tea, a light meal, we had a group huddle around the Philips valve radio, which soon gave way to the Bush television. That room also hosted the All-Star Hanrahan Family Revue, a concert performance for visiting relatives and friends, with each of us lined up for curtain call to perform our party piece. We all played an instrument or danced, so every available space in the house was taken for practice for our many musical endeavours. Mam and Dad were very much associated with Comhaltas Ceoltóirí Éireann, an organisation founded in the 1950s to preserve Irish culture and music. They attended local meetings and assisted at all local *fleadhs*, with my mother and her friends making hundreds of sandwiches, and Dad along with his mates preparing and cleaning halls and rooms for performance or competition. I sang and played tin whistle with my brothers Joe, Kieran, Ger and a couple of other neighbours in the St Michael's Céilí Band, performing at charity and village variety concerts. My sisters Gay and Jean along with other neighbours provided the dancing spectacle. Once a week we had music lessons with the great Frank Custy at the national school in Toonagh, where I won my first and only Fleadh Cheoil medal for singing the ballad 'Kevin Barry'. I must have been only eleven or twelve. One summer, the carnival came to town and we all entered the talent contest. One by one they went to the podium, belting out reels, jigs and hornpipes at a very high standard. I went up and blurted out a rickety version of 'Lily the Pink' and took the crown – well, a shilling, but it was as good as any crown to me. My very talented brothers and friends were not at all amused.

## PRAY FOR US

The living room was also a central room of prayer under the watchful eyes of the Sacred Heart, the child of Prague, the mother of Perpetual Succour and the Lord himself staring down from his crucifix. Every night we knelt to recite the longest Rosary in the history of the Catholic Church, with Hail Mary, Holy Mary, Hail Mary, Holy Mary, followed by the Glory Be into a litany of add-ons that included Prayers for the Faithful, blessings for the departed, those suffering sickness or hospitalised, relatives starting new jobs, sitting exams or heading off to foreign shores. We counted down the various mysteries on our fingers, keeping our eyes tightly shut to avoid any sibling contact for fear of the giggles and Dad's severe reprimand. The Angelus bells were respected twice a day, everything stopped as we recited a special Angelus prayer, and we always did the First Friday, a devotion that required you to attend Mass and receive Communion on nine consecutive First Fridays of the month. Miss one, and you had to start it all over again. Rewards included a ticket to eternal life, a peaceful home, comfort in affliction, mercy and a guarantee of grace, glory and sanctity in death. It was a heavenly-brownie-point feast day. I served as an altar boy for the Franciscan Friary and the Poor Clares, an enclosed monastery of beautifully serene, pious and, frankly, adorable nuns. They lived their lives behind mesh walls tending their little farm and they showered us with their love, smiles and, after every Christmas and Easter midnight Mass, with sweets and chocolate. My favourite religious service was evening benediction with its Latin prayers, beautiful hymns and the swinging of the thurible with its sweet scent of incense and charcoal.

## PORK CHOPS AND A CUPPA

Beneath the Sacred Heart of Jesus was our Stanley range, which was constantly on the go to produce the most amazing stews, roasts and Mum's famous pork chops. I loved her pork chops. After a slow pan-fry, she added sliced onions and a cup of leaf tea and allowed them to simmer for a while. It was a recipe passed down from her own mother, who maintained that it added flavour, keeping the pork moist while creating its own very distinct gravy. It was succulent, tasty and legendary. I always thought it was a family dish, and when I suggested Mum's method recently in reply to a recipe query on Twitter, the reaction was overwhelming. Turns out there's an ancient tradition of tea-brining, with a definite historic link to Ireland and Scotland.

# DAD

*Firefighter won't you come and take my pain away,*
*Firefighter bring me water, dampen down the flame.*
— 'Firefighter', *What You Know* (2002)

My dad, Jackie Hanrahan, was a powerful influence on my life, his great strengths being his solid character, great sense of humour and unyielding commitment to his wife and family. My parents shared a very deep love that certainly bound us all together as a family. I have often wondered how they remained intact through all the difficulties and pressures of raising eight children. I cannot recall ever hearing my mother and father argue or show disrespect to each other. If they did, it occurred in the dead of night, far away from our young eyes and ears.

He worked for the Clare County Council, initially in the supply stores and then as manager of the Ennis swimming pool, which was a great addition to the town and to our lives. We practically grew up in the water and came to be known to some as 'the Cousteaus'. Our instructor was Dad's great friend Tom Finnegan, who was the size of four very large men. To pass through the grades in water safety, you had to rescue him from the deep end of the pool. As you approached, he splashed, reached out his long arm, grabbed your tiny head in his hand and held you firmly underwater for seconds, raised you aloft and pronounced 'Failed!' before sending you back for another attempt. This went on until he was convinced that you had conquered the fear of approach, could swim round him and grab him from behind. He was a superb teacher who helped many of us to become very capable swimmers.

My father smoked a lot but never drank. At sixteen he was caught drinking at a neighbour's house party and a horrible uncle force-fed him beer slops until his face turned green. Some uncle! Dad never drank again, although in his last few months he confided that he sometimes regretted not going for a few pints with his family.

Dad was a home bird, and especially loved the garden, and most of all his shed. His shed housed everything imaginable for DIY, and was a great source of peace and fulfilment for him. One year, he made nine Christmas stables, one for each of the family, with hazel sticks collected from the crag at the back of our house. He painstakingly cut hundreds of sticks to size, fixed them side by side to form three walls, made a roof and thatched it. Each stable measured two feet by one foot with straw scattered on a flat sheeted floor, peopled with a set of religious figurines. A coloured bulb was pushed through the back wall with a lead and plug hidden from view. They were works of incredible patience, and without doubt the most beautiful Christmas gift I have ever received – and I a very lapsed Catholic.

When I was a kid, he helped my brother Kieran and friend Vinny McMahon to build a wooden table soccer game. As kids we often called to Carmel Healey's games room in town, and as Kieran had become quite the champion, he had taken the notion to build his own for home practice. Dad built the wooden stadium from a sheet of plywood, measured to perfection, with two goalkeepers and twenty outfielders all made from half-inch heavy black tubing, fixed firmly to wooden rods fed through holes perfectly measured on the table walls. Two goal mouths completed the scene. A box of table tennis balls gave the neighbourhood many great days of entertainment, and the very enterprising Kieran and Vinnie made a small fortune by charging everyone a penny a game.

I spent a lot of time in the garden with Dad, growing spuds, cabbages, carrots, rhubarb, lettuce and spring onions, forever planning for the following year. I read a gardening magazine piece on how to grow the perfect carrot by sifting all pebbles from the ground to allow the carrot free passage to grow to perfection, so I suggested it to Dad. I knew by the 'Oh holy God' look on his face what he really thought, but he replied, 'Whatever you think yourself, away with you *a stór* (a beautiful Clare term of endearment). I'll get the screed, and you can start sifting away.'

I dug the appointed plot and painstakingly sifted about a square metre area free of all pebbles and rocks. I was exhausted, but I think Dad was even more exhausted looking at me. However, my efforts were rewarded with perfectly straight carrots – which tasted exactly the same as regular ones. I think I missed the rugged shape of the old carrots, so the following year we reverted to the traditional method, stones and all. I have come to really appreciate and understand his attitude, and what stayed with me from my life with him was his constant encouragement to follow an idea or a dream. He never saw any harm in attempting the impossible, even if it meant spending needless hours and hours sifting pebbles from a patch of ground. It was all about making the effort and doing your best.

At twelve I started playing my brother Ger's nylon-strung guitar. A young Franciscan priest, Pat Coogan, had recently arrived in Ennis and was playing soccer with our local team, St Michael's FC. He played guitar and gave me my first lesson. One day, I sat down on my bed and heard a crack: I'd shattered my guitar. To the day he died, Dad was convinced that I did it on purpose to get myself a better instrument. I denied it at the time, but in hindsight he may have been right because I'd had my eye on an Egmond steel-string guitar in Tierney's music shop. I eventually bought the guitar, along with my first Leonard Cohen album and book of songs.

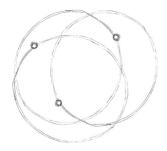

I was besotted with Cohen and started teaching myself his guitar technique from a system included in the songbook. Every day after that I flew through homework to get to my bedroom to sing his songs. After about six songs, Dad would shout up, 'Have you learned that song yet, Mikie?' Yeah, Dad, thanks … You just don't understand.

Despite the monotony, his encouragement never waned, and I even heard him reassure a mother distraught to hear that her son wanted to become a professional musician: 'Sure, Mary, as long as he has a guitar on his back, he won't go hungry.'

## STRAUSS AND THE TULLA CÉILÍ BAND

When we were very young Dad bought a Philips record player and the most curious, eclectic collection of records imaginable. There was Strauss with the shimmering strings of 'The Blue Danube', the Tulla Céilí Band, the Dubliners with 'Waxie's Dargle', Larry Cunningham, Donal Donnelly, Tom Jones, Doris Day, the Kilfenora Céilí Band and the Beatles. Our first record player was a turquoise blue, portable foldaway that looked like a suitcase. It had a turntable, a three-way speed switch for singles, albums and old 78s, two buttons, one for on/off and the other for volume, but that little box created the most incredible sounds that filled the entire house. I can still hear 'Take me back to the Black Hills, the Black Hills of Dakota' from Doris Day, with my mum's beautiful soft voice singing along. Later, Dad bought a very fancy console-style stereo all in one, with radio, turntable, storage racks and speakers encased in a beautiful mahogany cabinet. Our record players were hardly ever silent and our record collection grew every week.

## THE SUMMER JOBS

As soon as we reached our teenage years, we found gainful part-time employment at various shops in the town. I worked at Morgan McInerney's hardware store in the market square, which sold everything from teapots to bags of cement. I was entitled to a staff discount, so all birthday and Christmas gifts carried a hardware theme. Mum's were usually kitchen gadgets: a four-

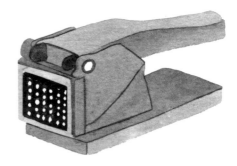

egg poaching pan complete with lid; a fancy cheese grater; a tomato slicer that required extra-special skills to avoid slicing fingers; and Dad's favourite kitchen mate, the potato chipper, which he used every Saturday for our eagerly anticipated special treat. He loved that chipper, and we devoured each and every equally-sized chip it cut, the smell rising from the sizzling basket of Mazola oil, chips drained and sprinkled with salt, soaked in malt vinegar and served up with a good dollop of ketchup. Now that's a food memory that's hard to beat – unless you add a soft-fried egg.

Going to work at an early age was good for us, and my mum was delighted with the extra few bob. We worked all summer, Christmas, Easter and every Saturday during school terms. My brothers Joe and Adrian also worked at the hardware store, and Ger and Kieran worked in a shoe shop, which made runners the thing for Christmas morning. My poor sisters Gay and Jean were confined to barracks-cleaning and sweeping the homestead.

Work was not at all taxing as I recall. I spent much of my time tidying the many stores of cement, timber, paint and plumbing pipes. On Saturdays I had to polish and shine the proprietor Jack Daly's silver Jaguar, and to this day I still want to own my own Jag. The rest of the day was spent serving behind the counter, or running errands for the staff, which took me to various locations around the town. One day I was taken by Mr Daly to see Joe Leyden, who had called in sick. Joe was a simple man who did odd jobs around the shop and spent the rest of his days sitting at the Daniel O'Connell monument in the middle of the town, watching the world go by. As we entered his house on Parnell Street a darkness like no other engulfed us. Mr Daly threw open the curtains and as my eyes readjusted, I reeled at the sight: hundreds of old newspapers piled high on an earthen cottage floor, a table in the corner with books, empty bottles, teacups and a vase of faded flowers. The kitchen was full of unwashed dishes and yet more newspapers and magazines. An open door led us to a bedroom where Joe lay moaning in pain. He was later moved to hospital and recovered to live another day.

Years later that visit was the inspiration for 'Indians and Aliens', a song about a very misunderstood young man who read accounts of the Trail of Tears march of American-Indian tribespeople across rough terrain that left many dead along the way, and of the massacre of the Lakota at Wounded Knee by the US Army. In a rage, he returned to his schoolhouse, a metaphor for those who instilled in him a deep-seated prejudice against the Indian nations. He burned it to the ground, and society, rather than seek to understand his troubled mind, shunned him and forced him into an institution. Joe, like the character in the song, was very misunderstood, and bore the brunt of many jibes from locals, young and old. I often wondered what went on in his mind as he sat on the monument looking down on the town. Many of us can relate to a degree; I was also that boy burning down the schoolhouse by the river. Mine had controlled my world through religious doctrine and fervour.

*He was a simple man who loved* Star Wars *and John Wayne,*
*Lived in a little house, a little down and out, but that was his way.*
*Nightmared on Geronimo and the Empires of Doom*
*All alone in a little town, all he ever knew*
*Was Indians and aliens, Indians and aliens, coming for me and you.*
      – 'Indians and Aliens', *What You Know* (2002)

## ARE YOU RIGHT THERE, MICHAEL, ARE YOU RIGHT?

On Sundays we jumped on an early bus to seaside Lahinch, which lies between Ennistymon and the majestic Cliffs of Moher. These days its ferocious waves attract thousands of surfers who want to test their skills on tough Atlantic breakers all year long. When we were kids, the great attractions were an amusement park of chair-o-planes, high swings, bumper cars, carousels and an outdoor swimming pool with a diving board that reached way up into the sky. The beach stretched for miles, and we crept through myriad sand dunes to spy on kissing couples. We ate boiled periwinkles and dried sea grass served in little chip bags from the vendors on the promenade, or instead settled on burgers and ice creams at the entertainment and games centre across the street.

## THE BALLROOM OF ROMANCE

At weekends my dad collected tickets at the local dance hall, Paddy Con's, later the Jet Club. The hall now operates as Madden's furniture shop, and Michele Madden and her daughters protect the history and heritage of the building with pride and dedication. Its balconies, stage and heavily sprung hardwood floor are still intact. The memories come flooding back every time I stroll from balcony to floor, feigning an avid interest in some nest of tables or chaise longue on display. As I climb the stairs to the stage, I inhale a welcome breath of nostalgia – but I never feel alone, as I'm well aware that some of Madden's other customers are doing the very same, soaking up the energy that lingers from this once vibrant ballroom of romance. I often helped Dad sweep the floors, stack chairs or clear out the dressing rooms, and constantly badgered him to bring me along to meet the bands as they arrived for the evening show. I remember meeting Butch Moore the year after he represented Ireland at the

Eurovision Song Contest singing 'Walking the Streets in the Rain'. I met all the stars of the day, Larry Cunningham, Brendan Bowyer, Dickie Rock, Margo, the Clipper Carlton, Gerry and the High-Lows, the Drifters, the Miami, the Cadets, the Premier Aces and my favourite of all, the Cotton Mill Boys. Of all the people I saw perform there, fiddler Sean McGuire stands apart. I still remember his breathtaking versions of 'Hungarian Gypsy Rhapsody' and 'The Mason's Apron'. I met him many times in later years and realised a dream when we shared a stage and a few tunes at the Ulster Hall in Belfast.

All I ever wanted was to be up there on that high stage. Whenever I call in to check out the latest furniture deals, I close my eyes and see a crowded hall, a sparkling mirror-ball casting its glitter across a pulsating dance floor. I can still feel that sinking sensation when a beautiful girl refuses or ignores your invitation to dance, or worse, when your pal beats you to the chase. As a young teenager I would play that hall on many occasions in a rock band called Effigy, and those nights at Paddy Cons ignited a flame within me that still burns.

## THE GARDEN OF ROSES

As a twelve-year-old I harboured ideas of a religious vocation, choosing the Order of St John of God following a visit by a brother to our school on a recruitment mission. Three of us were taken to a seminary in Celbridge, County Kildare, for a trial retreat. It was my first time being so far away from home, and I felt isolated in that seminary. Even though there were lots of people moving around, sports fields surrounded by beautiful tree-lined avenues, large dormitories, lovely food, altars and lots of prayers, I still felt alone.

On my return, my mother and I discussed the visit and she insisted that I really think about what I wanted to do. 'Mike, I hope you're not doing this for me or your father, because that would not be right. If you don't want to go, then please tell me, and that will be the end of it.' When I told her I wanted to stay at home she said, 'Good, that's that, then.'

We never spoke about it again until many years later when she confided she was thrilled with my decision, as she dreaded the prospect of me living away from home at such an early age. Crucially, though, she reiterated that she would have supported me either way. Mum and Dad often pointed out possible obstacles but never ever put one in our way.

As a young teen I was a true believer, and very dedicated to the Catholic Church. I spent a lot of time as an altar boy in the local Friary. It was a beautiful place and most of the Franciscans were wonderful people. We had many visiting priests and brothers who came to spend time at the centre, and when I was about fourteen, maybe fifteen, a regular visiting Franciscan brother came to our house to ask my mother for permission to take me to Galway for a weekend retreat. He sat with my mother and grandmother drinking tea, talking God and Church and praising my work at the Friary. He blessed them both and followed me out to the hallway, closing the door behind him. In the privacy of the hallway he enquired about my girlfriends, their names and which one I liked best. He began poking and feeling around my genital area, asking me if I liked it. I felt trapped, and was extremely uncomfortable. I didn't know what to do. He continued until I managed to get to the front door. I begged him to leave me alone. As he pushed past, I noticed a lot of dandruff on the collar of his brown robe. That's how I still remember him today. I felt ashamed, and almost dirty. I made up some excuse for turning down the trip to Galway, and I left it there in that hallway for years and years and tried not to think about it. Years later, I was walking down Abbey Street in Dublin when I spotted him coming towards me. I panicked, and hid in a doorway. As he walked by, all I noticed was the dandruff. It was still there. I wanted to scream at him, but I had no voice. I was still scared, or perhaps ashamed. I was twenty-one years of age. I never saw him again.

We all knew that certain priests in the parish were 'dodgy' – many altar boys relayed stories of hands slipping into their trousers. Some of us eleven- or twelve-year-olds were once brought into the office one by one by a Franciscan priest, who said he was to show us some 'personal hygiene' habits. He said our parents had requested it, but that we were bound to silence, as they were far too embarrassed to broach the subject further. Best keep it to ourselves. Yes, Father. Among ourselves we knew there was something wrong. We had our names for them, and we tried to steer clear of their advances and warn the younger boys, but the overriding reality was that we had a dedication to a church that controlled every aspect of our lives – and that's where their power lay.

I have never forgotten those instances of abuse, and unfortunately to this day I still harbour a deep sense of personal responsibility for allowing them to have occurred in the first place. I have had to wrestle with that guilt every time it finds its way to the surface. I certainly felt betrayed. Thankfully, I do not own that shame any more. Healing is powerful in that regard.

In 2001 I felt compelled to write and record a song called 'Garden of Roses' after all the harrowing accounts of cases of child abuse by religious orders, including one particular cleric close to home. Deep down I knew I had to speak to Mum about the song's imminent release, and if I could, talk about my own experience. Words will never truly describe that profound moment between a mother and her son. We talked and cried a little but together crossed over into a very special place of understanding. I felt such a deep sense of relief because I knew she understood my hurt, and I in turn empathised with her own very personal pain.

> *In the garden of roses where you came by,*
> *Beautiful roses, the eyes of a child*
> *In your secret desire you cut it all down.*
> *Now the petals lay scattered on tainted ground*
> *In the garden of roses, beautiful roses.*

Hot Press founder Jackie Hayden called me after hearing the song; he wanted permission to include it in his book *In Their Own Words*, a compilation of personal stories from abuse victims in the Wexford region to support the Wexford Rape Crisis Centre. I was invited to perform at a few very powerful and moving healing services where the song found its true home. The song continued to make an impression with listeners as the revelations kept coming, as it was included in a 2011 book, *The Rose and the Thorn* by Audrey Healy and Don Mullan. In the autumn of 2018, I was invited to perform the song once again, but this time at a day of remembrance for Ireland's lost children at the site of the mother-and-baby home in Tuam in County Galway. It seems we have come some way from those terrible days of darkness. I certainly hope so. May the healing continue.

> *Now your temple has fallen, the walls cave in.*
> *We witness the sanctum in their evil sin.*
> *But a river once frozen deep in the mind*
> *Flows on like a river should in the eyes of a child*
> *In the garden of roses, those beautiful roses.*
> — 'Garden of Roses', *What You Know* (2002)

# FAREWELL TO DAD

My dad died before the avalanche of abuse stories arrived, and I know he would have been shocked to the core. He was a very religious man, and like many of his generation lived by church rules and served without question. I have no doubt that I could have spoken openly to him about writing 'Garden of Roses'. He would have listened and offered comfort, of that I am certain. His death in June 2000 had a profound effect on my life and my songwriting. Two years later I released the album *What You Know*. The title of the album is an expression he used for almost everything that he could not instantly put a name to. If he wanted you to get a paintbrush from the shed he might say, 'Mikie, will you get the what-you-know from the shed, I want to finish that bit of painting. It's in the box beside the what-you-know, the screwdrivers.' You had to be on his wavelength, but we usually were.

A songwriter friend of mine once wrote of his dad's passing, 'The greatest man I never knew lived down the hall.' It was such a sad song. I am glad to say I knew mine very well and we shared many great times together. When he was diagnosed with cancer, he was given nine weeks to live. Such was his strength and determination he lasted almost two years and faced it with great courage. Thankfully, I never had a slate to clean with him so we carried on as normal and tried our best to make the journey comfortable. His funeral was one of the biggest Ennis has ever seen, a testament to his wonderful personality and selfless generosity. He sits on my shoulder for every gig and I love to talk about him. He never got to see me in chef whites but I have absolutely no doubt it would have pleased him and he may have turned to Mum and said, 'Sure, Mary, once he has a frying pan in his hand, he won't go hungry.'

*Take away the sad and lonely, all the trouble that surrounds him,*
*Firefighter won't you come . . .*

# CHAPTER 2

## DOOLIN

*See all the doors swing open,*
*Your life's unfolding before your very eyes,*
*Such a strange affair,*
*Walk in around, come into the sound,*
*Forget you're down, feel the air, beautiful affair.*
　　　　– 'Beautiful Affair', *Light in the Western Sky* (1982)

## McGANN'S PUB, DOOLIN, 2018

I'm sitting on an old bench in McGann's pub on the rugged north-west coast of County Clare. The walls of old faded photographs come to life, evoking powerful memories of a bygone era. I feel this swell of emotion, exalted and suddenly aware of the significance of these amazing colourful characters who taught me so much all those years ago. Doolin, my gateway from innocence, where the petals of youth opened wide to drink in their first rays of glorious sunshine.

Doolin sits on the edge of the Burren, that mystical landscape of limestone rock and rugged terrain where creative energy finds comfort and a true home. They say that Tolkien was inspired to write *The Lord of the Rings* after spending time here; Dylan Thomas married a local woman and lived in Doolin for a time; George Bernard Shaw and J. M. Synge often wrote of its beauty. In the early 1970s a new generation of free spirits arrived in Doolin from faraway places, and though some passed on through, many remained and integrated to develop a very special community. Today that community thrives and continues to provide a haven for travellers, lovers, dreamers, musicians, poets and singers. It feels so good to be back again, and it feels like I'm home.

## TOMMY McGANN

In 1976 Tommy and Tony McGann returned from America and bought a run-down pub in a very quiet and neglected area of Doolin about a mile east of the action on Fisher Street, where Micho Russell held court at O'Connor's pub, singing and playing the whistle, entertaining fans and visitors from all over Europe. The pub had been owned by two Americans who had run out of money, forcing the bank to take over, and within a couple of years the building had fallen into disrepair. Their father, Bernie McGann, sold a little plot of his land in Kilmaley to finance his sons' venture. Neither had any previous experience in the pub trade, which resulted in much trial and even more error in the early days. Although Tommy's management skills were almost non-existent at that time, he found a way through, with a charm that came to define him and set him apart throughout his short life.

In that same year as they took up the pub, my secondary schooling came to an end at Rice College on the banks of the river Fergus, not far away in Ennis. I was a reluctant student to say the least; I had no interest in school apart from history and economics, the latter receiving most of my academic attention. The enigmatic Jody Burns, with his appearance and antics of a nutty professor, was a gifted teacher who managed to corner my full attention on matters of supply and demand. I duly received an A in my Leaving Certificate examination in economics, which was a great shock to many – but not to Jody Burns. He was very proud of my achievement but expressed great disappointment on hearing that I would not be going on to study economics in college. These days third-level education is a natural progression for so many students, but back in the 70s the order of the day for the majority of us school-leavers was to secure a 'grand pensionable job', settle down, buy a house and raise a family.

Little did I know while sitting those last exams that as soon as the school books hit the waters of the river Fergus, I'd be in a car on my way up to Doolin to play music with my brother Kieran and first cousin Paul Roche, right here in this very room where I sit today in McGann's. During that first summer of freedom I shook off the shackles of a sheltered Catholic upbringing. I made many new friends, discovered love, expression and songwriting. I recognised early on that the fish and lamprey eels of the Fergus would benefit much more from my books than I ever did, while I concentrated my further education on the life and music of North Clare and beyond.

## MY FIRST KITCHEN JOB

Up to the mid-40s transatlantic flights – mainly seaplanes – had to stop to refuel at Foynes in West Limerick on their way to continental Europe. During the Second World War Foynes became the busiest airport in the world. Shannon Airport was then established in 1945 as Ireland's first international airport, and within a few years it became the world's first duty-free airport, operating as a gateway between North America and Europe, as most aircraft still required refuelling for long-haul flights.

In that summer of '76 I got a job as a kitchen porter in the airport's 'free-flow' restaurant, doing my best to get to Doolin for our Tuesday and Thursday night sessions and up again on Friday evening for a weekend of music and *craic*. The job was supposed to be a stepping stone either to a culinary career or to a more secure position in the airport or surrounding industrial hub. The busy kitchen served passengers, flights, all airport staff and stocked all duty-free restaurants. Most of my day was spent either on wash-up or working the conveyor belt, which delivered mounds of dirty dishes and cutlery to the sinks. Life as a kitchen porter was non-stop grief, thanks in particular to an ogre of a chef who barked and bellowed orders through an early-morning fug of stale alcohol. Stockpots and skillet missiles whizzed past my right ear to rattle against the sides of the stainless-steel basin before sinking into an angry, greasy ocean of bobbing and weaving pots and pans. The two of us manning the station were not allowed to speak a word, but we soon developed early warning signals for any incoming, including the main man himself, who would storm over with a badly washed pot, reload and fire it back at us again with bonus expletives. By the end of lunch, his anger grew as his hangover craved its afternoon cure. His venomous eyes have stayed with me, but it was a lesson to me to learn my surroundings inside out.

My next-door neighbour and childhood friend Ken Shaughnessy also worked in that kitchen as a commis chef. He went on to culinary college and became an executive head chef for an international hotel chain in Germany. On the very rare occasions we meet, we toast many schnapps to our wonderful childhood, that kitchen and good old Cerberus. Perhaps he was the making of us after all, as our love of food survived and neither of us have ever tolerated kitchen bullies, no matter how important they consider themselves. I will never understand how aggressive chefs get away with humiliating people in their place of work.

I moved quickly from the kitchen to the duty-free mail-order department, packing and posting Waterford crystal, Belleek china, shillelaghs and leprechauns to exotic-sounding destinations like Pine Ridge, Vermont, Wyoming, Montana and Biloxi. I finally left Shannon to work with my friend TV Honan at a newly opened drop-in centre for teenagers in the old refurbished National School in Ennis. It was the first of its kind in Ireland, the brainchild of Sean Sexton, a very proactive, clued-in priest. We called it the Green Door after a short story by American writer O. Henry, a tale of romance, adventure and fate

as we search for a door to opportunity. I often think that the story somehow reflected my decision to break free from that grand pensionable position to search for my own green door. With an unyielding determination to find a way to the music I convinced Mum and Dad by telling them my wages at the Green Door were higher than at Shannon, when in fact they were a lot lower, but I figured I could make up the loss from sessions and gigs.

## ROOM WITH SEA VIEW

On my weekend visits to Doolin I slept behind the pub in a caravan and in tents beside the beautiful Aille River, or found a sleeping space in the upstairs restaurant. Come the morning there was the usual scurry to clear the beds and clean up last night's fun to get ready for early lunch. One summer a group of German tourists found their way into a disused, dilapidated, roofless house at the entrance to Doolin pier, cleared it out, filled it with straw and hay and pinned a sign at the front entrance:

After closing time, we had some memorable nights at that waterfront Hilton. Everyone checked in, signed the guest book, played music, sang songs and listened to stories from all around the world. We heard about Aboriginal dream time, the Northern Lights, American Indians, Nordic folk tales and magical Dutch fairy stories, while smoking reefers and drinking beers on beds of straw beneath a blanket of sparkling stars. All strangers who entered left as friends. I fell in love there with Bebke Smits, a free-spirited young woman from Boxtel in the Brabant district of southern Holland. Bebke sang Dutch folk songs, wrote and recited deep and weird poetry, danced very freely and was extremely comfortable in her hippie skin. She introduced me to vegetarian food, and gave me my first Herman Hesse novel, *Narcissus and Goldmund*, a book I return to time and again. It's a poignant tale about young Goldmund, who develops a friendship with a slightly older and more committed monk, Narcissus, at a monastery somewhere in Germany. Goldmund strays into the woods one night, where he meets a beautiful young woman who seduces him. The confused novice seeks counsel from the older Narcissus, who encourages him to leave the monastery and embrace life beyond the walls rather than remain in search of salvation. On the journey that follows, Goldmund becomes a talented carver but refuses to join the carving guild, preferring to continue unbound on his road to understanding. He meets and loves many other women along the way, and survives the Black Death and all its ugliness. Eventually he returns to his friend Narcissus, where in the monastery the artist and philosopher speak freely about their lives in a beautifully written story.

Myself and Bebke ultimately drifted apart and she went home, got married and seemed quite content until suddenly, out of the blue, she contacted me around 1981. She was in Dublin, distressed following a very acrimonious break-up. We met at the People's Park in Dún Laoghaire and found our way to Walter's pub on the corner. As we entered, the barman called me aside to say it was men only in that section and he could not serve my girlfriend. We were stunned. Beb stood up and let him have it, refusing point-blank to leave without having a drink. He eventually poured her a glass of stout and we sat in a pub full of astonished old men either in awe or aghast at this feisty young lady dressed in purple, with beaded auburn hair, bedecked with all sorts of bangles and rings, speaking with a very strange accent.

It would be years before we met again, when she wrote to say she was taking her new partner on a trip to Clare to show him her place of youth and magic. We sat together for hours remembering the days of music and love, Narcissus and Goldmund again.

> *Her purple dress in slight decay,*
> *Winter weaving its weary tale.*
> *Outside swallows fly,*
> *Moving out on a twilight sky.*
>         – 'Black Hill', *The Crooked Rose* (1994)

# MICHO RUSSELL, STAR OF THE LISDOONVARNA FOLK FESTIVAL

One of Tommy's crazier notions was an open-air festival, in his mind's eye featuring us alongside Van Morrison. Though that never came to pass, he had been on to something; the Lisdoonvarna Folk Festival did happen two years later, and Tommy was right in the thick of it all, running the bar and dishing up his simple but legendary beef stew. He made so much stew that first year that every neighbourhood freezer was commandeered for storage, and it was so popular that it stayed on the specials board for most of that winter.

Over the fireplace in the pub hangs a motif that says, 'Everyone who visits this place brings happiness; Some by coming in . . . some by going out.' How

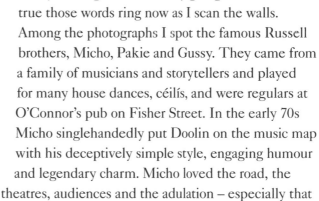

true those words ring now as I scan the walls. Among the photographs I spot the famous Russell brothers, Micho, Pakie and Gussy. They came from a family of musicians and storytellers and played for many house dances, céilís, and were regulars at O'Connor's pub on Fisher Street. In the early 70s Micho singlehandedly put Doolin on the music map with his deceptively simple style, engaging humour and legendary charm. Micho loved the road, the theatres, audiences and the adulation – especially that of the young European ladies, who were enchanted by his eccentricities. Their arrival in Doolin to visit him was well reported locally, often leading to much whispered speculation about the 'goings on' at the cottage by the sea.

For me, his crowning musical moment had to be an appearance on a beautiful sun-drenched Saturday afternoon at the Lisdoonvarna Folk Festival. Micho sat centre stage, nonchalantly playing away on the whistle, when suddenly, mid-tune, a beautiful young Swiss woman dressed in translucent pink chiffon sashayed onto the stage in a freestyle ballet, gliding around a seemingly oblivious Micho. She drifted effortlessly across the entire stage, looping back to Micho, now beaming and winking in her direction. A sleepy afternoon crowd quickly awoke to the emerging scene, and the noise grew as people clapped along and cat-called. When the dance finished, Micho stood hand in hand with the dancer, who gave a graceful ballerina curtsey, and they walked off the stage, leaving a festival in consternation. It was all people could talk about for weeks, with reviewers relegating headline acts into the 'also ran' bracket as they honed in on the spectacle of Micho Russell and the girl in the pink nightdress. It was the only show in town.

# TOMMY IN AMERICA

In early 1978 Tommy McGann, having spent a day in his pub drinking with a group of Americans, decided to join them on their return journey to Connecticut. He had neither luggage nor a passport. On his arrival in the US, he talked his way through customs. Back then, American customs and the world in general were a little less suspicious of the traveller. Tommy phoned his mother to announce that he was now living in America for a while and to please tell Tony to mind the pub while he was away. He would be home soon. Though it was a spur-of-the-moment move on his part, it proved to be the beginning of an adventure that lasted many years, a move that positively affected the lives of the thousands of people who connected with him directly or indirectly either in Doolin or on the shores of America.

He moved to Boston to work at the Purple Shamrock, a downtown Irish bar that was the first port of call for many Irish immigrants. He then opened his own bar in Cape Cod called the Irish Embassy, which quickly became a consular office of sorts for countless Irish visitors. He renamed it McGann's, then opened a second Irish Embassy in Easton, Massachusetts, and relocated back in downtown Boston on Friend Street, a short walk from the famous Boston Garden, home to the Bruins and the Celts. He settled in there for the rest of his short life.

A second McGann's pub was opened next door, which included two youth hostels. The hostels were an inspired addition and welcomed by many Irish immigrants, including my own brother-in-law Stan, who to this day regards Tommy as his saviour. Having arrived in America, almost penniless and jobless, Stan worked as the doorman and in true McGann fashion was available for any other duties that might arise. Tommy worked a very simple system for immigrants: new arrivals were taken in by Irish people and looked after; months later, you returned the favour to the next wave. It was an unwritten rule that was never questioned or considered, and everyone who came through was guaranteed a solid, friendly and dignified beginning to their new world far away from home.

Tommy was very particular about his menus in the pub. He used many local ingredients, but also imported Irish goods like sausages, beef, bacon, Tayto crisps and, at one stage, brown bread. I still recall our first visit to the Purple Shamrock all those years ago. When we arrived, Tommy had us leave all our bags down in the basement and then treated us to a feed of eggs, sausages and baked beans – Boston baked beans.

# Quick Boston baked beans
Serves about 8

Oil or butter, for frying
600g thick streaky bacon, chopped
1 small onion, peeled and diced
1 tsp mustard seeds
1 x 400g tin of cannellini beans
1 x 400g tin of kidney or pinto beans
200ml homemade tomato sauce or passata
3 tbsp molasses
1 tbsp maple or golden syrup
A pinch of dried oregano
Sea salt and freshly ground black pepper

1. Preheat the oven to 150°C/130°C fan/gas 2.
2. Heat the oil or butter in a frying pan. Add the bacon and onion and fry until golden, then add the mustard seeds.
3. When the seeds begin to pop, stir in the beans, tomato sauce or passata, molasses, syrup and oregano. Taste for seasoning.
4. Place in an ovenproof dish, and bake in the oven for 40 minutes.

*Note: The traditional method is a very slow cook using fresh beans or part-boiled beans. Traditional recipes also use either molasses or syrup, but I added both to keep everyone happy.*

Tommy's pubs on the Cape and in Boston also played host to countless touring Irish musicians, who regarded them as recharge stations during long, arduous tours. He was well established as a businessman there, and, crucially for someone dealing with a lot of young messers far from home, he was also well connected to the authorities. I remember one occasion when a member of our band decided to go for a midnight swim at a Quincy motel, only to be arrested for trespassing and taken away in his soaking underpants to spend the night freezing in a local cell. The following morning, he was arraigned in the same attire, but Tommy's successful plea for clemency meant we could carry on with our tour, as long as our swimmer remained on dry land and donated a few dollars to a local church fund.

## SAD FAREWELL

Clearly, Tommy's greatest legacy is his generosity to friends and strangers; there was no dividing line between the two for him.

He died tragically in a car accident in County Clare in 1998 when he was only forty-five, having already survived cancer. The city of Boston and the people of Clare alike wept in each other's arms at his passing. For one St Patrick's Day, the city named a street in his honour. I, like thousands more, owe much to his friendship, spirit and character. The years pass swiftly now, but every time I return to Doolin memories are still strong, and Tommy is always present in my thoughts, audacious as ever, smiling, jibing and dreaming up his next crazy adventure.

## TOMMY PEOPLES AND CHRISTY BARRY'S FLUTE

One particular set of photographs on the wall in McGann's really caught my eye. There's cockney Tom Thomson, driving his old red bus with an engine that constantly howled in pain, almost longing to be decommissioned. Next to Tom, fiddle supremo Tommy Peoples, who worked with my dad at the County Council and toured with the ground-breaking Bothy Band. Tommy's playing was on another level, from a different place, sometimes dark, sometimes melancholic, but always exciting and performed with such panache. He was an introverted character and, in those days, insisted on taking me along to play guitar at all his gigs. I was only a novice with very few chords, but he said he loved my rhythm and the way I accompanied tunes. That meant more than I could ever express in words, and unfortunately he'll never know the effect he had on my confidence as a young musician.

Next to Tommy is Christy Barry, who played concert flute and whistle from morning to the late hours, regaling tourists with countless tales. When a crowd had gathered, Christy dipped the flute in his pint, proclaiming to the young ladies gathered round that the Guinness was very good for his flute. Christy had a glint in his eyes that could woo a stone. I hear he still plays wonderful music at house concerts around the county. I also hear the Guinness has been replaced by large pots of tea.

# THE THREE AMIGOS

I scan along the wall and stop at three delightful characters. I immediately break into laughter. It's the formidable Donegal/Dublin trio of Skippy, the Sheriff and Rory O'Connor. They arrived in Doolin in the late 70s and held court daily at McGann's, entertaining the masses with their wit and beguiling charm, snaring many tourists for free drinks and food. They easily passed a day's drinking without spending a penny. Tony 'Skippy' Reid had that acerbic Dublin sense of humour delivered with impeccable timing, sparing no one in the process. One day a customer enquired about McGann's 'world-famous Irish stew'. The barman talked up the stew, explaining its popularity among locals and tourists alike. 'Some say it's the best stew in the world,' he boasted. At the time Tony McGann ran the kitchen and he was very proud of his stew, and with Tony well within earshot, Skippy stood up from the stool, turned to the customer and said, 'Stew me arse . . . they should have called it Aran Islands stew, 'cause it's just three small pieces of meat surrounded by fuckin' water.' He may have been barred on that occasion but his expulsions were never long served. On another occasion Skippy hurt his knee and was walking around on crutches. The locals organised a benefit dance to cover medical expenses under the banner 'The Needy Knee' at the Hydro Hotel in Lisdoonvarna. As the evening wore on, the music got the better of him and he rose to his feet and started dancing. The Sheriff grabbed him and sat him back down: 'Will you sit down, you eejit, we'll get lynched!'

He is literally part of the furniture at the Hydro, where a bar stool engraved 'Skippy's Seat' stands proud in his preferred position at the end of the bar with a full view of all proceedings.

Whenever I stayed at McGann's, I mainly played music and when required, I served beer, made the sandwiches, soups, stews, swept the floor, collected glasses or carried out whatever task was presented. There was no question of any kind of demarcation, which was in total contrast to my job at Shannon Airport. Everyone just got on with it. On occasion when customers wished to speak directly to the chef, Tommy chose whichever one of us looked the most respectable, and urged us to say by way of an opener that we were trained as chefs at the Ritz in London and gave it all up to live the life here in Doolin.

# McGann's world-famous Irish stew
Serves about 4 to 6

I often cooked their stew, and in later years included it on several of my menus.
I like a simple stew, but good meat, veg stock and herbs are essential. I use lamb
neck or shoulder pieces, but I have used gigot chops. I like to use lamb stock if
I have some stored in the freezer, though chicken stock is fine too. Fresh thyme
is essential.

Olive oil
1 large onion, peeled and finely chopped
1kg neck of lamb, chopped into bite-size chunks, lightly salted and set aside
2 large carrots, peeled and chopped
2 celery sticks, peeled and chopped
1 parsnip, peeled and chopped
500ml well-seasoned stock (see below)
1 dsp fresh thyme leaves
I tsp chopped fresh rosemary
1 bay leaf
2 large potatoes, peeled and chopped into bite-size chunks
Sea salt and freshly ground black pepper
Extra fresh herbs, finely chopped, for garnish

1. In a medium-sized pot, heat a little oil and fry the onion gently for about
   3 minutes.
2. Add the lamb pieces and let them get a slight colour, about 6 minutes.
3. Add the carrots, celery and parsnip and mix.
4. Add the stock and herbs and bring to the boil, then lower the heat and
   simmer for 40 minutes.
5. Add the potatoes and cook for a further 25 minutes. Taste for seasoning.
   Serve garnished with the chopped herbs.

*Lamb stock is easy to make yourself. Get a few lamb bones with a little meat
on them into a large pot with 2 litres of water, a carrot, some celery, thyme, a
bay leaf, an onion and a few black peppercorns. Boil for about 2 hours, stirring
every so often, then strain and return to the heat until reduced to about half.
When cold, remove the layer of solid fat. You can freeze what you don't need,
ready for other recipes later.*

# McGANN'S EQUALLY WORLD-FAMOUS TOASTIE

Under the mantelpiece by the old kitchen I spot a photo of a very young Davy Spillane with his long, flowing curly hair, taken just before he conquered the folk world with his incredible piping and innovative, modern and progressive approach to writing and arranging music for the uilleann pipes. We played many sessions together back in the day, and we both practically lived on the house toasted sandwich special of ham, cheese, onion and tomato. The hams, or occasional corned beef, were boiled in large pots in the kitchen, we sliced the red Cheddar from a massive block, the onions and tomatoes were either sliced or very roughly chopped according to the skill set of the appointed 'chef' on duty. The ham caused us the most trouble, as we tended to eat more than we filled, and on top of that our slices were always very thick. 'Ah, for fuck's sake, lads!' Tony would moan, followed by a lecture on the values of portion control. But the trick to the toasted special was the magic toastie bags: two slices of liberally buttered bread filled with fresh ham, onions, cheese and tomatoes, wrapped in a special heatproof plastic bag and toasted on a double-sided grill. The bag blackened in the intense heat, causing the cheese to caramelise at the edges. You had to allow a minute for cooling, to avoid second-degree lip burns, before cutting through to a waft of warmed ham, tomato and onion soaked in the burnt liquid Cheddar. A sensorial symphony filled your nostrils, a symphony like no other from our fine-dining days at McGann's.

The toaster is still in operation today, and I was brought into the kitchen to say hello. The chef says it has acquired a mind of its own in old age and only works when it feels like it. I think it has earned that right.

## THE STINGER

It was in McGann's pub in 1976 where myself and cousin Paul discovered the joys and tribulations of alcohol. I was reared in a teetotal house, so the only time we ever saw whiskey was at Christmas, when in the name of a festive welcome, Dad unwittingly attempted to poison guest after guest with tumblers filled to the brim. It took deft skill to get glass to mouth. In Doolin I tasted stout, beer, lager, shorts and all sorts of fancy drinks, all for the first time. Steve Birge, a friend of Tommy's from Vermont, introduced us to his list of exotic American cocktails, including the Sombrero, a mix of Kahlua, crushed ice and fresh milk, and the Killer Stinger, a potent mix of brandy and crème de menthe poured into a glass of crushed ice. The Doolin twist was to crush the ice by taking a tea towel full of it and battering it against a wall. Paul and I settled on the Stinger as our drink of choice, and I can safely say it is firmly etched in our hangover memory.

## THE MG

Somewhere in a mounted collage I recognise the old pub MG convertible, and I'm right back in the driver's seat accompanied by concertina ace Noel Hill, on our way back from Garrihy's shop with the morning supply of milk and eggs. I had never driven a car before that summer, so the excitement was palpable every time I turned the key. On our way back down the hill towards the pub, a tractor suddenly appeared around the corner. In a fit of panic, I swerved to avoid it but ended up sideways in the ditch with the wheels spinning in the air. The farmer was highly amused as he tied a rope to the car and brought the MG back onto the dirt road, bidding us well on the rest of our journey. As we continued on down, we noticed a group of people gathered outside the pub pointing in our direction. The village wire service had notified base of our little escapade, and as we rounded the rear of the pub some of the lads guided us into our parking spot like a Formula 1 pit signals team. 'Well done, lads. Emerson Fittipaldi called there, looking for yer details!' shouted one. 'I hear Evel Knievel is gonna jump the Grand Canyon, boys – sure ye might have a go at the Cliffs!' laughed another. For days, we heard nothing else, and all the locals made sure we were never going to forget how we were run off the road by a tractor – chugging its way UP a hill. Years later, at the Irish Embassy pub in Boston, Tommy introduced me to a TV host friend whose first words were, 'I've heard a lot about you. Tommy tells me you could have made it in Formula One. We could set you up for Nascar while you're here – or maybe you'd prefer the demolition derby?'

# THE ORIGINS OF 'BEAUTIFUL AFFAIR'

*There comes a time when you look around*
*And you see the ocean rise before your eyes, showing no surprise.*
*So you make your way down to the shore,*
*And you climb aboard and give yourself a smile, it makes you feel alive.*
   – 'Beautiful Affair', *Light in the Western Sky* (1982)

The imagery of 'Beautiful Affair' is Doolin and neighbouring Lahinch, where I spent many Sundays of my youth on the sprawling beach and sandy dunes, playing on chair-o-planes and dodgem cars and swimming in the wild Atlantic Ocean.

Today as I sit in my old haunt, I think I finally understand the song it gave to me. I certainly know more than that seventeen-year-old boy who arrived at his first major crossroads not really sure which direction to take. Whatever road he chose, it was guaranteed to turn upside down his sheltered and wonderful childhood – but it was time. Nights were now filled with the dreams I would often realise the following day, as I played music, sang my songs and discovered writers, philosophers and poets.

I close my eyes and summon the spirits of the music to fill each crack and crevice with their wonderful tunes and laughter – I can hear the notes bounce from hand to bow, feet firmly stomping out the beat as tourists and travellers alike are drenched in the atmosphere of the moment. I see postcard snippets of the world flutter before me: I see Rome, Amsterdam, Sydney, Boston, Calgary, all the smaller towns and villages and those wonderful faces who embraced and cheered the Wing's effervescent musical swagger. It all began here in this room at McGann's Pub in Doolin – the place where I belong.

# CHAPTER 3

---

# MAURA O'CONNELL

*Mell and Colly lay down by the water to watch the stars collide.*
*He takes her by the hand, says*
*'I can't understand this fear we keep inside.*
*Take a look along that empty shore.*
*If we walk that lonely road*
*I'll pick you up when you fall down.*
*You'll be there when I fall down.'*

        – 'From the Blue', *What You Know* (2002)

By 1977 I was writing a lot, singing at sessions and playing the odd support gig. As with all gigs, it helps to have a professional in your corner; at a Clive Collins Hobo Junction gig, I met up with local sound engineer TV Honan, whom I'd first met in our teens at the Friary Hall Youth Club. TV (Thomas Vincent, in case you were wondering) was meticulous in his efforts to ensure I had a good sound. This was all new to me, as in my younger days, sound engineers rarely acknowledged our band's presence, let alone offered a sound check.

TV called a few weeks later, suggesting I should hook up with Maura O'Connell for a few songs. I knew Maura from the family fish shop in Ennis right across the street from where I worked as a teenager, and I heard her sing many times at the Pro Cathedral. Her mother Amby was a great singer who instilled in Maura a love of old Irish music-hall ballads, light opera and the emotional dynamics of the great musicals. We met at TV's flat on Abbey Street in Ennis, which was the third floor of a house owned by his parents, Derry and Tras Honan. Tras was a very strong-willed Fianna Fáil politician who had the distinction of being the first woman to chair the Irish Senate. She loved a good debate and I was always the willing young agitator full of youthful notions, itching for a political row. Some might say I haven't changed much apart from the odd grey hair or two.

## GARLICKED

I was completely taken in by Maura's voice right from that very first rehearsal, unique with a rich, velvet timbre that weaves and meanders through each lyric line – so authentic, so full of emotion. We spent a lot of our evenings singing and listening to new music. Way down in the basement stood an old Aga, which fed and kept us warm during cold winter evenings. If you walk through the alley at Cruises Bar in Ennis today you will see remnants of that old cooking wonder, rusted and worn but still able to conjure a good memory or two. These days it seems to function as a drinks table and perhaps a quaint decorative reminder of a bygone era. If it could talk . . .

Cooking was a communal event in the flat, especially at the weekends when feasts were planned sometimes days in advance. One Saturday myself and TV were on duty to cook a spaghetti bolognese, which required, among other things, a clove of garlic. We were not familiar with garlic, and Ennis was not renowned for its stock of 'exotic' veg, but we managed to find garlic somewhere and returned very excited to prepare our new dish. What follows has been recounted several times by Maura O'Connell – in fact, I would go so far as to say she has made a career out of this story, filling up many minutes of air and stage time with it, particularly if I am anywhere within range. TV and I busied ourselves preparing the ingredients, carefully following the ragù recipe to the letter while Maura and our friend Paddy O'Brien sat upstairs listening to music. We sautéed the onions, followed by diced carrots, celery and then the clove of garlic. We added the beef, and as we poured in the wine, there was a sizzle and the room began to choke with the smell of garlic.

'Jesus, it's strong stuff, TV!'

'Yea, it surely is. Sure, it might settle down with the wine.'

We kept going, but the smell was soon catching the backs of our throats.

'Open up the window there, Jaysus,' I said as we coughed and spluttered.

The aroma had made its way out into the hall, and up around the three flights of stairs to Paddy and Maura. There was a clatter of feet on the wooden stairwell and the kitchen door swung open.

'Jesus, lads, the smell of garlic would kill you! How much did ye put in? It's very strong.'

'Only one clove,' I replied. 'The recipe said just one, but it's very strong stuff.'

'And where is the rest of it?' she asked.

'There is no more. We only got one clove, and that's all we put in.'

Maura looked from one of us to the other. 'Ye pair of eejits! Ye put the full bulb of garlic in, not a clove . . . oh, Holy Mother . . . I'm going to Johnny Griffin's for chips.'

Years later, my poor mum made the same mistake after I suggested she try a little garlic in her stew. Her friends threatened to throw her from the bingo bus and leave her at the side of the road, miles from Ennis. My poor dad suffered with stomach ulcers, so he put down a tough few days for it too. He claimed the garlic was seeping through his pores. Needless to say, he was very wary of the clove after that. Poor Mum, only trying to spice up their life.

# A CLAREMAN'S RAGÙ

I am not a fan of complicated menus. Why on earth would you want to cook pork fifteen ways in an apple and cider reduction, with a chargrilled peach salsa, served with honeyed baby carrots in a macadamia nut pesto, wasabi-soaked roasted cauliflower, kimchi-coated thrice-fried sweet potato chips with an essence of artichoke velouté, nasturtium leaves and a port jus? Honest to goodness.

Because I like to keep things simple, I love to cook Italian food; it's the simplicity that's the key, and the greatest challenge in cooking is to keep it simple – and seasonal. A few years ago, my brother-in-law married his Italian-Irish girlfriend, Rosa, in a beautiful castle at the foot of Castellabate on the Amalfi Coast. We spent the two weeks feasting on local food, including their famous mozzarella, produced at many local buffalo farms. In a small family-run restaurant up in the mountains we tasted the best ragù ever. It was delicious, rich and so full of flavour.

Rosa was born in Ireland, but her family maintains a very strong connection to her parents' homeland. Over the years, she has been my go-to Italian foodie, particularly for clarity on Azzurri cooking, and she didn't lick it off the ground, as her mum is never out of the kitchen. Naturally, each region of Italy boasts the best ragù, but they all seem agreed on one aspect – the pasta is hardly ever spaghetti, preferring instead wider, flatter pappardelle or tagliatelle, which is a better vehicle for the sauce. Ragù freezes really well, so if you have a little left over, save it for another day. It also works really well on a barbecued or roast potato, although I'm not sure Rosa would appreciate me suggesting the humble spud, she might just disown me for that idea alone. Some recipes use tomato paste but I find it far too intense a flavour.

# A Clareman's ragù
Serves 6 to 8

1kg good-quality beef mince with about 10 per cent fat content
2 tbsp rapeseed oil
1 medium onion, peeled and diced
1 celery stick, trimmed and finely diced
1 medium carrot, cleaned and diced
1 large clove of garlic, crushed
2 glasses of good red wine
400g tinned tomatoes, passata or homemade tomato sauce
200ml beef or chicken stock
1 dsp finely chopped fresh marjoram, sage, rosemary and a bay leaf
Sea salt and freshly ground black pepper

1. Break up the mince with your fingers and season with salt. Leave aside at room temperature.
2. In a wide-bottomed sauté pan, heat the oil and add the onion and celery. Slow-cook on a low heat for 3 minutes, then add the carrot and garlic. Cook for a further minute – do not burn.
3. Cover the veg entirely with a layer of mince, and leave it to cook for 6 minutes on a low heat. The underside should be browned but not burned, so a low heat is essential. Use a heat diffuser below your pan, if required. You may need to add a little extra oil.
4. Mix well and cook for 10 minutes, stirring constantly.
5. When the meat is cooked through, add the wine and reduce until it is almost dry. Be brave.
6. Add the tomatoes, stock and herbs. Cook at a low heat for 1 to 1½ hours, stirring often. Add a little water if it seems to be drying out.

# JOE GALLIGAN'S FOLK CLUB

We had a very active and vibrant folk club outside Ennis in the little village of Crusheen, called the Highway Inn, owned and run by a wispy-bearded Cavan man called Joe Galligan, whose accent certainly softened from the few years in the Clare air. No PA system, no frills, just a small stage in a house full of listeners. Joe usually sat at the back of the room guarding the silence vigilantly, ready to pounce at the mere hint of a whisper.

He had the foresight to help set up a national grid of folk clubs, which allowed artists to pull together a series of gigs around the country. Folk clubs on the circuit usually met in January to discuss regular touring artists, listen to recommendations or requests from new acts, and set out a tour plan for the year ahead. Clubs from Clonmel, Limerick, Carrick-on-Shannon, Carrick-on-Suir, Roscrea, Dublin, Waterford, Kerry and several others were linked into a rolling schedule from Tuesday to Saturday, which meant relatively little travel time between shows. In that little room in Crusheen we heard a very young Barry Moore (aka Luka Bloom), Henry McCullough, Hobo Junction, Dolores Keane and so many more wonderful Irish and international artists. Such was the high standard set by the grid that emerging or new talents were always assured of a reasonably full house of dedicated club members who loved their music and embraced the opportunity to hear new tunes.

Joe gave myself and Maura our first gig, and we were so excited – but we had no name, and for some reason back then you had to have a band name. While flipping through our album collection, we came across a Dan Hicks and His Hot Licks song called 'The Tumbling Tumbleweeds'. 'Tumbleweed' it was to be. I still remember that first gig, as both of us, extremely nervous, stumbled through our first song, but the audience cheered us loud and long – not a tumbleweed in sight. Such a great feeling. Joe invited us back many times, all the while encouraging us to spread our wings and get out on to the club circuit. We spent weeks writing and learning new material, and soon were playing at the National Institute for Higher Education in Limerick with a very young Stockton's Wing, who were beginning to cause quite a musical stir around Ireland.

# PJ CURTIS

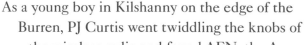

As a young boy in Kilshanny on the edge of the
Burren, PJ Curtis went twiddling the knobs of
the wireless radio and found AFN, the Armed
Forces Network radio station broadcasting
from Stuttgart. There he heard the sounds
of the Grand Ole Opry, rock and roll and
the Mississippi blues. His family was
steeped in traditional music; his mother
played fiddle and was part of the great Lynch
family, who were, and still are, at the core of
the Kilfenora Céilí Band. But when the likes of
Muddy Waters and Sonny Boy Williamson came
seeping through the walls of the Old Forge cottage,
PJ's world changed forever. His mother eventually found a guitar for him in
Limerick, and PJ was on his way.

At sixteen he found his way to Belfast, joined the RAF and was stationed
outside Bath. In 1962 he was playing with beat group Rod Starr and the
Stereos, gigging regularly around the area. The Beatles were coming to Bath
and the Stereos were booked to play support. A few days before the gig, their
slot was given to another band, and to compensate the promoter put them on
with Jerry Lee Lewis. PJ was delighted, as he was a fan of the great man.
He got to see the Beatles play and be on the same stage the following week
with Jerry Lee.

He was sent to Borneo to work as a radio technician. On his return to
Ireland he met with a young Bothy Band, who were creating innovative Irish
music, with guitarist Mícheál Ó Domhnaill, Paddy Keenan on pipes, Tríona
Ní Dhomhnaill on clavinet, Matt Molloy on flute, Donal
Lunny and Tommy Peoples on fiddle. Tommy was
soon replaced by Kevin Burke. PJ worked as a driver
and roadie for the Bothy Band while producing
albums for Mulligan Records in Dublin.

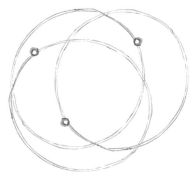

When we met PJ Curtis, he had recently
finished touring with the Bothy Band and was
back living at his Old Forge cottage while
producing the first of his many iconic Irish folk
music albums in Dublin studios. PJ introduced us

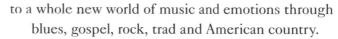

to a whole new world of music and emotions through blues, gospel, rock, trad and American country. We discovered Mahalia Jackson, Richard Thomson, the Mills Brothers, Mississippi John Hurt, John Coltrane, Robert Johnson and Lightnin' Slim. None of these artists were available at local record shops, so I bought most of my music from a Welsh mail order store called Cob Records, and my order sheet grew with each visit to PJ's cottage. Cob stocked thousands of albums and sent out weekly catalogues of old and new releases, all sold at discount prices. It was my brother Ger, an avid collector, who had originally discovered Cob, and when the latest brown package with the green par avion sticker arrived, we'd tear it open to give it its first spin on our turntable as fast as we could. Many years later, while on tour in Wales with Ronnie Drew, I went in search of Cob Records. I found it in Porthmadog, where I met an old man who remembered sending lots of records to a house in the west of Ireland. He said he loved to see our catalogues arrive back with some of the oddest of requests. I think Ger and myself kept his international business going for a few years.

PJ would go on to record some of the great Irish albums of that era with Scullion, Freddie White, Maura O'Connell, Sean Keane, Mary Black, Altan, Dolores Keane, Mick Hanley, and of course two great albums with Stockton's Wing, including our two big hits. These days PJ splits his life between Clare and Spain. He has been part of my music life since the early days, and I owe him thanks and respect for his constant support down all of these years. He saw something in myself and Maura O'Connell way back in the day, and gave us both great encouragement to get out there and fly. When he heard my songs for Stockton's Wing he built a wonderful platform so that the world could listen.

# Maura's salmon chanted evening
Serves 4

Maura O'Connell is an exceptional cook, dedicated to good produce and great recipes – and she always hosts a mighty fine shindig. She spent most of her youth handling and selling fish at her family shop, so you are always guaranteed a tasty fishy dish.

2 large fillets of salmon, with skin (about 300g each)
120g baby spinach leaves
150g crumbled feta cheese
Oil, to grease
1 tsp lemon zest
4 large tomatoes, finely chopped
4 cloves of garlic (not a bulb!), crushed
Boiled rice and salad, to serve

1. Preheat the oven to 170°C/150°C fan/gas 3.
2. Wash and dry the salmon on kitchen paper.
3. Blanch the spinach by plunging it into boiling water and removing immediately. Place it in a colander to drain. Coarsely chop the drained spinach, and mix with the feta cheese and lemon zest.
4. Place one salmon fillet skin side down on an oiled baking tray or oven-safe dish. Spread over all the spinach mixture. Place the second salmon fillet on top, skin side up.
5. Mix the tomatoes and garlic together and spread over the salmon, completely covering the top and sides.
6. Bake in the oven for 40 to 45 minutes.
7. Serve with boiled rice and salad.

## ON TOUR WITH BETSY

TV owned a beautiful 1965 black Morris Minor with wing indicators that flicked out like a pair of hands when engaged. Maura christened the car Betsy prior to our first tour around the folk clubs of Ireland. After months of writing, learning new songs, rehearsals, planning, playing support gigs and sessions, we were now out there on our own, with our names on our posters, playing our music on our very own stage. It was a very exciting time. We played in Carrick-on-Shannon with a very young Charlie McGettigan, and we also played at the famous Clonmel Folk Club, still going to this day with Ken Horne at the helm.

## BOBBY CLANCY

Bobby Clancy and his wife Moira ran a folk club in the basement bar at their hotel in Carrick-on-Suir in Tipperary. Bobby and Moira loved our music and sat with us for hours after the show Maura and I played, passing on some hard-earned experience from Bobby's days with the Clancy Brothers. 'Guys, it's not just a performance, y'know; it's a show as well. You can both sing and play well enough, but you need to tidy up between the numbers. There's far too little going on, and you need to keep the audience's attention. Talk to them, and have a little fun. In the early years of the Clancys we learned to keep the show going by adding little snippets of poetry, or a few funny stories.'

'And you, my dear Maura. You need to stop looking at your feet. Look up, and smile at them.' Such a lovely man.

## THE NATURAL DISASTER BAND

On St Stephen's Day 1978, Tumbleweed played a one-off charity gig at the Green Door Youth Centre with a full band aptly named the Natural Disaster Band, for very obvious reasons. The gig was a nightmare to set up, with so many obstacles put in our way, PA problems with cable issues, not enough microphones or stands, amps breaking down, all sorts of buzzing sounds, electricity failure and no time at all for rehearsals, but we got through it – and I think most of the musicians in Ennis participated in some way or other to make that a very special day. On the back of it, PJ Curtis encouraged us to start putting songs down on tape so that he might spread it about the Dublin music scene, where he worked as a producer with a couple of record labels. A month later, TV set up a recording studio in his parents' house and we made our first demo cassette recording. I found the old cassette sleeve only recently, which was drawn in multicoloured crayon by my then girlfriend Bebke Smits of Doolin Hilton fame. Bebbie designed individual sleeves for many of our friends, and this was called 'The Sea of My Imagination'. Nothing much came from that particular demo, but we did enjoy a few great gigs around the country and one in particular at Smokey Joe's Café in Galway.

## SMOKEY JOE'S CAFÉ

In the late 70s the Students' Union set up Smokey Joe's Café as an alternative lunchtime eatery for the Students' Union in a prefab building behind Ma Craven's coffee shop, close to the popular Aula Maxima at University College Galway. It was run by student activist Ollie Jennings, an energetic, selfless promoter of the arts who later created the Galway Arts Festival, put De Dannan firmly on the popular map and introduced us to the wonderful music of the Saw Doctors.

Smokey Joe's really caught the imagination of the students. Lunch was simple fare: homemade soups with large chunks of red and white Cheddar on brown bread baguettes from Griffin's bakery in the city, all served by the students, and occasionally grains and pulses made an appearance on the menu as our generation began to embrace vegetarian and macrobiotic diets. Although I distinctly remember one particular 'chef' at Joe's, a real character who I discovered had a different slant on the menu. One day I plucked up enough courage to approach him, hoping for some tips on cooking. 'You seem very dedicated to this food yourself. It's really beautiful. Any tips?' 'Ah Jaysus no, Mike,' he spluttered, surprised. 'I only sell the feicin' stuff. I'm purely a burgers and chips man meself.'

The music was cool, with the likes of Emmylou Harris and Gram Parsons regularly featured by spinners Tom Prendergast and Mike Kilduff, and the UCG Arts Society set up a weekly Sunday folk club from October to March. Admission was a mere 50 pence and the café seated 200 people. The sale of alcohol was prohibited, so the audience usually arrived with their flagons of cider from nearby Kelehan's bar. For those who came without, there was always the house special, a potent and highly illegal wine punch, served in discreet paper teacups. If discovered, the college authorities would certainly have closed down the folk club.

Our first Smokey Joe's gig was well received, and Ollie invited us back again and again, on one occasion to support a Loudon Wainwright III gig in Galway city. Loudon toured Ireland quite a lot in those years. His hallmark, apart from being an excellent songwriter, was his ability to ad lib songs, reacting to issues in the news or those people unlucky enough to be seated in his immediate vicinity. Walking to the bar or the toilet was worth at least two good lines of verse. To acknowledge our support slot he sang out, 'And what about the music from the two lovely slickers, the Shannon Shitkickers? Yeah you, Shannon Shitkickers!' Whenever we met at festivals, he'd always greet us with, 'Hey! The Shannon Shitkickers. How you guys doin'?'

## THE RELUCTANT VEGGIE

Some of our friends moved to London to study nursing at Whipps Cross University Hospital in Leytonstone. Whenever they were home, they'd hang out and eat with us at the flat, go to all the gigs and never missed a session. We were a good solid crew. We went to London and stayed at their tiny house on Chadwick Road in Leytonstone. They introduced us to London life, jumping the tube station barriers to head into Portobello Market, to fill up on albums from Honest Jon's record store, catch gigs at Dingwall's, the Marquee Club or the Hammersmith Palais. A couple of the girls presented me with my first cookbook, *The Bean Book* by Rose Elliot – it was a revelation. I quickly developed a taste for veggie cuisine, although I never could proclaim to be a complete vegetarian, preferring to keep my options open.

Back at home I started to branch out and cook from the book. Dad had great difficulty understanding what was actually sitting on my plate, as I stubbornly refused Mum's crispy pork chops and spuds in favour of kidney bean moussaka, toasted chickpea salad or a plate of lentil mush. He once remarked that even Dinky, our lovely dog, wouldn't touch that stuff – or a word to that effect.

With Rose Elliot's help, I persevered as a reluctant vegetarian for a few years until my journey ended abruptly at a hotel restaurant in Kilkenny. Ireland was not renowned at the time for multiple-choice vegetarian menus, so it was hit and miss. Having ordered the usual hotel chef's go-to veggie option, 'the vegetarian salad special', I sat back, waiting in anticipation, ever the optimist. Unfortunately, back in the day veggie options were more than likely put together by the kitchen porter while the cooking crew concentrated on the real stuff. A veggie salad plate was often a respite home for bewildered greens and miscellaneous garnishes intended for other dishes, all smothered in a blanket of salad cream. Occasionally a tin of kidney beans might find its way on to the plate for added texture, and it seemed a great repository for jars of beetroot and burger gherkins, with a bonus fistful of Tayto. I patiently waited as steaks, burgers and stews were served to the rest of the band, imagining all sorts of lovely things: 'He's probably in there roasting the cumin-spiced vegetables, or frying homemade lentil fritters while waiting for the brown rice to boil.' Soon I was eyeing the service hatch. The waiter quickly scampered off through the swinging doors, followed by the sound of kitchen discontent. He returned far too quickly with a few apologetic words and presented me with my salad: a mountain of oil-drenched wilted lettuce leaves, a badly sliced hard-boiled egg coated in a Marie Rose sauce, tomatoes and cucumber that had clearly spent the morning atop a dressed salmon. The gherkins made their scheduled appearance, along with a few black olives to keep them company. Mixed herbs were pebble-dashed around the rim, with the obligatory series of little red paprika mole mounds dotted about at random intervals. But the centrepiece, the main event, was a pair of honeydew melon wedges, unsegmented, sitting like two ships bobbing on a very stormy ocean. I searched around for any specks of hidden Italian ham, but the kitchen porter had clearly been very clinical in its extraction. Game over, I called the waiter, ordered the roast beef and said, 'Tell the chef not to spare the gravy.'

## BETSY IN SHOW

Bebke returned to finish her studies in Holland, so TV and I decided to travel over for a couple of weeks to say hello. Betsy the black Morris Minor was readied for the great adventure, and on a bright, brisk September morning we left for Rosslare, taking the ferry across to Le Havre, chugging past Calais, Dunkirk and on into Belgium. We had never seen such scenery, vast tracts of land presenting an array of stunning blooms, from brown to blue to orange to purple, then on to large fields of maize, beets, corn and wheat all growing in perfect symmetry. Betsy caused more than a little excitement on the journey. While her sleek black form should have been a spectacular sight as it cut through the beautifully manicured Ardennes countryside, the reality was quite different. She had taken a shine to oil and was burning it at a ferocious rate. The view through the rear window was of a long black vapour trail stretching for miles as it obliterated the beautiful vista. We eventually found a garage and with some very animated sign language, broken French and lots of charm, we managed to get Betsy a new filter. We set off once again, heading into southern Holland, and soon hit a major traffic jam on the outskirts of a small town. There was a lot of commotion from what looked like a convoy of farm machinery heading towards the centre. 'Maybe it's a protest,' we wondered. As we rounded a bend into the town square, we were met with hundreds of happy faces waving flags and banners and the sound of a very large brass band. The entire area was covered in bright orange bunting. As Betsy came into view a wave of excitement grew from the crowd as they clapped our every chugging move, until we came to a stop in front of a viewing stand, where the dignitaries stood to applaud. There we were, in the middle of a municipal parade, looking and feeling like the main attraction. Betsy was Best in Show. We rolled down the windows and waved in a royal fashion, shouting, 'Come on, Ireland! Viva Irlande!' with our Dutch hosts responding in kind.

## ZANGER, GITARIST

Bebke lived in Boxtel, a small town in the Brabant district of southern Holland, and she had organised a gig for me at the local youth club. The council handed over a section of one of its buildings to the youth service to host events and provide a place for young people to gather. Deal-breaking conditions applied, and one of the more innovative ones allowed for the use of cannabis within its walls – as long as they refrained from smoking in public places. Open-minded though they can be, the Dutch love their rules, and I don't think that rule was ever broken. Bebke, having acquired financial support for the gig, had to justify the sponsorship by presenting it as a promotional event for the youth of Boxtel. She contacted the Irish tourist office in Amsterdam and requested some help and support for the special Irish night she was organising for the young people of the town. They were delighted, and sent reams of Irish posters and bunting. It was suggested that she offer some food, so she decided on bacon and cabbage to remind her of her time in Doolin. With no bacon in Boxtel, she settled on pork sausages, and sauerkraut replaced the cabbage. The room was decorated with large posters of the Killarney lakes, Blarney Castle and the Cliffs of Moher. In bright lights a banner read, 'Mike Hanrahan: Zanger, Gitarist, liedjesschrijver uit Ierland' – singer, guitarist and songwriter from Ireland. I had arrived . . . well, in Boxtel at least.

## WE THOUGHT WE COULD DRINK

On our way back home to Ireland we stopped outside Louvain in search of a campsite. We met a family on the roadside who gave us directions and off we went, but somehow ended up right back where we started and met them

again. They took pity on us and invited us to follow them up along a dirt track to spend the night at their farmhouse. The mother, who spoke no English whatsoever, ushered us to a table where we ate a bowl of hearty, warm carbonnade flamande – the first of many. It is without doubt one of the tastiest stews you will ever eat. Beef, brown beer and vegetables cooked very slowly and washed down with some strong Belgian ale. Oh, and there's bread in the stew as well. Belgian food is well worth an investigation; traditional restaurants produce very special local dishes with influences from a variety of cuisines. I will always remember this particular dish for the flavour and the warmth of Flemish family hospitality.

# Carbonnade flamande
Serves 4

This is my take on carbonnade. I have tried all sorts of cuts of meat, but my favourite is short ribs with a portion of oxtail. If I have time, I will marinate the beef overnight in beer, herbs and bay. You could also dust the beef with seasoned flour for a thicker sauce. I cook this in stages, and the bread is optional and not always used, but when you try it once there is no coming back. I think it is essential to the dish. Close your eyes to the calorie count and enjoy.

1 tbsp rapeseed oil
2 small onions, peeled and quartered
500g stewing beef
1 butcher's portion of oxtail (about 8cm)
A knob of butter
2 carrots, chopped (optional)
2 celery sticks, chopped
A pinch of brown sugar
2 tsp apple cider vinegar
1 glug or about 1 tbsp red wine
1 bay leaf
2 cloves of garlic, roughly chopped
100ml good beef stock
250ml good dark ale
1 tbsp chopped fresh herbs (parsley/ thyme and/or marjoram)
Lots of Dijon mustard
1 French loaf, cut into thickish slices
Sea salt and freshly ground black pepper

1. Preheat the oven to 160°C/140°C fan/gas 3.
2. Heat a deep pan, and fry the onions in a little oil until coloured. Transfer to a casserole dish.
3. Season the beef and oxtail, then fry in batches, transferring them to the casserole dish as you go.
4. Add a knob of butter to the pan, fry the carrots and celery, then transfer to the casserole dish.
5. Add the sugar, vinegar, red wine, bay leaf and chopped garlic. Cook for a minute to reduce the vinegar and wine, and to dissolve the sugar.
6. Add the beef stock, ale and herbs. Continue to cook rapidly for another 5 minutes.
7. Transfer everything from the pan into the casserole dish and mix well.
8. Spread the mustard liberally onto the bread slices and place them on top of the stew, mustard side up. The bread softens and soaks in all of the flavours and the mustard creates an extra flavour layer sensation.
9. Cook in the oven for about 3 hours. You could serve this with herbed boiled potatoes; some roasted carrots would be nice, kale colcannon and, dare I say, the remainder of the bread.

# BELGIAN BEER

After this almighty feed we were taken on a tour of the farmyard. It was littered with old and new machinery. The entire family were dedicated fans of racing, particularly Formula 1, motocross and hot rod. We were brought into their world, looking at photos of international events, pics of the great Belgian Formula 1 Grand Prix and proud moments from their various success stories. The yard was like a bikers' museum, with vintage machines proudly on show alongside the latest models, and we even got to sit in a hot rod.

They showed us to our sleeping quarters in the barn, where we sat talking, drinking beer, and I even sang a few songs. The eldest son, Jean, then announced, 'So, we now go to the city to drink some beers, yeah? We hear you Irish can drink, yeah?' We both looked at each other – more drink, Jaysus . . . At that stage we were well settled in, feeling comfortable and thinking of a good night's rest, but the boys were obviously only starting. They brought us into Louvain, sampling various local brews, visiting many bars while soaking up the student atmosphere. The city was full of life. Years later, I returned to marvel at the stunning architecture in Louvain's beautiful squares. By all accounts, after much drinking, walking and drunken versions of 'Molly Malone' and 'The Irish Rover', we fell asleep at one of the bars and awoke in the back of the pickup truck, bouncing up the dirt track heading for the comforts of our barn – that part I remember well. The following morning, we were greeted by the mother, who was in convulsions as she listened to her sons recall our hapless adventure with the local brew. She prepared an array of breads and cheeses which we just about managed to taste. Jean leaned across the table, closely inspecting our hungover eyes, wagging his forefinger.

'Hey, you Irish, I think you no can drink, no?' The room erupted once again.

# A PICCOLO

We packed up and said our goodbyes. An hour into the journey I needed the loo. TV suggested I go into one of the fields for now, and we could stop somewhere further down the road for a cure later. Still being a God-fearing man, I said I might get arrested, so we took the next turn, found our way to the outskirts of a very small town and stopped at a café. It was all a-glitter with flashing lights and looking quite odd out there in the noonday sunshine. We made our way through a doorway of multicoloured plastic strip blinds to be greeted by a scantily dressed peroxide blonde with bright purple lipstick and a beaming smile. I was bursting, so in my best broken French I asked if we could use la toilette, si vu play.

'Yes, of course . . . Mmm, and after . . . err, maybe you like a piccolo when you come back, ya?'

TV threw me a startled look and nodded at the door. We made a swift exit and found a bush across the street. A brothel? In a little village in the middle of nowhere? In the middle of the day? Well, I never . . .

## CARNSORE POINT

For a couple of years in the late 70s the Anti-Nuclear Festival was held at Carnsore Point, in a field in Yola on the Wexford coast, the proposed site for Ireland's first nuclear power plant. The anti-nuclear movement was well organised, with groups developing in all the major towns across Ireland, creating a powerful network of information and organised protest. Speakers travelled the country to address local meetings, distributing information and advice. Some were dedicated Greens, some hippies, some extreme lefties, but all had one common wish: no nuclear power, please. We signed up for the Ennis branch and were actively involved in fund-raising for the festival. There were international speakers too, and I was very moved by a speech from a young German activist called Petra Kelly, a founding member of the German Green Party, who caused a sensation whenever she spoke.

It was a great time to be young and conscientious, with a real sense of purpose, and it was empowering to be involved in a movement that challenged government policy. There was a definite sense of belonging at Carnsore Point, a sense that we, as a young nation, could engage and force change. Despite the efforts of government ministers and some sections of the media to downplay the numbers, the crowds were vast, peaceful and very focused. The plans for the power plant were abandoned, and whether it was down to the younger generation's campaign, we will never know for sure – but we are certainly due some credit for the government's volte-face. Tumbleweed were not on the bill, but we played a few sessions around the campsite, where we were overheard by one of the organisers, Eilis Moore, who had organised a few gigs for us up in Dublin earlier that year. She told us to find her brother Christy, who was on security backstage in the main concert tent. So we did, and there was Mr Planxty himself, and he only the headline act at the festival – manning the backstage barricade of hay bales. He would have done whatever necessary to make the festival a success as it was dear to his heart. It was that kind of a family movement; inclusive and very welcoming. Christy ushered us through to the holding area, where we were introduced to other artists, given a beer and waited for our stage call. In the end, we had a wonderful gig at Carnsore.

A few months later, Christy invited us along to his Sunday afternoon show at the Meeting Place in Dublin. After we finished, TV's sister Anne, who was nursing at St Vincent's and had to start her shift, drove at speed across town to make the opening slot at the beautiful old Oscar Theatre in Ballsbridge, where Christy's brother Barry was playing. Christy arrived over much later and handed us a fiver for the Meeting Place gig, adding, 'Never, ever leave a gig without getting paid, lads. Ye'll never make any money that way.' Sound advice from the man, and advice Maura took to heart in her role as bag woman for all future Tumbleweed gigs.

By the end of that summer there were whispers that all was not well in the Stockton's Wing camp, and that they might be looking for a new singer. Eyes were beginning to focus in my direction. My heart was yearning for the road, but I was dedicated to Tumbleweed. Yet deep down, the draw to Stockton's Wing was very real. I found myself in something of a quandary.

# CHAPTER 4

---

# TAKE A CHANCE ON ME

*Would you take a chance?*
*Meet me wherever you please.*
*Leave your cares for a while.*
*If we could walk the miles that keep us apart*
*Then we could free these dreams locked inside.*
— 'Take a Chance', *Take a Chance* (1980)

Stockton's Wing's second album was set for release in late 1979, but singer Tony Callinan announced he was leaving in the spring. The search was on for a replacement. They asked myself and Maura O'Connell if we were interested, but she was not at all ready to make that kind of commitment, preferring to stay in Ennis with her mum in the family fish business. Maura and I sat on the steps in the hallway of TV's flat as she insisted that moving on to the Wing was the right thing for me to do. 'Besides,' she added, 'I don't really want to join a trad band.' Thankfully, it didn't turn out to be anything of the kind, but her instincts were otherwise bang on. I accepted the offer and my first gig with the band was scheduled for March 1980.

Tumbleweed was a solid foundation bolstered by all that is good in music and friendship. A year later, I met Maura at Logan Airport in Boston as she set off on her first American tour with, would you believe it, Stockton's great music rivals, De Dannan, a force in traditional Irish music led by Frankie Gavin and Alec Finn. The irony was not lost on us as we drank a beer and toasted our good fortunes. I reminded her that not too long ago she'd intimated that she had no wish at all to join a trad band, yet here she was about to embark on an American tour with one of the greatest trad bands ever to grace a stage. We wished each other well as we set off on the journey. On her return to Ireland she had her first major hit single with De Dannan singing 'My Irish Molly'. She met American five-string banjo ace Béla Fleck and moved to Nashville in 1986 to work with his friends in Newgrass Revival. She has been twice nominated for a Grammy and enjoys an extremely successful career, working with some of the finest musicians in Nashville, including the incredible dobro maestro Gerry Douglas, producing several hit records of powerful songs with that beautiful sublime velvet voice. We continue to toast each other's good fortune.

# A SENSE OF IRELAND

In January 1980, PJ Curtis offered me a job for a few weeks as a roadie with sound engineer John Munnis for the Sense of Ireland Festival in London. PJ was music director for the most ambitious event ever staged to promote Irish culture at various locations around the city, from 1 February to 20 March. I went to Dublin a few days before the festival to meet John and his partner Niall Shortall at the rented basement of a Georgian house on Northumberland Road. In the middle of the night we loaded the van with twenty-two Bose 800 speakers, leads, stands, mics and a desk, then headed for the early-morning ferry from Dún Laoghaire to Holyhead. The Sense of Ireland was a feast of Irish entertainment, with concerts, art and photographic exhibitions, theatre, ballet, lectures and seminars, showcasing the works of Séamus Ennis, John Banville, U2, the Chieftains, Van Morrison, Robert Ballagh, the Abbey Theatre, Jim Sheridan, the Virgin Prunes, Louis Stewart, Rory Gallagher, John A. Murphy – and Stockton's Wing. I spent three weeks there moving from venue to venue: Battersea Arts, the Camden Centre, the Fairfield Hall in Croydon, and the truly majestic Albert Hall, where we hung sixty-four Bose 800s speakers from various trusses around the room, having to hire in an extra forty-two speakers from a local PA company to ensure the entire room was covered. It was an incredible feat, not helped at all when John discovered every lead provided by the hire company was fitted with the wrong plugs, so each had to be painstakingly rewired on site. As it turned out, the stand-out moment of that Albert Hall gig was equipment-related: Séamus Ennis walked onto the stage, sat down with his pipes, and with a flick of his wrist turned all the mics out to the audience. Under no circumstances was he going to play into those mics. All our hard work meant nought to the wily Séamus.

A few gigs later, I met my heroes, the Dubliners, who gave an outstanding performance at the Wembley Conference Centre. At the Fairfield Hall in Croydon, we worked with the Chieftains, who invited us back to Festival Central, the Royal Tara Hotel in Kensington, for drinks and a great session that brought us through the night. Early the following morning, John woke me from my hotel foyer couch to make our way out to the Gaumont State theatre in Kilburn for the gig with Stockton's Wing. That was an uncomfortable experience, given that I was about to replace singer Tony Callinan in a matter of weeks. There was a very strange energy on that stage, and I recall one nervy moment when I had to readjust a microphone for Tony. It must have been a very difficult time for him also. A few days later I kept my distance at the gig in the Civic Hall in Wimbledon, where they played with a host of trad musicians including the legendary Peter O'Loughlin and Paddy Murphy. Like he'd taken a cue from Séamus Ennis, Paddy would retreat every time I put the microphone close to his concertina. John Munnis joked that Paddy might very well end up playing his gig from the backstage wall if he kept going.

The festival was a resounding success. Days were long, and I was sleeping out at Leytonstone with my nursing friends unless I hit the jackpot with empty musicians' rooms at Festival Central. To me, those rooms were palatial, with hot water, clean towels, television, a very full mini bar and a huge bonus breakfast.

After my stint at the festival I jumped on the Magic Bus to Amsterdam for a few days of R & R. That bus company was a remnant of the famous hippie trail of the 50s, 60s and early 70s, when psychedelic coloured buses transported thousands overland from Europe to Asia, stopping at all the major cities, which all came to an abrupt end as a result of the Iranian Revolution. The bus I jumped on was a regular scheduled trip, very cheap and offering a list of recommended hostels in Amsterdam.

I went to a couple of gigs at the famous Melkweg and found an amazing vegetarian restaurant that opened my eyes to the endless possibilities of veggie food. All sorts of grains, salads and dishes I had never known before, bulgur wheat, quinoa and my first taste of hummus. I bought a copy of the *Friends of the Earth Cookbook* that was worn out within a year.

I discovered a letter in my attic, a note I sent from Amsterdam to TV, who was soon to emigrate to London. Although it is quite naive, there's a certain charm to the words:

*I'm sitting here in a youth hostel, positively you know what, but I'm in the mood to write . . .*

Money was very poor in London, but I think I learned a lot looking at managers, stage crew, sound men and of course musicians. The Chieftains were really professional – their whole attitude was really good . . . The Wing didn't have any good gigs really, they were not in great form. The situation with Tony was not good at all. I think the pressure is beginning to show . . . I'm looking forward to doing a bit of work now. I wrote some new songs in London. There's two worth mentioning, I think . . .

The note stops short of mentioning the songs but I am sure it was 'Beneath the Shade' and possibly an early 'Beautiful Affair'. Both songs have always been linked, almost like brothers.

# SMUTTERNAGH KNOCKVICAR [BASH THE BISHOP]

*The birds were singing all around him,*
*Trees gently swaying in the breeze,*
*The answer lies here somewhere, he thought,*
*As he found his way through those falling leaves*
　　　　　– 'Beneath the Shade', *Light in the Western Sky* (1982)

Smutternagh is a townland of Knockvicar, a few miles from Boyle in County Roscommon. In the late 70s the Land Commission purchased many derelict houses around the country and put them back on the market at reasonable prices in a bid to regenerate the community. A group of English New Age travellers moved into the area, buying and renovating some of the properties in their bid to create a self-sufficient community based on the principles of environmentalist John Seymour. His book, *The Complete Book of Self-sufficiency*, became a bible for many young English and Irish couples seeking an alternative lifestyle. On his farm in Wales and a later one in Wexford, Seymour freely shared his vision of a sustainable environment. In addition to his environmental work, he was also a musician, a singer and a fine collector of English folk songs, particularly those relating to water and canal life.

In 1978 Dermot and Gill Wickham moved from Doolin to one of those cottages in Smutternagh, armed with John Seymour's book. They were good friends with Stockton's Wing bodhrán player, Tommy Hayes, and kindly offered the band an opportunity to stay with them and rehearse for a couple of weeks in the run-up to my first tour with them and again just before we went to the studio to record our first album together, *Take a Chance*.

The photograph on the back of *Take a Chance* was taken in the barn at Smutternagh, with Dibbles, their lovely dog, at my side. The cottage had no electricity and the water was drawn from a neighbour's well or from two large rain barrels that collected from the roof, just as my grandparents did, back in the day. Gill cooked amazing vegetarian food on a black Stanley range: beanburgers, homemade pizzas, colcannon with wild nettles, a variety of pies, daily wholemeal and white yeast breads with incredible soups from their vegetable garden. We foraged berries for elderberry wine and jams from the woodside, where a piebald horse shared grazing space with the hens and a few goats that provided milk for homemade yogurts. We ate the occasional meat stew, but Jill always sat out that chore. A large pot was on permanent simmer for fresh leaf tea or washing-up and was regularly used to fill the wonder bath,

an impressive oval tin bath that was placed in
front of a red-hot range for a luxurious soak.

The house was full of antiques: oil
lamps, dressers, mirrors, and an old couch,
all giving the appearance of a small museum.
The band slept in sleeping bags on a
wooden floor in an upstairs loft and generally
helped with any chores around the house
or garden. It was a beautiful place, a rich
creative environment for my songwriting. In
the evenings we often made the journey –
sometimes in a pony and trap – to Clancy's
pub in the village, where the irrepressible
Mrs Donnellan left her bar duties to join us
for a few tunes on her fiddle.

With no television I also read lots of good books there, from Richard
Brautigan's *Trout Fishing in America* to Luke Rhinehart's *The Dice Man* or
Kahlil Gibran's *The Prophet*, books that had a profound effect on my thinking
back then. It was a time of awakening.

# MY DEBUT

My debut with Stockton's Wing was on 20 March 1980 in Clonmel. Clonmel
Folk Club was one of the best around, and a good place to start. I had played
there a couple of times with Tumbleweed, and club organiser Ken Horne
has remained a friend ever since. Two days later I was at the Savoy Theatre
in Cork supporting Ralph McTell, a gentle man and a wonderful performer.
We'd soon have some good times together at the Half Moon in Putney, his
local in London and one of our favourite UK gigs by a mile. The promoter
there was none other than the inimitable cockney wheeler-dealer Doe Rae
Fuck Me Johnny 'Jonah' Jones, a long and deserved name for one of the most
colourful characters in the English music scene. He was a true Del Boy, and
the only place to have him was on your side, as his tours were strictly cash-
only affairs: no accounts, no letters and no contracts. His cockney slang, quick
wit and funny stories kept us on our toes, as there never was a dull moment
in Jonah's company. The Half Moon was a memorable place, as occasional
staff also included the great English wrestler and TV icon Giant Haystacks,

who sometimes manned the door during our shows. His mere presence was enough to keep the peace, but in truth he was a gentle giant, who loved music and telling stories with the rest of us over a few beers after the show.

# THE NORTH

After the Savoy gig we spent a week in Northern Ireland. To this day I still remember the anxiety and dread that kept me sitting in my room, refusing to venture out, until sound check and show. It was my first time being confronted with such fear, yet all around me people were carrying on with their lives – but there was a palpable tension in the air. Our daily news reported of atrocities, internment, torture and death. It was only a few years since the Miami Showband massacre, and that too was constant in my thoughts.

We feared the daily checkpoints and were extremely unnerved at night-time as we approached the flashing lights, uniforms with their guns, hovering as we emptied the contents of the van onto the roadside, knowing many more suspicious army eyes were monitoring our every move from a short distance, ready for any action. Those events were a constant reminder that we were working in a war zone. Thankfully, it never stopped many of us from touring, because the reward, paradoxically, was a warm, friendly and welcoming audience who genuinely appreciated our music and presence.

# THE GREAT MEETING PLACE

Back in Dublin, I recorded 'Take a Chance' at Lombard Studios and invited Maura to sing backing vocals – Tumbleweed had finally made it to the studio. Stockton's Wing then secured a Tuesday night residency at the famous Meeting Place on Dorset Street, where I had played on a few occasions with Maura the previous year. It certainly was the place to be; upstairs, people packed in seven nights a week to hear Paul Brady, Christy Moore, Red Peters, Jimmy Faulkner, Barry Moore – and now Stockton's Wing.

The Meeting Place was owned by brothers Shay, Paddy and Sean Spillane. We became friends, and the downstairs bar became our favourite Dublin haunt, the chosen venue for many of our Christmas parties, birthdays and even the odd stag night. The bar was like a community centre, full of colourful local characters, including a few small-time cons who quite openly offered you contraband of all sorts – you could procure anything from weed to gallons of paint and on occasion a brand-new instrument, right there at the bar.

Each week, without fail, we introduced a new tune or song to a packed room. We met some of the great Dublin musicians, including our first bassist, the wily Declan McNelis, who normally played with guitar virtuoso Jimmy Faulkner. We also met a certain young Aussie called Steve Cooney, who introduced us to the sound of the didgeridoo. After most gigs we went to the third floor for late-night drinks and I don't know how many times we were caught by the guards for after-hours, but we made a lot of court appearances as witnesses for the three brothers, proclaiming our innocence and insisting that technically, we were staff finishing a day's shift. As far as I remember they never received an endorsement on their licence and there were no convictions.

Around that time, we secured another residency at the Baggot Inn down on Baggot Street and, combined, these two standing gigs were to prove crucial to our development and success. The public started to take notice.

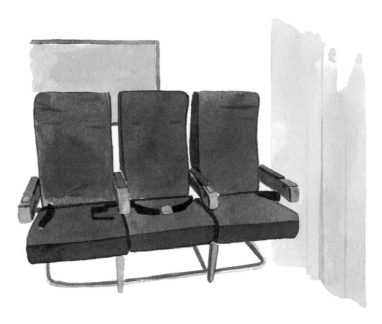

## THE COACH HOUSE

The van was home for so much of our time on the road. So, with the help of an uncle, we procured two rows of aeroplane seats from a decommissioned aircraft at Shannon Airport to make life on the road a more comfortable experience. Complete with armrests and ashtrays, the seats were bolted to the floor, two seats facing three. A wooden panel was erected to separate the PA, instruments and bags. Windows and the driver's section were kitted out with brand-new curtains, and stereo speakers built into the walls. It was quite a cosy set-up.

The van doubled as our hotel on numerous tours, with the addition of a tent. Far from today's touring buses, equipped with air con, running water, full bathrooms, bunk beds, reading lights, WiFi, games consoles, TVs, a full bar and espresso machines, ours was basic. There were only three really comfortable sleeping areas: a mattress on the floor (the deluxe); the two rows of aeroplane seats (the mini suites); and a small floor area between the back row and the wooden panel (economy twin). This entire bedroom area enjoyed privacy and shade, thanks to the curtains. The front passenger seat certainly looked like a nice spacious area to lay one's head, but as dawn approached and the sun rose, the vast windscreen turned the front seat into a veritable sauna. It was the bogey seat, hardly warranting a single star (budget).

Card games passed the endless hours in the van, but one particularly divisive game called 'Lives' decided all the sleeping arrangements. It was not for the faint-hearted nor indeed the slow-witted, as fierce cheating and chicanery were always at the heart of play. Rules were altered by the dealer, so you had to be on high alert. If you broke a rule, missed your turn, or were caught cheating, a series of hefty fines were levied, including at least one overnight stay on the dreaded front passenger seat. It was dog eat dog.

On occasion we hit the jackpot and were offered complimentary hotel rooms, of which we always took full advantage. The luxury of fresh towels, clean sheets, a hot bath and a continental breakfast were hard to match, especially since they also presented an opportunity for lunch. A pillow case was often filled with breads, rolls, pâtés, jams and whatever else was within range on the breakfast buffet table and smuggled out to the van, to be distributed down the road to a bunch of hungry but very happy campers. In the early days, gigs were at small folk clubs or local festivals, which paid very little, but we accepted every invitation to play our music. We were living the dream.

Despite our efforts to make each of our vans into a second home, they proved to be our Achilles heel. Between breakdowns and bad luck, they were a constant drain on our resources – some of which followed us. Driving from Limerick city on our way to Adare, we heard frantic beeping from behind, and saw headlights flashing in our rear-view, so we pulled over, thinking flat tyre. Much to our surprise, our bank manager came running to the window, demanding money and threatening all sorts, so we had to give him a sweetener with a promise to do better. Needless to say, banks chasing you down is not a new phenomenon.

On one Swedish tour, having fitted a new exhaust and a complete set of tyres, the Merc van collapsed just outside Malmö, which ironically is home to one of Mercedes' biggest service centres. However, all the Merc service stations in the world could not save our poor bus, as the engine gave up the ghost and our tour profits went on flights home and a tow truck to get the van across to Denmark, then England and finally back home to Dublin. On another day, in pouring rain, we crashed into the wall of the hospital in Castlerea in Roscommon, on our way to a festival in Donegal. On that occasion, thankfully, Dermot called his friends from Knockvicar and half a dozen vehicles of all shapes and sizes arrived from Boyle, to take us up through the hills of Donegal to play the gig, and later that night, bring us back to the comforts of Smutternagh once again.

# A RAINY NIGHT IN BIRKENHEAD

Coming back from another festival on the Isle of Islay, we stopped in Birkenhead for a few pints to kill a few hours before the ferry sailing from Holyhead. We were only a few miles back on the road when a wheel came off the rented van. Our own wheels were in for yet more repairs, so our regular Dublin rental company had provided a replacement for that particular trip – not that it helped. We were stranded in the Welsh countryside in total darkness, in the rain. Our sound engineer and driver, Mick Barry, the only sober one among us, hitched a lift back into Birkenhead to rally some help. He was gone for hours.

In the back of the van among the equipment sat a case of Bowmore Scottish Single Malt whisky. We were transporting it safely back to Dublin for Tara Records boss John Cooke. After a very short meeting, a sample bottle was opened, the contents of a large plastic Coke bottle emptied into a saucepan, cut in two, and *voilà*, a pair of drinkable beakers. When the Coke ran out, someone suggested the vitamin C soluble tablets we'd once used with a bottle of duty-free vodka, but they proved no match for pure malt – we went neat. We sang lots of songs and then I played a new song from Shane McGowan called 'Rainy Night in Soho'. We played it over and over again, and as we contemplated the third bottle, a very wet, weary and frustrated Mick Barry arrived back with a tow truck and driver.

We poured ourselves into a very small cab for the trip to Holyhead. I often think about that poor misfortunate Welsh tow-truck driver who had to endure a couple of hours of very drunken Irishmen singing into his ear as he tried to concentrate on the road. Mick told us later that we probably got through about a hundred ballads, as we could only remember a line or two from each. John Cooke was none too pleased to be without a few bottles of his favourite tipple, and the person who'd rented the van told us never to come near him again, as this was the third time we'd returned a vehicle in bad shape. It was hardly fair; like we told him, 'The wheel actually fell off the van. We didn't take it off ourselves, you know.'

He wasn't interested. The following week I learned the rest of the words to 'Rainy Night', performed it at a gig in the Harcourt Hotel, and have been singing it ever since.

# THE DINING CAR

The band covered all accommodation and travel costs as well as the severe hire purchase costs, beyond which we managed to pay ourselves a minimum wage to cover our rent and expenses. Economics dictated that we not eat out, so for a couple of hours each day the van was transformed into the Wing family restaurant. A pressure-cooker – a one-time Christmas present to my mother – was borrowed and, as she reminded us for many years, never returned. A two-ring camping gas stove was rooted out of my dad's shed, and someone else provided a bunch of plastic plates. The cutlery was . . . borrowed from somewhere or other, likewise with the salt, pepper and an array of condiments in sachets . . . we were all set. We cooked inside the van and, weather permitting, dined al fresco, a habit we picked up on our travels to warmer climes. I have a vivid memory of our percussionist Tommy Hayes on a beautiful summer's day in a Saint-Jean-de-Maurienne car park at the foot of the French Alps, stirring a bucket full of spuds with a brush handle in the hope of dislodging the brown earth. Health and safety rules did not apply, though we developed a detailed knowledge of good butcher's shops back in Ireland. With a bit of practice, we turned ourselves into a one-pot-wonder band of brothers, producing delightful stews, bacon and cabbage, soups and casseroles.

The position of chef was rotated to those who had the inclination, so I cooked often. Clean-up duties were distributed among the rest, except for the drivers, who had special dispensation. On occasion, one of us had to leave the stage mid-set to fire up a prepared pot for the starving onslaught of musicians immediately after the gig. In winter, the windows steamed up and the smell of simmering stew wafted out through the open skylight, attracting hungry locals wondering if we were a takeaway, something we joked about as a possible sideline.

# FOOD, GLORIOUS FOOD

Sometimes the road wasn't so kind to the hungry travellers. We were on our way to a festival from a gig in northern Italy, heading through the Alps via the impressive Mont Blanc tunnel, then turning south at the border town of Chamonix for a further two-hour journey to our hotel, where we could look forward to a shower, some grub and some relaxation. We'd been driving along narrow snow-filled roads through spectacular scenery for some time when someone said the terrain looked very familiar. There were a few mumbles of concern from the back of the bus as the pack got interested. Questions were put to Mick at the wheel, who was now nervously shifting in his seat as the navigator pulled at the road map. The driver and his cohort tended to stick together on all travel matters. Mick finally announced, 'We're not lost, lads. We're just travelling parallel to the main road, which is over there. We're fine.' You'd have to admire his tenacity. No one believed him, of course.

'You're going parallel all right, Mick. Parallel to the road we were just on, except going the opposite way.'

Outside, the mountains were throwing up a blizzard. The anxious pack was getting hungry. We eventually pulled into a lay-by, where Mick admitted they'd missed a small turn a couple of miles back – 'just a slight mistake'. Three hours later we arrived, cold, miserable, argumentative and very hungry.

The hotel reception ushered us into the heat of the dining room and rattled off a list of French dishes. Someone recognised the term 'cassoulet', repeated in his finest West of Ireland French brogue. 'It's a shtew . . . Grand. We'll all have the shtew.' I have never known a bowl of food to transform such a grumpy mob of whingeing musicians into a brood of satisfied bantam hens, clucking away to their hearts' content after feeding time. Mick asked the woman of the house for the bathroom, and was met with a chorus: 'It's over there, Mick – parallel to the bar . . .'

# WINGING A CASSOULET

Cassoulet is the perfect centrepiece dish for all to dig in, share a nice bottle and a good conversation. I serve it with a crisp salad, a few baked potatoes, some real butter, and wine – although a beer helps the process along very nicely also. It all starts with a duck cooked very slowly; 'confit' means slow-cooked in either fat, salted water or sweet syrup. You can buy confit duck nowadays, but I prefer to make my own (see opposite). You can buy the extra duck fat you'll need to cook it, or you can render your own by slow-roasting a breast or carcass in advance. NB: You need to start 24 hours before you want to serve.

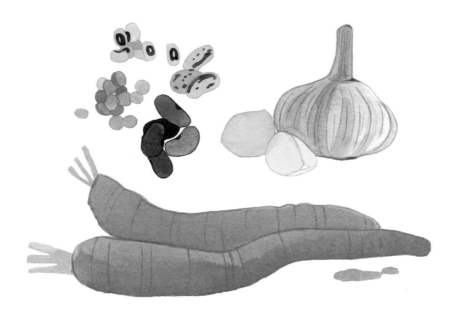

# Duck confit

1 tsp each cumin and coriander seeds, roasted and crushed (optional)
4 juniper berries, crushed (optional)
2 cloves of garlic, crushed
A pinch of sea salt
1 tsp chopped fresh thyme and rosemary leaves
4 duck legs
Duck fat, enough to cover the duck legs
1 bay leaf, crunched
8 whole peppercorns

1. The day before, mix together the roasted spices, juniper, garlic, salt and half the herbs, and rub into the duck flesh. Leave in the fridge for 24 to 36 hours.
2. The next day, wipe the duck legs dry but DO NOT wash.
3. Transfer the duck, duck fat, the rest of the herbs, the bay leaf and peppercorns into a pot and cook very slowly for 3 hours on the hob.
4. Allow to cool, then transfer to a Kilner clip-top jar or an earthenware pot. The meat has to be completely submerged in the liquid.
5. When completely cold and set, place in the fridge until required.

*Once you've eaten the duck, the fat can be used for future confit. The dark jus or liquid gold at the bottom of the jar brings a whole new meaning to a duck stew, soup or casserole. It's also a beautiful addition to a good duck-based risotto.*

# Cassoulet
Feeds 6 to 8 hungry musicians

We cooked a few different versions of this in the van. The word 'cassoulet' comes from the terracotta dish it is traditionally cooked in, called a cassole. This is either stove-top or oven cooking. I believe French people get as animated about cassoulet as the Dubs over coddle, or Leitrim folk and their boxty.

2 tbsp rapeseed oil
300g streaky bacon, chopped
1 onion, peeled and diced
2 cloves of garlic, crushed
3 carrots, diced
2 celery sticks, trimmed and diced
3 fresh Toulouse sausages or good large Irish ones, whole or chopped
4 confit duck legs (see page 93), with the liquid from the confit jar
800g tinned chopped tomatoes
800g cannellini beans, drained and rinsed
2 tsp each of fresh sage and marjoram leaves
500ml chicken stock
2 sprigs of fresh thyme
1 bay leaf (optional)
Sea salt and freshly ground black pepper

1. Use a wide pan, maybe a sauté pan if you are cooking the cassoulet right through on the stove. If planning to cook in the oven, use an oven-safe pan.
2. Preheat the oven to 170°C/150°C fan/gas 3.
3. Heat the oil and fry the bacon for 5 minutes, then add the onion, garlic, carrots and celery, and cook for a couple of minutes until soft. Set aside in a separate dish while you brown the sausages, then set them aside while you crisp the confit.
4. Return everything to the pan and add the tomatoes, beans, chopped herbs, confit liquid, seasoning and chicken stock. Heat gently, then stir for a few minutes. Place the sprigs of thyme and bay leaf, if using, on top and cook on the stove top over a medium heat, or transfer to an oven and bake for 45 minutes.

Some people add a layer of breadcrumbs to the oven version, which crisps beautifully. I once used a recipe that whizzed up breadcrumbs with chickpeas, parsley, marjoram and, of course, butter. I have made my own sausages, plain or flavoured with herbs and fennel, but the simple taste of a Toulouse works really well and it's authentic.

I've had this served with the addition of lamb and pork. I've also heard of a veggie cassoulet, but I am not a fan of tofu or Quorn, so I don't really see the point. Besides, there are plenty of tasty veggie casserole dishes available. For me a cassoulet is a hearty mix of duck, sausage, bacon and beans, and it always reminds me of gigs down in the South of France, surrounded by beautiful mountains, sitting in the sunshine hoping for a glimpse of the Tour de France riders as they go whizzing by.

## THE PLANXTY WING BIG BAND

On that continental trip we played a series of festival gigs with Planxty, performing alternate nights at Brosella Folk in Brussels, followed by a gruelling journey south to Mussolini's old mansion in Rome, and another gig in Cesena near the Adriatic coast, until we finally met again at the Neon Folk Festival in Switzerland to enjoy two days of music and fun. As both bands were enjoying a few beers, the instruments were produced and a session started. The festival organiser arrived in the bar and asked if we'd be up for transferring the session to the now-vacant John Martyn slot on the main stage, as he was fog-bound in Shannon after his appearance at the Lisdoonvarna Folk Festival, and we duly obliged. Punters were treated to Planxty with their sound man Matt Kelligan sitting in on drums, Stockton's Wing and a few stray musicians picked up at the session – and what a day it was.

# Wing Kitchen goulash
Feeds 4 hungry musicians

Goulash very much kept us alive during our early German tours. Whether as a soup or a stew, it certainly gets the job done. Years later, I was delighted to hear Ronnie Drew order a bowl of goulash on our first trip together in Germany. He turned to me and said, 'This has everything you need, Mikie.' So true.

1 tbsp rapeseed oil
2 onions, peeled and chopped
1kg stewing beef, round or chump
2 carrots, diced
1–2 pinches of caraway seeds, crushed
1 clove of garlic, chopped
1 tbsp tomato paste
1 glass of red wine
1 litre beef stock
1 x 400g tin of tomatoes
1 tsp paprika
1 tsp smoked paprika
1 bay leaf
1 sprig of fresh thyme and 1 sprig of fresh rosemary
2 red peppers, cored and diced
2 potatoes, peeled and diced
A pinch of cayenne pepper

1. Heat half the oil in a high-sided pot. Add the onions and cook slowly until caramelised, about 12 minutes. Essential for flavour. Set aside.
2. Heat the rest of the oil in a casserole dish and brown the meat. You may have to do this in batches to get a good colour on it.
3. Add the carrots, caraway and garlic and cook for a few minutes. Add the tomato paste, then the wine and caramelised onions and reduce for a few more minutes.
4. Add the stock, tomatoes, paprika, bay leaf and herbs and cook on a medium heat for 1 hour.
5. Add the peppers, potatoes and cayenne and cook for a further 30 minutes, until the beef is tender and falling from the fork.
6. Serve in bowls, maybe with some extra boiled buttered potatoes on the side.

## OUR FIRST FLAT IN THE BIG SMOKE

Myself, Paul and Maurice moved into our first flat in Ranelagh, where every available space was utilised by the landlord to get the best return on his investment. My bedroom doubled as a sitting room, while Paul's 'box room' was the hallway to a box toilet and hand-held shower. Upstairs, three lads from Wexford paid their rent from the profits of hashish, and the top floor housed a few lads from the Horslips road crew. A communal bathroom for the lot of us on the middle floor just about survived the daily onslaught. It was an experience to say the least, but we had lots of good times there. The Wexford boys had broken the electricity seal, so each day for a few hours the little ignition hook was disarmed, thus reducing our ESB bills to the bare minimum. The public phone outside my room was in constant use and we were educated in the art of phone-tapping. Day and night, I'd hear the constant ratatatatatatat from the old black coin phone on the wall outside my door as tenants nabbed their free calls. The old phones used what was called a Strowger pulse system: as you dialled a number you would hear a series of clicks as each digit registered with the exchange until you were put through. The art of tapping required swift and precise movements to replicate the procedure, with each digit tapped out at speed – you listened for the clicking and moved to the next digit, eight taps for 8, six for 6 and ten for 0. Those phone boxes had two buttons: Button A accepted your coins, and Button B returned them if you could not get through. Neither button got much use at Elm Park Avenue. The landlord eventually came to investigate the enormous discrepancy between his bills and the contents of the coin box, but no one said a word. A note was pinned to the wall threatening the removal of the phone if tapping continued. It continued.

## OUR FIRST HIT SINGLE

PJ Curtis urged us to shift up to another level musically for the follow-up album to *Take a Chance*. I presented a very raw version of 'Beautiful Affair', Kieran and Maurice had written a beautiful piece called 'The Belltable', and it all started from there. Over the following year we wrote and arranged a whole new sound for Stockton's Wing.

Intrigued by the beautiful Gregorian chant emanating from the monks at Glenstal Abbey in County Limerick, PJ suggested we consider a similar approach to the opening stages of 'Beautiful Affair': a huge choral introduction announcing the arrival of this new Wing sound. We worked tirelessly in Ennis, later retreating to the quiet of a fish farm in Wicklow run by a friend of bassist Steve Cooney, where we fine-tuned vocal harmonies and developed a variety of rhythmic patterns. We were introduced to an array of odd percussion instruments, a guiro, a cabasa and a pair of claves – and a cowbell mounted onto an old céilí band clog box. Kieran, Paul and Maurice branched out and joined Tommy as the percussion section. Fran Breen was invited in on drums to give a solid reggae-style structure alongside Steve's bass guitar.

We recorded the song in the autumn of 1981 at Lombard Street Studios with the great Fred Meyer as engineer, assisted by the talented Philip Begley, with Carlos Villa working as tape op. A brilliant engineer, Fred loved his whiskey but was prone to the odd fit of sleep – mid-recording. Philip was young, with an extremely sharp ear. I think Phil manned that desk for many of the thirty-five hours we spent recording 'Beautiful Affair'.

As soon as the basic track was down, all our concentration and effort was spent on that vocal block of sound. Each session produced new layers of expression. Harmonies, counter-melodies, vocal drones all moulded together, rising and falling, sweeping in and out, creating this huge towering wall of voices. It was unlike any other sound in Irish music, and although it lacked the almost angelic sound of its influential monks, it stood out proudly.

'Beautiful Affair' was released towards the end of 1981, but was very slow to take hold. At that time, you had a window of six to eight weeks for a single to filter through radio stations, record shops and then on to the charts. As soon as you hit the charts the workload increased dramatically, as you canvassed DJs, music magazines and TV for extra exposure. It was a crucial few weeks that could make or break a record.

On the first week of release we were playing a few shows in the UK when word came that our manager, for some unearthly reason, had panicked and switched to the B-side, a ditty called 'Céilí Swing', without any consultation with the band. Maurice Lennon and myself flew back to Dublin on the Saturday morning and reversed his decision after a very fiery confrontation at the office. Thankfully, little damage had been done in such a short space of time, but it could have been disastrous. Radio 2, now 2FM, was up and running, and most of the DJs loved 'Beautiful Affair': Declan Meehan, Maxi, Jimmy Greeley, Ronan Collins, Larry Gogan all played the song, and especially Mark Cagney, who had a very popular late-night show called 'Night Train', and raved about it every night. 'It's a sleeper,' he said. 'Give it time, folks. This will be a hit.'

The success brought interest from the UK publisher Dick James Music, and we soon signed to their record label. Terry Wogan started playing it on his morning BBC radio show, declaring, 'I will keep playing this song until you lot make it a hit!' Some weeks later, according to the record company, the song was hovering at number 44 in the British charts and on the verge of breaking through. If it went any higher that week, we were to ready ourselves for an appearance on *Top of the Pops*. Alas, the song peaked that week, and as it went tumbling back down the charts so too did our dreams of sparkly suits from the imaginary *Top of the Pops* costume department. Despite that, we signed with a UK agency and toured extensively on the success of the song, appearing on many TV shows, including our first *Val Doonican Music Show* on the BBC. Back at home, audience numbers increased dramatically practically overnight, and our humble little PA system had to be replaced to cope with the larger venues. We certainly had stepped up to another level.

# A LIGHT IN THE WESTERN SKY

In 1982 work began on the most important album of our career, *Light in the Western Sky*. It had its origins in that beautiful cottage in Smutternagh, Roscommon, Brogan's bar in Ennis, Doolin and the fish farm in Wicklow. To this day, it remains my absolute favourite album, mainly because our young band had so much creative energy, honed beautifully by producer PJ Curtis and engineer Brian Masterson, both men at the top of their game. Their approach was innovative, and this was a time well before push-button digital technology opened us to so many new studio tricks. Editing required incredible skill and concentration, as the engineer painstakingly identified the edit spot, spliced the tape with a razor blade and joined it all together again. These days it's a simple copy and paste. PJ and Brian were like magicians, who conjured up their genius to help us create original classic pieces like 'The Golden Stud', which opens with the eerie sounds of a didgeridoo, moving into the voice of actor Jonathan Ryan quoting the great writer Thoreau: 'There was a time when the music and the beauty were all within.' I look back on those incredible times when the music of Stockton's Wing was no longer within, it was flowing freely all around the studios at Windmill Lane.

We used many special effects and odd instruments like wind chimes, African percussion and piano strings, and odd locations too. Kieran's banjo was tested all over the studio, both inside and out, until PJ settled on a bathroom cubicle. Microphone and playback were set up, and that's where Kieran spent the entire album playing the banjo, sitting on his throne.

The album proved to be well before its time and caused quite a stir among the music press. At the launch, a journalist from Hot Press commented to PJ, 'It's not trad, but it is trad; it's not rock, but it is rock; it's pop, it's new, it's fresh – but what bracket do we fit it into?'

## ALEX 'HURRICANE' HIGGINS

'The Belltable', composed by Maurice and Kieran, is a lengthy, intricate arrangement, beginning with a beautiful waltz that morphs into a lively jig and then goes back to its origins. The switch from 3/4 time to 6/8 jig-time and back proved tricky. We spent hour after hour trying to lay it down, but failed and grew frustrated so we decided to take a break and relax for a while in the green room.

The final of the World Snooker Championship was on TV, between Alex Higgins and veteran Ray Reardon. We were fans of the game and played quite a lot on tour. Higgins was our hero, as he constantly challenged the norms of his world. It was a thrilling final, and from fifteen frames each, Higgins took the next three, to be crowned world champion. The green room was on fire as we leapt and hollered at his success. Elated, we headed straight back into the studio – and, unbelievably, nailed it on the first take. Every time I listen to the track, I am transported back to that green room, the entire band screaming with joy. Good man, Alex.

# 'WALK AWAY'

*I can hear a lonely minstrel on a crowded street,*
*No one stands to listen, they turn and look discreet,*
*See him with his head held high, the music starts to flow*
*He can hear a distant cry reaching out to know.*
— 'Walk Away', *Light in the Western Sky* (1982)

Following the success of 'Beautiful Affair', we released 'Walk Away' in August 1982. The song was inspired by an outrageous and ill-thought-out Dublin City County Council motion to clear the streets of all buskers. At the time of its release, a minor dispute had erupted at RTÉ Radio and they went out on strike. Unsure when music would be back on the national broadcaster, we panicked, and, along with many others, used the illegal pirate stations to promote the single. Pirate radio was tolerated to a large extent by the authorities, who turned a blind eye and every so often organised cosmetic raids, confiscating the equipment, which was later returned intact. Unlike the authorities, however, RTÉ were far more proactive, regularly jamming signals, a practice eventually outlawed by the government. While RTÉ was quiet, hundreds of local radio stations flourished from their disused offices, factory floors, trucks, kitchens and bedsits. In Dublin, Radio Nova, Capital and Sunshine were beginning to take hold and attract serious advertising money, and were proving to be a credible threat to RTÉ's business. When the strike was settled, rumour went around that RTÉ was privately putting an embargo on artists who used alternative radio to promote their music. We came on to their radar for whatever reason and they were not playing 'Walk Away'. Our manager went to the press and caused a little stir. We hit the headlines, and of course RTÉ denied it, explaining in a newspaper interview that the song just wasn't good enough.

Larry Gogan, RTÉ DJ and national treasure, had a Top-30 chart show on Sunday afternoons. Our priority was made very clear: chart entry, whatever the cost. It was well known that it was the sales figures of specific record shops throughout Ireland that made up a large percentage of the music charts, so off we went on a shopping spree. I know . . . it was very bold, but desperate times and all that. We got the news on the Wednesday that we limped into the charts at number 23, and on the Sunday, huddled around the radio to hear Larry announce 'Walk Away', the new single from Stockton's Wing. We spent a few more weeks in the charts, and though we may have privately claimed some sort of moral – if very expensive – victory, we were realistic enough to understand that we really didn't need a continued spat with RTÉ. Bridges were quickly mended, and the positive relationship got back on track, and remains strong to this day. But, my memento of those stormy weeks is what might be the world's largest collection of that single – in my attic.

*We walk away, talk away, looking for someone to blame,*
*Feeling fine, singing a line, I can see no other way –*
*Walk away.*

## AU REVOIR, NICE TO BE HERE

*So, if you have been born to be a rambler,*
*You've taken to that highway for a home,*
*Never let that world fall around you*
*And never fall around the world you own.*
     – 'No Worries', *Celtic Roots Revival* (1988)

No one handed us a book of etiquette as we left Ennis to make our way around the highways and byways of Europe. We had no yardstick and knew little about the various customs or eating habits of our many host countries, each presenting its own new and sometimes hilarious challenges.

Kieran and Maurice had basic French, which certainly got us in the front door. I understood a little Dutch, but had zero German, Swedish or Italian. We quickly learnt the rudiments of each language: hello, goodbye, thanks and two beers please. Our agent suggested very early on that I should use the local language for all introductions, which I duly did, arriving at the gigs searching for a local to help me write down each intro phonetically, adding little snippets of regional dialect along the way. I noticed that outrageous grammatical errors were always very well received, so I worked hard to mix my metaphors, tenses and genders. It certainly helped me to connect with the audience, as I'd greet the room with a warm, 'Au revoir! Nice to be here.'

# MR PASTIS

Cultural differences accounted for other faux pas. We arrived in the historic port town of Brest in north-west Brittany to be greeted by the Lord Mayor, who hosted a civic reception in our honour. At the town hall we were greeted by the dignitaries and offered a glass of pastis, a liqueur with a distinctive aniseed flavour. Watered down and served with ice, it was offered as an aperitif. Thinking it was like one of those weak German schnapps we'd tried the previous week, we had no idea as to its potency. We gladly accepted a refill and then another before we were ushered into the stately room, where a reasonable crowd applauded our entrance. There was a huge oval table brimming with beautiful, colourful dishes: duck salads, pasta salads, artichokes, poached eggs on leaves, green beans, mangetout, Puy lentils, corn, mixed leaves, brown and white rice salads, couscous, olive oils and baskets of fresh bread. Our hosts encouraged us to sit and eat, and, starving as usual, we got stuck in and filled our plates high. By contrast, our host and the other guests took very conservative servings and placed them gently on their plates as they chatted. They seemed amused by our approach. Suddenly, a team of waiters cleared all dishes and left, passing another team with trays of piping-hot food, which we attacked with the same gusto. There was squid, prawns, mussels, flat fish, round fish, smoked fish and lobster. Again, our hosts only ate morsels, as us Irish boys went hell for leather.

Halfway through, someone paused long enough to ask, 'I wonder is there more, lads? Maybe we should calm down and see?' Our appetites were all but sorted when the clearing team reappeared, only to be followed by a regiment bearing platters of steaming chicken, duck and steaks. Finally, and with a little fanfare, the head chef emerged in a very tall hat to carve an enormous beef roast. With much hand signalling and very broken English, someone had finally gotten through to Maurice. 'We Bretons like to eat . . . A little, but many times, no? You understand?' As they giggled good-naturedly, we realised we'd made a balls of it.

We passed on that course, nibbled at the cheese, and kept a little room for pudding. As my dad used to say, we were 'well bate' by the end of the dinner. How we managed to get up from the table and perform a half-hour set for the Lord Mayor is beyond me. Photographs of that session show us playing away, beaming, our feet tapping away beside several glasses of pastis. We retired to the van for a much-needed hour's rest before the evening concert at the local hall, where we played a full set. We managed it, but perhaps we weren't at our sharpest. 'Take a Chance' opens with Paul playing a beautiful, low whistle, followed by two long verses and choruses before he re-enters with a second solo. Halfway through the second chorus, I spotted him sound asleep on the chair, head bowed onto his chest, whistle on his lap. Maurice gave him a kick in the shin, and he jumped to attention and broke into the solo, almost in perfect time. The audience were watching it all, cheering with laughter.

Afterwards, there was an extremely positive review in the local paper, which our agent sent on to us. Unbeknown to us, the reviewer had been with us all day and wrote a brilliant piece on the concert, the earlier session for the Lord Mayor, and had a laugh at our new-found love of pastis, not to mention our eating and drinking habits, which he rated as legendary. He wasn't wrong.

## STARS TO THE FRONT

Back in Ireland, our life was studded with certain events that left indelible marks on our music business education. One was a protest march to Dáil Éireann, organised by the Lombard Street band managers to put pressure on the government to increase radio play for Irish bands. Everyone gathered outside the Unitarian church on Stephen's Green on a brisk morning. Band manager Jim Hand went through the crowd to organise the group, shouting, 'OK, listen up now. Stars to the front, stars to front, now, lads,' taking Joe Dolan's arm and pulling him through to the vanguard. Being fresh country boys, we didn't want to be left out in case there was any publicity to be had. 'Let's get up there, lads, up where the action is,' Kieran said. As we made our way forward, another famous showband manager stopped us in our tracks. 'Did ye not hear what Big Jim said, boys? Stars to the front. Hold back there a while, lads, we have to get the stars to the front first.' We melted back into the lower ranks suitably humbled, but from that moment on 'stars to the front' took on a whole new meaning – it almost became our battle cry.

# SMOKE OUT

After the release of *Light in the Western Sky* we introduced drums and a bass guitar to the line-up. The live show also had the addition of 'The Light Revue', a pyrotechnic lighting presentation designed to match the dynamics of the music. It featured a state-of-the-art hydraulic lighting rig, which if truth be known probably spent most of its early days in the van, being far too big for some of the venues we played.

The live show opened with the gentle sounds of Stravinsky's 'Firebird' suite as slow-release coloured smoke bombs rose from the floor, filling the stage, lights beaming, swirling and flashing to the tune. We crept into our positions and six flash-bombs exploded as the final note reached its crescendo. It was spectacular for its time and certainly very different for most of the venues we were playing. Unfortunately, not all stages were built for such an extravaganza. Queens Hotel in Ennis had a tiny box stage, so as soon as the coloured smoke rose, it had nowhere else to go. A cloud rolled out and engulfed the entire room, creating a cacophony of spluttering, choking, moans and lots of laughter. As we walked out onto the clear stage, we looked down at a scene so dense with smoke you could barely pick out a human form. To make matters worse, it was our hometown gig, so we heard about it for weeks afterwards. 'Jaysus, where on earth are ye going with all that smoke? Ye nearly suffocated the entire town!'

# CHAPTER 5

# BAND OF BROTHERS

# AMERICA

In 1984 we signed with American agency Herschel Freeman and embarked on a mammoth tour of Canada and the US, with our first performance at the Orange Hall in Edmonton, home to the local folk club. The gig was organised by Big Jim McLaughlin, a Scottish nationalist immigrant piper and great friend of our mates the Tannahill Weavers, whose singer Dougie McClean went on to write that iconic ballad 'Caledonia'. Behind us onstage hung a photograph of the Queen Mother, and every now and then Paul turned to place the whistle to her mouth so she could join in on a few jigs and reels. The *craic* was great that night and we had a wonderful time with Big Jim. From there we went to Calgary, where mercifully, we experienced the wonder of the Chinook winds, a warm Pacific phenomenon that sweeps in from the mountains and clears the snow from the ground in a matter of hours. Chinook is the name of the local tribe and translates as 'ice eater'.

We then flew south across the US border to Spokane, on to Oregon and during the four weeks covered over twenty states, including gigs in California, Texas, Michigan, Ohio and the first of some memorable visits to Louisiana. How I loved the energy on Bourbon Street in New Orleans, with its music, dancers and constant smell of Louisiana cooking. We spent a few days there, which gave us time to take in the atmosphere of the city. I befriended a local music shop owner who brought me to his family home out in the bayou, where his wife introduced me to her blackened shrimp and gumbo pie.

# BOSTON

From New Orleans, we travelled to Madison, Wisconsin; Iowa City; Chicago; Louisville, where we played with Béla Fleck; eventually landing at Logan Airport in Boston for a couple of gigs with Tommy McGann at the Purple Shamrock. Tommy collected us from Logan in a battered pickup truck – seven tired bodies, two in the front and five in the back, crushed together with a collection of instruments, freezing cold as we drove through the Kojak skyline. On our next visit, Tommy arrived with a few of the girls from his new bar on the Cape, in a stretch limo complete with beers, champagne and a box of Tayto crisps. It was back to the pickup the time after that, because you never really knew with Tommy, though it was better than the few times he completely forgot we were arriving, but hey, that was just how it worked with him.

# 'THRILLER' AT MILWAUKEE IRISH FEST

The American audience really took to the sound and energy of Stockton's Wing. There were very few bands developing new Irish music at the time, and we were bringing new levels of syncopation into intricate arrangements of traditional tunes, as well as writing contemporary pop songs. While we may have upset a few purists with our approach, the audiences, particularly the younger ones, relished our style of music and came out in droves. By the time we played Milwaukee Irish Fest in 1984, we had a very exciting electric sound. It was a reasonably conservative Irish-American family affair, with plenty of young kids wandering around the festival listening to the music of their parents' generation, primed for something exciting to happen. After the first of four shows, word had spread about a new young Irish band who played Michael Jackson's 'Thriller' in the middle of a set of reels. By Sunday, we were the only game in town.

In that summer of '84 we certainly blazed a trail through America. Over the next few years we played the folk, bluegrass and Irish festivals during the summer months; autumn brought us on the theatre and college circuit; and March was almost exclusively Irish-American celebrations of Paddy's Day. Some of the college radios had taken to 'Beautiful Affair', which certainly helped our profile in America, while at home our profile grew with each week, as RTÉ played our music constantly and the band appeared on the *Late Late* at least twice each season. We were regulars with Mike Murphy, Bibi Baskin and boxer Barry McGuigan, who had a run of chat shows on RTÉ.

There was one thing we did a bit differently, which I believe really helped us build our profile and keep our engagement with the audiences fresh. We made it a policy, whenever possible, to play concerts at secondary schools the afternoon before the evening event in any town we were visiting. I loved these gigs, and so did the students. It surprises me that very few of the current crop of artists play the school circuit, as it's such a rewarding thing to do, and the kids never forget the excitement of the gig.

## THE PURPLE RAIN GIGS

We played a few gigs at the First Avenue Club in Minneapolis, home of Prince. On our first night, the crew, all African-American, stood watching us inquisitively, wondering what on earth was going on with banjos, fiddles, flutes, guitars and drums. As we played our first sound check piece they gathered around side stage and front of house to listen to this weird music; they'd clearly never heard too many jigs and reels. When we finished, they clapped and whistled with all thumbs up in our direction, which meant a lot. It was plain sailing after that – the gig was a sell-out, and the room was heaving. First Avenue was a very special place to perform; some venues just have that extra energy, it's in the walls and in the air. I'm sure the Prince connection helped, as the club featured in the movie *Purple Rain*. We went back there a few times to that same lovely warm welcome and great crew. In 1990 we'd play support to Prince in Cork and meet some of that same crew again, who stood side stage with members of Prince's band to hear us play.

## NEW YORK, NEW YORK

Our final gig on that first trip was New York, and I couldn't wait to see the Big Apple: so big, bold, brash and in your face. From the moment you walk through arrivals at Kennedy, it's all action, everyone in a hurry: passengers, security, bag handlers, cabbies chasing fares as they fire abuse at each other, sirens wailing and honking horns. We managed to get two cabs and on the first journey into town we were like children at the zoo, and shared that moment of, 'Oh, so that's why they're called "skyscrapers".' Yet as our cab hit every pothole in the street, you got the first sense that maybe this place wasn't all it was cracked up to be.

On our journey in we spoke in broken Irish about the infamous American tipping system. The two cabs arrived together, and had clocked fees of $23.50 and $24.60, respectively. We settled on $25 each – 'that should be grand' – we all agreed, except the two cabbies, who returned the compliment with a string of abuse, New York style.

The Iroquois in midtown Manhattan would be our New York HQ for many years. As the disgruntled taxi men peeled off, a man in a fancy coat and hat arrived out of the hotel with a team of helpers and trolleys, packed up our bags and delivered them to the reception area, where they stood around while we checked in. Though already relatively cheap, the real attraction of the Iroquois was the unlimited number of bodies we could fit into two rooms. At reception, we were immediately informed that the great Hollywood star James Dean had lived there for almost two years, and that back in the 30s, one of the bellboys famously murdered a guest. Unfortunately, the loitering doorman and his assistants didn't fare much better than the cabbies. What did we know? We were Paddies, just over from the west of Ireland. But come to think of it, I wonder was that bellboy so irritated by the size of a tip that he took it out on the unfortunate guest?

We'd eaten everything on that trip from Tex-Mex chilli to Boston shrimps, Maryland crabs, jambalaya, steaks and all sorts of breakfast dishes, but the one we were all looking forward to was a Big Apple . . . Big Mac. After settling into the rooms, we met at the bar and headed out in search of the Great One. We located the Golden Arches a couple of blocks away, ordered and sat back in anticipation. We were convinced it would be so big we'd have difficulty sinking our teeth into it. After all, this is New York, right? We were so disappointed when we opened the boxes to discover they were the exact same size as the ones back in Dublin.

## ALL YOU CAN EAT

The steaks, however, hang over the side of your plate, they're so big. Some restaurants offer a free steak if you manage to eat one the size of a cow. All-you-can-eat diners and truck stops are a godsend to tired, cranky, hungry bands on a long tour. My friends, singer Roy Buckley and accordionist Dominic Leech – both men who love the grub – recently recalled a very funny incident in a New York steakhouse. They ordered and cleaned two T-bones, and when the waitress asked if they wanted dessert, Dominic pointed to the bone on the plate and said, 'We'll have two more of them please, thanks very much.' She hesitated for a second until she realised they were for real. As the two lads made their way through the second helping, the kitchen staff gathered at the counter to witness this incredible event. The sign did say 'All you can eat'.

# THE RISE AND FALL OF THE MAGNIFICENT SEVEN, 1989

In 1989 we ended a gruelling run of gigs from Ireland to the UK, back to Ireland and then straight over to Gaelic Park in Chicago to begin a ten-day trip that included Boston, New York and LA. We finished with an afternoon gig in the sunshine at a crazy bar called Lunny's in Orange County, California, owned by an old family friend, Clare man Ray Tubridy. Ray was a former professional pool player and hustler who, believe it or not, won the pub in a game of pool. We badly needed some downtime, so Tubs gave us his very large Winnebago RV and sent us south of the border into Tijuana. There we spent a few hours soaking up the atmosphere and drinking margaritas on a sunlit veranda before heading down along the beautiful Pacific coastline. We pulled into a small hotel just outside Ensenada in darkness, checked in and decided to ramble up the street for some food. We stopped by a traditional-looking Mexican bar and settled in for the evening. We were hardened fans of Mexican food, having tasted our share of tacos, enchiladas, quesadillas and all sorts of chillies, but this somehow felt more than special. A group of local musicians came into the restaurant and started playing. When they discovered we were musicians, the party really started, and we got to know that infamous swimming worm in the bottom of a couple of bottles of tequila.

The following morning, someone suggested we hire seven ponies and race along the beach to clear the heads. What a cure for a tough night it proved to be, as the Magnificent Seven readied themselves to ride again. We all loved horses, but keyboard player Peter was an

# Chilli Paddy Carney

Serves 4

A glug of rapeseed oil
1 large onion, peeled and diced
500g top-quality beef, diced
2 cloves of garlic, crushed
2 tbsp ground spice mix: cumin, coriander, garam masala and chilli flakes
1 tbsp ground chipotle chilli, or use paste
1 tbsp fresh marjoram, chopped
400g tinned tomatoes or passata
250ml good red wine
250ml beef or chicken stock
25g dark chocolate (optional)
1 lime, zested and juiced
400g tinned kidney, pinto or cannellini beans, drained and rinsed
1 courgette, diced
1 yellow pepper, cored and diced
1 red pepper, cored and diced
1 tbsp balsamic vinegar
Rice, quinoa, salsa and lime wedges, to serve (optional)

1. Preheat the oven to 160°C/140°C fan/gas 2.
2. Put a little oil into a heavy, ovenproof casserole dish and fry the onion.
3. Add the beef and cook in batches until coloured.
4. Tip all the meat back into the pan and add the garlic, spices, chipotle and half the marjoram. Mix well.
5. Add the tomatoes or passata, wine, stock, chocolate and half the lime juice, and bring to the boil.
6. Cook in the oven for 1½ hours. Stir in the beans, courgette, peppers and vinegar and continue to cook on the hob for 40 minutes, stirring occasionally.
7. Sprinkle with the lime zest and the remaining herbs and lime juice. Serve with rice or a flavoured quinoa, tomato and avocado salsa and some lime wedges.

exceptional horseman. My love of horses goes back to Charlie, my granddad's trusty steed, and had been rekindled when a friend of mine set up a horse-riding school at her farm in the Dublin mountains and suggested I take a few lessons.

After my first morning, I was hooked and went out at least once a week. At first, bumping along at a gentle trot, until I had the confidence to canter through the woods and fields – oh, that feeling of freedom, excitement and a little dread as you rose into the air over fence or ditch at the total mercy of your cob. Set up in our comfy American saddles, we revelled in that beach race, then headed back to our friends at the restaurant and had another right hooley, instruments in hand.

Horses reappeared in our touring life the following year on a weekend of gigs in Reykjavík. Our hosts brought us out to the wonderful hot springs for a dip before introducing us to those little darlings, Icelandic ponies. After our Mexican success, myself and Peter were excited for a pony ride, but the rest of the lads decided to stay on solid ground. We saddled up, confident that nothing could go wrong. They were only small little things after all, no bother. We were given a few quick lessons which we didn't really take in, and as soon as the farmer smacked their behinds, the ponies flew into a canter. Their speed increased with each stride, and squeezing the reins just made them run faster and faster and faster and faster. We quickly lost control, as these little guys clearly knew they were in charge of our fate. Peter took his chances and jettisoned safely onto soft ground, but I came to an abrupt halt a minute later, ditched unceremoniously to the hard volcanic ground. I hit the earth with an unmerciful thud that sent me rolling towards a wall of black lava, but I stopped short. The farmer came running to our aid as we rose gingerly in terrible pain. As we limped back to the paddock he explained – like we needed an explanation – that our manoeuvres had only urged the ponies on. The rest of the lads were doubled over, screeching with laughter. 'Four faults there, Mikie! Disqualified!' On the way back to the hotel someone started humming 'Two

Little Boys' – it was relentless. The bodies were well bruised, but not as badly as our egos.

We discovered lots of new food, flavours and traditions while touring America, but I particularly fell in love with Mexican cuisine. The chilli on page 112 is not authentic Mexican food by any stretch – I serve it up in honour of those magnificent seven Irishmen who rode down that Ensenada beach and off into the Pacific sunset.

## DEF LEPPARD AND LEITRIM SOCCER

The Pink Elephant on Molesworth Street in Dublin was the nightclub of choice for many in the music business, usually followed by a trip over to Suesey Street on Leeson Street until the wee hours of the morning, where the only grub was a packet of Hula Hoops washed down by very low-grade but highly priced wine. We hung out there with a few English bands who were over to record at Windmill Lane Studios. We met the Bay City Rollers, the Thompson Twins and the wonderful Def Leppard, who were working on the album *Hysteria* with Mutt Lange. We struck up a great friendship with Def Leppard and met often at launches, charity dinners, house parties and of course the nightclubs. On one occasion they boasted of their prowess on the football pitch, claiming they could all have been professional footballers after their successful trials with Sheffield United. We had our own team of sorts and played a few celebrity charity matches, including some memorable battles with Hot Press staff, offering the perfect opportunity to right a negative review. We were well ready to take on some would-be pros when the Leppards laid down the gauntlet to the Wing. We beat them every single time, and enjoyed plenty of victory pints at the Galloping Green pub in Stillorgan. One game out in Mounttown in Dun Laoghaire turned dirty, when guitarist Steve spent the first half running rings around Maurice with fancy hip movements, nutmegs and far too many giggles – uncalled for in a gentlemen's game. Maurice eventually had enough and decided to employ a move from the Leitrim school of defending. Steve was just about to pirouette when Maurice lunged and sent him into the air, hitting the ground with a clatter. A litany of abuse followed. The game carried on until minutes later, Steve was on the rampage again, headed straight for Maurice, but somehow hit a brick wall and lay there writhing in pain. He was forced to limp off to the side and sit out the remainder of the game. Back in the pub for post-match pints, we reminded Steve, as is the Irish custom, of his inability to round a humble amateur Leitrim man – and he nearly after signing for the English first division.

# DEF LEPPARD IN BALLYBUNION

On New Year's Day in 1985 we got news of Leppard drummer Rick Allen's terrible car accident outside Sheffield. He miraculously survived, but lost his left arm. He was determined to play again, spending the next year and a half developing a new system and technique which involved increased use of his feet to play a specially designed kit. It was an incredible feat of courage and determination. A world tour was announced, but the band wanted to play some low-key gigs, without the stadium fuss to test the stage and Rick's new drum system. We called a few of our regular venues to set up a weekend of shows. The band charged very nominal fees, but unfortunately, someone in their London office sent out the world tour contracts and caused all sorts of consternation and confusion, particularly with John Kissane down at the Atlantic Ballroom in Ballybunion. John called us asking if they were mad, looking for all that stuff in the rider. 'Jaysus, they're only short of asking me to take out the purple Smarties!' he said. The regular rider included specific foods, whiskies, champagne, PA specs and all the rest that is required for a 10,000-seater venue. I'm sure it floored John, but everything was soon sorted and the band set out on their mini-tour of Ireland.

We played Ballybunion on that Friday night and hung around all day Saturday to welcome the boys to town. The articulated trucks roared into the sleepy seaside town shortly after breakfast, drawing locals and holidaymakers out to view the spectacle. The stage was built, PA rigged, enormous lighting trusses put in place. Poor John was losing the will to live as he watched most of his venue disappear into the performance space. At capacity the hall would normally fit about 2,000 people standing. That was well halved. 'How in Jaysus's name will I fit all the crowd into that small spot?'

Rick arrived with another drummer on back-up duty and they started their sound check. We had to leave for another show. By all accounts the gig was incredible, with many people standing outside in the courtyard listening to the sounds of Def Leppard beneath a Ballybunion sky. I have the cutting from the Kerryman. The list of the weekend performers ran: Friday, Stockton's Wing; Saturday, Def Leppard; and Sunday, Chuckwagon, a local duo. I often wondered what they made of all the fuss and commotion.

## A NICE CUPPA TEA

In 1985, myself and Anne Burke organised a GOAL gig for Sudan at the National Stadium on South Circular Road in Dublin. Anne had been working as a nurse in various famine-torn countries serviced by GOAL. We pulled together a fine line-up that included the Wing, the Dubliners, Mary Coughlan, Mary Black and Chris de Burgh. I called Chris's London agent to see if he had any special backstage requirements. He started to list off a variety of hot and cold foods, water, fruit juices, salads . . . I soon stopped writing and waited for him to finish. 'You know this is a charity gig, and all proceeds go to Sudan. The only people getting paid a nominal fee will be the PA company. Fitzers Restaurant are throwing in free grub in the afternoon, some sandwiches later, we'll have a few cases of soft drinks and beers from a local cash and carry and that's about it.'

'Oh, I know,' he replied, 'but these are the requirements for all his tours . . . ' And he started in on another rant about pianos and lights.

I cut him off. 'Sorry to butt in here: this rider alone could probably feed half the population of Sudan for a week. I'll get back to you.' And I hung up.

I called Anne and said I could not possibly agree with these requests. She phoned back later to say all was sorted, and then Chris called to apologise for the insensitive requests, begging forgiveness for the guy in London. When I asked what he really required, he replied, 'A nice cuppa tea would be lovely, Mike.' He gave a powerful performance and was everything you could expect from a gentleman.

## HAUGHEY'S LITTLE IRELANDER

*See him on the TV take a shadow for a substance,*
*Lead us blindly down the road to ruin,*
*With no rhyme or reason still believin', still deceivin',*
*He's building walls that keep on falling down,*
*Why wait until tomorrow, why wait at all?*
　　　　　　　　– 'Why Wait Until Tomorrow', *Full Flight* (1986)

Very early on Sunday 28 July 1985 we flew into Cork from a festival in Porto in Portugal and were given a police escort out to Páirc Uí Chaoimh for Siamsa Cois Laoi, an annual music event which attracted thousands of visitors. There

is nothing quite like the feeling of self-importance as the police escort speeds its way through the streets, breaking red lights, sirens blaring, motor bikes whizzing by – well, as long as it's not taking you to court. Kris Kristofferson was headlining that year, and Charles J. Haughey was hovering around, filming for his soon-to-be-released self-absorbed video, *Charles Haughey's Ireland*, lauding his own greatness and flaunting his wealth. I had recently read *The Boss* by Joe Joyce and Peter Murtagh, a true and detailed account of the corrupt government between March and November 1983, including a glance at Haughey's early years, his influences and an insight into his thirst for absolute power at whatever cost.

I supported Fianna Fáil on occasion, and the band recorded an election song for them at one point called 'There is a Better Way', but that book had shaken my political views to the core. I was sitting in the dressing room when word came through that Charlie was on his way to say hello to the band as part of his video recording. I brushed past his entourage out onto the pitch until the meet-and-greet ended. On my return, I was asked for an interview, as I was the main spokesman for the band. It is one of the few Stockton's Wing interviews I ever missed – and I never regretted it once. Despite my bowing out, Haughey's narcissistic video does contain the music of Stockton's Wing on the soundtrack, but there's nothing much more I could have done about that, being the only member of the band riled by his presence. We lived in a democracy after all.

*Destiny will come to those who scorn the path of reason,*
*Lead them to the flames of burning pride.*
*We'll see the cloak of deception cast into the ocean,*
*In the morning watch a new day rise.*
*Why wait until tomorrow, why wait at all?*
  – 'Why Wait Until Tomorrow', *Full Flight* (1986)

## WACKO JACKO

We returned to Páirc Uí Chaoimh in 1988 to play support for both of the
*Michael Jackson Thriller World Tour* gigs. We played before Kim Wilde,
and as far as I know we were the only local act to appear at any of his gigs.
Memorable days, and although we never met the man himself, we spent a
good few hours in the company of his band, who were more than generous
with their support and time. I can still remember the cheer that went up as
we were announced out onto the stage. Cork was very proud to welcome one
of their own that day, and the gig was timely, as our profile was beginning to
wane after a few years in vogue.

## FROM PRINCES TO PAUPERS

We appeared at that stadium once again in 1990 as support to Prince, though we
never met him then either, nor did we see his performance, as we had another
gig already booked that evening at the Salthill Festival in Galway. Life threw us
a great lesson that day, a humbling one that comes around every now and again
to keep you somewhat grounded, and in our case to remind us just how fickle
the entire music scene can be at times.

The Salthill show was an annual event for us and always guaranteed a lively
promenade packed with people enjoying live music in the evening sunshine.
One of the best gigs in our calendar. We accepted the Prince invitation after
securing a helicopter ride from Cork to Galway. Whatever fee we received went
to cover our transport. When the Cork show ended, we ran from the stage to a
waiting chopper that soon rose majestically above a beautiful sun-drenched Páirc
Uí Chaoimh, waving to its crowd of more than 30,000 people as we set off on the
short journey to Salthill. It felt very rock and roll and we were all a-buzz after a
brilliant gig in front of a very vocal and supportive crowd.

As we crossed the Shannon the rain arrived, then the heavens opened, and by the time we hit Galway it was pelting down as we circled a rainy windswept promenade that was completely isolated apart from the stage crew, who were huddled under a canopy. As we ran from the chopper we heard a few cars beeping from the nearby car park. In the space of one hour we had gone from the high of sun-drenched Páirc Uí Chaoimh to the very dramatic low of Salthill in the drowning rain. The weather eased eventually, and we performed to a very sparse crowd who braved the uncertain conditions. Some remained in the comfort and warmth of their cars, showing appreciation by tooting their car horns. It was a day when you understood the saying, 'You are only as good as your last gig.'

> *Share a little laughter, a little shelter from the pain,*
> *And when you're feeling low you know you've got*
> *No worries, because sunshine will always follow rain.*
> — 'No Worries', *Celtic Roots Revival* (1988)

## IT'S THE JOE DUFFY SHOW

Around that time Marian Finucane was hosting a very popular RTÉ Radio 1 afternoon talk show called *Liveline*. Her producer Julian Vignoles called to ask if they could use one of our tracks as the signature tune to a revamped programme. We were delighted and listened in regularly – only to hear the tune, not the country's gossip, of course. When Joe Duffy replaced Marian, we were sure the tune would follow suit, but it's still there Monday to Friday, welcoming the country to air their views and problems on the *Joe Duffy Liveline*.

## MR BOJANGLES

Our manager Oliver Barry was also a major concert promoter, whose events had included all the Siamsa Cois Laoi gigs in Cork, and Michael Jackson and a host of other major stars who performed in Ireland during the 80s. In 1989 he promoted the 'Ultimate Event', featuring Frank Sinatra, Liza Minnelli and Sammy Davis Jr., for two nights at Lansdowne Road. Oliver called to offer us a gig at a pre-concert private party for the show's stars and entourage, to be held on the night before at the old Horseshoe House pub in Ballsbridge. We were delighted. When we arrived, we were led upstairs to a blacked-out room, where we met the tour manager – I think his name was Bob – who gave us a list of instructions for the evening, performance times, etiquette while meeting the guests, and an absolute ban on any photographs with the stars. If any were taken, our film would be confiscated. The official photographer, Charlie Collins, was instructed to hand up all his rolls at the end of the night to be vetted by the crew.

We were no strangers to corporate events, which required you to play as the guests arrived and chatted, often quite loudly. You might be required to perform in between the courses at dinner, with a final concert-style presentation before dessert. These gigs can be hard on musicians, but sometimes they lead to better things. I learned to get through the tough ones with advice received from Ronnie Drew: 'Keep the head down, smile and collect the readies.'

At about 7.30 we were asked to begin, as the guests had left the hotel and were expected quite soon. About twenty minutes into our set a commotion began, men and women on full alert, frantically running about with walkie-talkies. 'The guests have arrived, over.' 'On the way . . . over.' It was all very American, presidential-style, organised and controlled by Bob, the tour manager.

Just then, Frank Sinatra appeared through a black curtain, walked by, lifted his glass in salute and sent that iconic look of approval in our direction. Wow. Frank Sinatra is in the house. Not as tall as I expected, impeccably groomed and looking extremely agile. Liza Minnelli soon followed, beautifully dressed with a bright, broad, sparkling smile. 'Hi guys, thank you so much for the lovely music.' Oh my word, Liza Minnelli, *Cabaret* star performer, Judy Garland's daughter and she's in the house.

Then a tiny figure appeared, the great Sammy Davis Jr. How many times had we watched him on the television growing up in Ennis? How many times had we played 'Mr Bojangles' from one of Dad's random collections? Sammy stopped and listened to us play. When we finished, he sat with us for a long time, talking about Dublin, Ireland, his excitement for the two shows, and he was mesmerised by Paul's tin whistle playing. He could not believe the sound he was producing: 'How can you get so much music from that little penny whistle?' Himself and Paul then got into a conversation about his 150-year-old concert flute. He talked about the various rhythms of our music, about the links between Irish dancing and American tap, he understood the connection to bluegrass, spoke about the Irish influence in jazz, big band and rhythm and blues. All the time referring to the music of the people, the folk music. It

seemed to me that his entire being was consumed by the rhythm of music. He wished us well and made his way to his table.

We played through dinner and left the stage to Brendan Grace, who delivered a powerful set that would prove to be one of the most important of his career, as it led to many successful shows in Las Vegas and beyond. When dinner finished, Sammy Davis made his way back over to our table and specifically asked about a set of tunes that had caught his ear called 'The Golden Stud'. After a short conversation he turned to us and said, 'Guys, I would really like you to join me on stage tomorrow night to play while I tap. Do you think that would work for you guys?' We were aghast. 'Of course we will – thank you so much.'

'Well,' he continued, 'I guess tap has its origins in Scotland and Ireland, right? So it makes sense that you guys play with me tomorrow night. Bob will sort out all the details. Hey, thanks for the great music, you guys can really play.'

Bob suggested we get to the stadium about 2 p.m. for a run-through with Sammy. The following day we walked up to the gates to get backstage when Bob came towards us. 'Hey guys, what you doin' here?'

Our hearts sank. 'We're here to play with Sammy, he invited us last night.'

'Ah, guys. Sorry about that, he's always doing things like that. That's not going to happen. I forgot about it myself . . . So sorry, guys.'

He turned and started to walk away. We looked at each other in disbelief. We'd called the office earlier that morning to confirm the gig, and told all our

families and friends. Someone suggested it must have been the drink talking, and we all agreed. Just then we heard bellows of laughter. 'Hey guys, only jokin'. Got you guys goin' though, hey! Mr Davis will see you now . . . come on, follow me and we'll get you settled in. We're all so excited that you're doing the show. You guys were awesome last night. Sammy has been talking about you all morning.'

He brought us into one of the mobile homes parked along the walkway to the stage. 'This is yours for the two nights, make yourselves at home. Sound check in about thirty, and Sammy wants to see you guys beforehand, so don't go anywhere.' Hardly.

Sammy greeted us, brought us to the stage and introduced us to the orchestra, who applauded our entrance – that was a lovely moment. We went through a few tunes until we settled on a set of reels to suit his dance routine. In the wings, Liza Minnelli was tapping her feet and smiling. To her right stood composer and conductor Frank Sinatra, Jr. It was all surreal. After two rehearsals, Sammy announced, 'That's going to be great, guys. We need to keep some of that energy for the show, right? See you later.' The orchestra cheered us off the stage as we passed Liza and Frank Jr. along the way – and that was just the sound check.

## A TWO-WAY STREET

The welcoming Lansdowne roar was deafening as Sammy called us out on to his stage. The performance was magnificent, and how he danced – the energy. After his show he stopped by our dressing room. 'Guys, that was so great. Did you hear that crowd? They loved it. Same time tomorrow?' The newspapers were full of photographs and positive reviews of our performance. On the second night, Sammy stopped by our dressing room with his lovely wife, Altovise, and this time stayed a while to chat with each of us. Paul presented him with a brown paper bag of whistles in a variety of keys. He was thrilled. I told him how much the shows had meant to everyone, to our fans, but most of all to our parents and families.

'You know, Mike, life is a two-way street. You're here with me, but you know what, Mike? I'm also here with you. I have one of the great Irish bands playing with me on my Dublin show. That works for me as much as it works for you. The audience loved what we did these past two nights, so don't ever forget that, son. It's always a two-way street – it's the only way it works.'

I have never forgotten that and I pass it on to whoever will listen. My Ultimate Experience was beautifully captured in a photograph that somehow crept through Bob's well-manned photographic cordon. Charlie Collins had hidden a roll of film in his sock.

# COME ON THE BULL

In the winter of 1989 *The Field* was filmed in and around the beautiful village of Leenane in County Galway. It featured Richard Harris, John Hurt, Brenda Fricker, Sean Bean, Sara Jane Scaife, Jenny Conroy and Tom Berenger. We were invited to screen-test for the role of local musicians playing for the American Wake in the film, a parish hall hooley in honour of young villagers soon to emigrate.

Maurice, Paul, Kieran and myself met with director Jim Sheridan at a hotel on Amiens Street in Dublin. Jim suggested I bring along a bodhrán, as the guitar never featured at a session in rural 1950s Ireland. I had never played a bodhrán, but I borrowed one and started practising a little at home. I had no idea what I was doing, to be honest. Jim put us through our paces, explaining his vision for this crucial scene where Bull McCabe confronts the Yank during a crazy dance scene. He had us going in all directions, sitting, standing, moving, even dancing as we played. At one point we were sent charging forward, shouting and screaming, still playing as he whipped us into a frenzy. 'Hup! Come on! Hup!' By the time we finished the test I thought my right hand had left my body, but we landed the gig.

On arrival at the beautiful Renvyle House Hotel on the shores of the wild Atlantic, we were introduced to some of the cast and crew. The following morning at six our driver, Louis O'Connor, who has remained a dear friend, brought us to an old disused building in the village of Leenane, the once-upon-a-time Greene's Dance Hall. After a brief run-through we were sent to the costume department at a house further down the village, emerging all decked out in heavy brown tweed trousers, collarless shirts and waistcoats. We were a sight to behold as we made our way back down the street. For the following two and a half weeks we arrived, courtesy of Louis, each morning for wardrobe and make-up, played for hours, and sat around for far more as we waited for Jim to call the next take. Days were long but never boring.

The main dance scene between Bull McCabe and Katie the Tinker Lady (Jenny Conroy) opens to our music, with the young emigrants entering the dance hall for their American Wake. As we shift keys, the Bull's mood changes. The door opens and in walks the Yank – the Bull's nemesis – played by Tom Berenger. In the silence that follows you hear our whispered voices, 'There's the Yank. Oh, he's going to ask her to dance,' as he walks the length of the hall to take position in front of the musicians. Katie taunts the floor: 'Is there any one of ye man enough to dance with the tinker's daughter? Who's the biggest man among ye?' Fearing his hapless son Tadgh will take the bait, the Bull ups and shouts, 'I'll dance with you, redhead. Come on. Come on!' As the music picks up, Richard Harris skips across the hall while John Hurt screams, 'Come on the Bull! Come on the Bull!'

Harris had a fierce presence in that room, constantly in character. It is hard to forget the intensity of that stare. He had a peculiar dance step; certainly not from the Irish tradition, it was all of his own creation, and his timing was a little suspect. At one point he came down to us, suggesting we had changed the tune to a different rhythm, which we innocently denied. He then insisted that we had changed it, and stormed off to the other end of the hall to talk to Jim, who came down and whispered, 'Just agree, and everything will be fine.' And so it was. 'Yes, Mr Harris, sorry about that.' We played the same tune, and he danced away in delight.

The final two minutes of that scene is still very powerful to watch, the music driving the frenzy of the dance to its frantic crescendo, and then sudden silence as the McRoarty girl, played by Sara Jane Scaife, is flung to the floor by Tadgh McCabe, played by a very young and wonderful Sean Bean.

Some days my right hand was numb from beating the skin of that bodhrán, and I lost the stick several times, often to be returned by an ever-alert Bull McCabe with a wink and a smile. It's funny now to watch that scene, because I begin with a stick but end up without. Best actor in the role of a bodhrán player – no contest.

It was an incredible experience to see how *The Field* was all put together, hanging out with John Hurt, Sara Jane Scaife, Sean Bean and the gentleman that was Tom Berenger. Seventeen days for a four-minute, fifty-second scene certainly took the tinsel out of tinsel town.

We played a final session at Hamilton's Bar on the last night of filming. The place was packed to the rafters when the guards arrived to close the pub. It certainly has to go down as the most uncool raid ever. The bar and the village had hosted Hollywood for months, and this was to be their last major hooray. As the owner remarked later, 'A full house, Stockton's Wing playing for free and the feckers raid us! Nothing better to be doing with their time.'

The film was released in September 1990 and we all met again for a very special night in Dublin, when we walked on the famous red carpet. *The Field* is a very dark but extremely powerful movie about land possession and obsession. Richard Harris received an Oscar nomination. I was overlooked.

Some years later, while celebrating Christmas with my wife Donna at Dromoland Castle, we met Richard again and he invited us to join his family for a drink. We had a lovely evening at the bar, as he sang Limerick rugby songs and I replied with a few songs from Clare. We met him again the following year and reprised the few songs. A lovely, and funny man. He lived out his final years at the Savoy Hotel in London and was extremely ill towards the end. As they wheeled him out through the lobby, he lifted his head from the gurney and shouted, 'It was the food! Don't eat in here, it will kill you!' Come on, de Bull.

# SOMEONE LIKE YOU

*The light had almost faded,*
*A river all but dry,*
*Constantly invaded*
*By the thought of passing time.*
— 'Someone Like You', *Someone Like You* (1994)

I met Donna Barnes in 1989 at a gig in Bad Bobs in Temple Bar. She changed the course of my life in so many positive ways, and together we have sailed through plenty of rough and smooth waters. I knew on that first meeting there was a connection, and our relationship developed into something special. At thirty I had no expectations, and was quite content living my life as an aimless bachelor. What did I know? We continue to enjoy our life together, offering support, love and a ton of respect.

Stockton's Wing carried on for some time, and in 1992 we managed to record a great album with producer Bill Whelan and engineer Andrew Boland called *The Crooked Rose*. I think those songs were the best I wrote for the band, and it's an album I love to revisit, as we all had a memorable time in the studio.

Yet the gigs were becoming a chore, and in the end I finally left Stockton's Wing in 1994, which was quite a moving year for me. I recorded my first solo album, and myself and Donna married in September with a wonderful reception out at Comhaltas headquarters in Monkstown in Dublin, attended by so many friends and musicians.

# CHAPTER 6

## FINBAR FUREY

# 'WE HAD IT ALL'

My first solo album, *Someone Like You*, included 'We Had It All', and was recorded in Dublin by Karsten Linde's German label, Wundertutte. I needed to write a song to mark the end of a very creative period of my life, but songwriting is rarely a straight path. In the studio, the words 'we had it all' kept coming back to me, so I put together a few scribbles about all the places we had been. Ultimately, I ditched that approach – it was beginning to sound like 'trad music, I gave you all the best years of my life' – so I sat alone in the studio one night and used characters and scenes as a metaphor for remembering past joys while embracing change and new beginnings. Within a few days, the song came together. I've never written a song so quickly, particularly as I tend to mull over a project for weeks, sometimes months on end. For whatever reason, I called Ronnie Drew and Stockton's Wing and asked them to come in and record with me. Ronnie and I had become very close friends and it somehow seemed right that he should sing on this song. He had such an influence on my life, and was always there in the early days of the Wing, hand outstretched in friendship. I left the band on really good terms, and invited keyboard player and long-time roommate Peter Keenan to co-produce. I asked Kieran, Paul and Maurice to play on the song. I now see that particular recording as creatively closing one door on a wonderful period, while knocking gently on another.

# SOLO

I embarked on my first of many intensive solo tours. It was a whole new world for me, moving on my own from city to city with my thoughts, a guitar, suitcase and a train schedule. It was difficult at first to get used to my own company, the silence of the dressing room and the sound of a near-empty stage. Travelling and playing solo encouraged me to engage more with the people and to explore the local culture. At a gig at Mulligan's in Amsterdam my friend and great songwriter Francie Conway introduced me to Mark Gilligan, a young Dublin musician who had a small music agency in Holland. Mark signed me, and I was soon touring Holland, Belgium and Denmark. The gigs were mainly listening folk clubs, supplemented with a few awful Irish-bar diary-fillers. The Irish bars sell a concept of Ireland that has little to do with our culture, and the nightly live music is just another layer of the decor that requires four performances to an ever-transient audience, culminating in a final 1.30 a.m. set to a crowd that resembles the extras from Michael Jackson's 'Thriller' video.

A sound-engineer friend presented me with a solution to cope with those particularly loud venues. He gave me a prototype in-ear monitor system designed to block out noise pollution. That particular set-up was far removed from today's fancy personalised models, which are now measured to your own specifications, very comfortable to wear and digitally enhanced to give you the best sound possible. My early model was not so flash, with an uncomfortable earpiece, delicate wiring and a pocket transistor that only ranged fifty yards from stage to desk. It was a game-changer, though, allowing me to concentrate much more on improving my technique oblivious to the chaos and noise that reigned in the Irish bar around me. I treated all those type of gigs as dress rehearsals for the wonderful folk clubs.

## THE LODGER INSIDE OF ME

Miriam Feuth, the lady of the house at Mulligan's bar on Amstel in Amsterdam, lent me her old flat as a base during my Dutch gigs. It was my comfort zone, and much-needed. There was a farmers' market around the corner, where I got the best of fresh ingredients so that I could cook, eat well and build my resistance for the next series of gigs.

I came to love the country, its people and its welcoming heart, as I played so many beautiful venues in Holland. Mulligan's was central to the Dutch Irish folk scene, where many musicians still hang out, including my friend Siard De Jong, who lives around the corner from Mulligan's on his canal boat while working at the local music shop in between his gigs. He recorded and played on many of my solo projects, as well as a memorable tour with Ronnie Drew, which was tour managed by Mark Gilligan. Mark also played clarinet, whistles and bodhrán and sang with many immigrant Irish bands, and has worked for years with the Irish songwriter Danny Guinan. In recent years Mark was struck with multiple sclerosis, and his approach to living with the disease is truly inspirational. As I write, he is working on his own memoir, *The Lodger Inside of Me*, from the title of a song he wrote in response to his condition. His playing ability finally left him earlier this year, but true to form as a hardworking musician he set himself up as a DJ on local radio and plays at various clubs around Europe. On my last catch-up visit to Mulligan's, Mark joined me on stage along with Siard to play whistle on 'Beautiful Affair'. I admire Mark so much, particularly since I heard his reaction to the doctor advising him how to live with MS – 'Doctor, you should be asking MS how it will live with Mark Gilligan.'

## I NEVER WILL SING 'THE WILD ROVER' NO MORE

Mark Gilligan's tours allowed me a platform to perform my own songs, so I never felt it necessary to play cover songs – although I always had a few in reserve, just in case of emergencies. However, I refused point-blank to sing 'The Wild Rover', despite it being requested at so many gigs. To me some songs are so overplayed, they've been hung, drawn and quartered, and are best left alone or possibly laid to rest. I had a eureka moment on a long train journey when I started writing new verses to the ballad, slowly but surely killing him off by the last few lines before the final chorus of 'I never will sing "The Wild Rover" no more'. I was very pleased with myself, and sang it that night to modest reaction.

The following night I was at Mick Gillan's famous Shamrock Bar in Hamburg, which was renowned for good music, poetry readings and live theatre. That night, a local guy came up to the stage and asked me to play 'The Wild Rover'. I ignored him at first, as it wasn't one of those rousing-ballad-type gigs. I carried on singing the set I'd planned, but he was very persistent. I finally gave in and introduced my latest work, a Hamburg premier for the final days of the Irish Rover. I dedicated it to my new German friend, adding that while it may be a sad day for the Rover himself, it would prove a much better one for us long-suffering balladeers. I had the entire pub singing the final chorus, 'I never will sing "The Wild Rover" no more'. As I was soaking up the applause, he stormed up to the stage, indignant that I had 'destroyed a truly beautiful Irish song'. He went on and on, until I called him closer and whispered in his ear, 'Could you please fuck off now, and don't be annoying me, please. Thank you.'

He turned and walked back down to Mick, who was seated by the front door. From the stage it looked like a heated exchange, but I carried on. Mick explained later that the guy had complained bitterly about the gig, and was astonished by my use of bad language, saying, 'And he told me to fuck off!

My God, how insulting!'

Mick simply replied, 'And what's keeping you, son?'

## THE END OF THE TURKEY TOURS

I christened my annual three-week December tour of Europe 'the Turkey Tour', as it brought me back home a couple of days before the big day with plenty of paper money to get us through the festive season. Mainland Europe really knows how to celebrate Christmas, with beautiful markets, hot food stalls and tumblers of Glühwein, which really took the edge off the cold and loneliness of winter tours. Despite the seasonal perks and the adventures at home and abroad, after a few years of slogging it out I tired of my own company and the bustle of train stations. I was ready for a new challenge.

> *Share a little laughter, a little shelter from the rain,*
> *And when you're feeling low you know you've got no worries,*
> *'Cause sunshine will always follow rain.*
> — 'No Worries', *Celtic Roots Revival* (1988)

## THE BATTLE OF BALLYSHANNON

Legend has it that backstage at the Ballyshannon Folk Festival in the summer of 1979, Stockton's Wing and the Furey Brothers had words over something or other and a minor skirmish ensued. By all accounts, it was more shapes than action. Finbar Furey was nowhere to be seen for the duration of the shemozzle, and all agreed that was probably for the best, given his reputation as a boxer with a tough street-fighting attitude.

As it turned out, he was in fact back at home in Dunmore East, with tour manager Aidan 'Aido' Hand. Two critical factors sent him home early: a severe storm was brewing, threatening to cancel the event in Donegal; and Ireland was in the middle of a fuel crisis, so petrol was in very short supply. Having finished a gig in Galway, Finbar scoured the city's petrol stations but couldn't find the juice to take him north. He had just about enough to get him home to Waterford. He weighed up his options: home safe and sound in Dunmore, or up in Ballyshannon, where he could easy as not end up with no gig, no petrol, and very much stranded in the aftermath of a storm.

'That storm was so bad, wild winds and rain swarming in from the Atlantic. I could never see the gig going ahead – and that tent . . . we might have started the gig in Donegal, but we could have finished it in New York.' So Finn made his way south-east to the comfort and safety of home, and thankfully missed a rare chance to try out his boxing skills on the lads. I was not in the band just yet, and sometimes I liked to dream that the Furies were in fact the lucky ones in that regard.

# CHOOSE YER WEAPONS

The following year I was on my way to Adare Manor for my first TV appearance as a member of Stockton's Wing. The series, hosted by RTÉ personality Donncha Ó Dúlaing, was called *Donncha at Adare* and featured many Irish artists including the Fureys and Davy Arthur. As we approached Adare, we wondered how this meeting of the bands would pan out after the infamous battle of Ballyshannon, and although we were slightly nervous, we gave ourselves a good County Clare pep talk. There was of course the Finbar factor – he wasn't stranded at home this time – but we tried not to dwell on it for too long.

As we entered the great hall at Adare Manor, we were struck by its grandiose display. A spectacular chandelier hung from a large oak beam, glistening in the sunlight that shot through the stained-glass windows, its colours illuminating ancient walls heavy with portraits and tapestries of pomp and ceremony from days of yore. On the mantel of a blazing open fire stood two stunning turquoise porcelain vases, protected either side by marble pillars and suits of armour – one bearing a shield with the symbol of the Cross, the other wielding a ferocious mace. A perfectly aligned row of spears adorned a side wall. To the right was a wide and winding oak staircase, and all along its curved walls hung swords, mallets, shields, crossbows and a brace of lances. It was the ultimate medieval war museum.

Just then, a jovial group of Fureys descended the stairs, and a palpable tension filled the hall as we eyed each other nervously. Suddenly Finbar rushed forward, eyes wide and raging like a warrior going into battle. He stopped short before us, shoulders back, and shouted, 'Right, lads. Choose your weapons, we'll sort it all out here, now, once and for all!' A beat, and his face broke into the widest grin I had ever seen.

'How're ye, lads!' And that was it. The 'war' had ended right there among the ghost warriors of our ancient past. From that moment on, a bond was sealed between us, never to be broken.

Our newfound truce nearly crumbled as fast as it had been agreed, however, when we were set to meet for a pint at Chalke's pub down in the village when the day's recording was done. That evening as planned, Finbar and the lads went to Chalke's pub but there was no sign of us anywhere. They were drinking away, with a few mumbles of discontent from the brothers, when Finbar casually mentioned to the barman that he was supposed to meet Stockton's for a pint. 'Ah, shur,' replied the barman, 'they're probably in the other Chalke's. There's two in the village. This is Bill Chalke's, they're probably over at Lena's around the corner.' Two pubs with the same name in a small village – only in Ireland. Finbar duly arrived, and the session started. It's been going ever since.

# FINBAR AND EDDIE

In the 1960s Finbar and his brother Eddie were playing gigs in Dublin with their brother Paul on accordion and first cousin Johnny Keenan on the banjo. O'Donoghue's pub on Dublin's Baggot Street was the place to be, and Paddy and Maureen O'Donoghue welcomed all musicians and singers to a haven for the city's creative community. Paddy Kavanagh, the Clancy Brothers, Brendan Behan, John Kelly, Ronnie Drew, Barney McKenna and Luke Kelly all found a spot there to play, drink, eat, rest and meet the elder statesmen of Irish music in what was for all intents and purposes a school of music.

One of those senior figures was the great *sean nós* singer Joe Heaney, who spent most of his life touring and recording albums of the songs collected on his travels. In postwar England he worked with Peggy Seeger and Ewan McColl; he was invited to America by the Clancy Brothers to perform in all the concert halls; he toured Europe with the Dubliners. Ronnie Drew often spoke of his talent, and Joe often stayed with Ronnie and Deirdre whenever he was back in Ireland.

Unfortunately, even though he was highly respected among his peers, he never seemed to reach such lofty heights at home. Some say that after his tremendous success abroad he returned to a mid-sixties Dublin music scene, one that was shifting to more rousing ballads, with audiences a little more boisterous and a little less keen on listening to *sean nós* solo performances. Joe had a hugely successful career on the concert circuit across the US and the UK, and his reputation lived on in the next generation, particularly in trad music circles, despite the change in tastes. At O'Donoghue's and at the Furey house, he passed on the melodies, lilts and nuances of the old airs. Joe had a very willing pupil in Finbar; to this day, when Finbar plays slow airs you can hear the pipes sing the tunes rather than playing them through reed and chanter, imbued with all the feeling and inflection of Joe's *sean nós* style.

## THE OLD FIRM

In 1967 Joe Heaney asked Finbar and Eddie to cover a tour of Scotland for him, as he needed to be with his ailing brother over in Connemara. Eddie had been playing with a rock band called the Spartans who were causing a little sensation in the Irish rock scene. Unlike his brothers, Eddie's true love was rock and roll; consequently he knew very few ballads, so he had to hastily learn a few for the tour. There was great excitement in O'Donoghue's as Finbar and Eddie Furey took the cattle boat to Scotland, waved off by family and friends with only a few pounds in their pocket, a parting gift from Maureen and Paddy. They arrived in Glasgow and made their way to the main station to jump on a train bound for Edinburgh. There, they were to meet their hosts before their first show in Aberdeen, scheduled for the following night.

They were laden down with instruments – guitar, banjo, pipes, mandolin, their suitcases and a bodhrán with the words 'Erin Go Bragh' emblazoned across its skin strapped to Eddie's back. A police car shadowed them for a few yards before coming to a halt. 'It's the shades,' said Finbar.

'Good morning, boys. Where are you two off to now? Are ye over for the match?'

'No, we're going off on tour,' replied Eddie. 'We won't be going to the match, we've no time. Who's playing, anyway?'

'Don't you know? There's a big match on today, a soccer match, boy – between Rangers and Celtic.'

'OK. Never heard of them, but the best of luck to both of them anyway. Thanks.'

Baffled, the coppers turned to them and said, 'Would you two lads mind jumping into the car? It's not safe for you to be walking these streets here. Have you any idea where you are right now? In a short while this'll be a battle zone and you two are heading straight for trouble.' The police drove them to the train station and sent them safely on their way to a warm welcome at Sandy Bell's – the O'Donoghue's of Edinburgh.

## FLOWER OF SCOTLAND

Word had spread of their arrival and the pub duly filled with an eager crowd. Later that evening, the two Furies were introduced to Roy Williamson from Scottish folk group the Corries. Roy asked Finbar to play a few tunes on the pipes, but they weren't ready yet. So Roy passed him a whistle and said, 'Give us a tune on the whistle. Let's see if you're any good.' Finbar played a tune very badly, missing several notes. Roy took the whistle and played a Scottish tune, flawlessly, and handed the whistle back. 'Keep practising, son,' he said gleefully, adding, 'I hope you're a better piper than you are a whistle player.' As he turned away Finbar took the whistle again and broke into a set of reels that stopped Roy in his tracks. That first encounter sealed a friendship that lasted until Roy's untimely death in 1990.

Roy gave the world that iconic song, 'Flower of Scotland', and each time I hear it, I think of Finbar sitting in our Ford transit van driving through the

Scottish countryside, regaling us with stories of the good times at Sandy Bell's with singers Paddie Bell, Barbara Dickson, Dave Stewart and the Humblebums, a Scottish folk rock band featuring comedian Billy Connolly on banjo and Gerry Rafferty on guitar. Paddie Bell would go on to tour and record with Finbar and Eddie; years later, Barbara Dickson became the queen of the West End, a very successful recording artist and award-winning actress of both stage and screen. Dave Stewart went on to create Eurythmics with Annie Lennox, Gerry Rafferty became one of the greatest songwriters of his generation with hits like 'Stuck in the Middle' for Stealers Wheel, 'Baker Street' and the Furey Brothers' hit 'Her Father Didn't Like Me Anyway'. Billy Connolly, well, we all know what happened to him – he's been a comic, actor and banjo-player for decades, and Finbar might just say he gave him his first start on the banjo. Billy was also a great friend of Ronnie Drew, and visited often to say hello or called in to the odd gig.

Finbar met local girl Sheila Peebles at Sandy Bell's one evening, fell in love and they married soon thereafter. Roy Williamson was best man. Finbar often speaks about his friends in Scotland, how much he treasured their love and support all throughout his career, but whenever he speaks about Roy his expression portrays a much deeper affection. Of all the photos Finn has shown me of Roy and his Corries sidekick, Ronnie Brown, one stands out: it's the pair of them holding two of the oddest-looking instruments you are ever likely to see: combolins, which Roy invented. Ronnie's combolin had a regular guitar neck alongside a mandolin neck, and a sliding bass mechanism complete with strings that ran parallel to the guitar neck. Roy's was a combination of acoustic guitar, sitar-like drone strings, and a Spanish bandura, which is akin to a twelve-string mandolin. Having studied art in college, he finished the instruments with an exquisite inlay of mother-of-pearl and ivory. The bodies of both instruments were large and bulbous, like a Greek bouzouki, and his daughters nicknamed them 'angry eyes' and 'sad eyes' due to the differing shapes to the soundholes.

As you'd expect, they each had a unique sound and required specialised skills and techniques. Apparently, Roy and Ronnie took months off to create a new Corries show that took advantage of the versatility of the combolins, and during songs they alternated between the many sounds available from each instrument, creating an incredibly colourful musical backdrop for their vocals. It's been suggested by some folk that Roy only invented them to ease the luggage count on the road, and we're certainly all for that.

Finbar and Eddie relaxed into their new life in Scotland learning songs and tunes, building a solid platform from which to tour the UK, Europe and America, recording their first album in early 1968 with Scottish singer Paddie Bell, and later that year releasing their first duet album. The following year *The Lonesome Boatman* was released and then 'October', a song written by Robin Williamson from the Incredible String Band. In 1972 BBC DJ John Peel latched on to 'Her Father Didn't Like Me Anyway' and named it the Folk Song of the Year. In 1976 their version of the Ralph McTell song 'Clare to Here' became a major hit. By that stage they had several albums to their credit and had spent three years touring America with the Clancy Brothers. 'That was amazing,' said Finbar. 'One day we're drinking pints in Sandy Bell's, and the next thing we're in a room with Bob Dylan and Doug McClure, yer man from *The Virginian*.'

# NIGEL KENNEDY

In 1993 our UK agent Ron Welsh from Malvern suggested that Stockton's Wing tour with Finbar as a double-header, which was an inspired move. We played the first half of the show, and then I joined Finbar for his set, as one by one the rest of the band filled the stage, culminating in a pulsating finale. We all travelled together in one bus and there were very few nights without a session, but some were spectacular. During the tour, Ron Welsh invited us to his local restaurant, where we were joined by local violin virtuoso Nigel Kennedy. We were treated to a stunning fiddle duet with Maurice Lennon and Nigel Kennedy in the wee hours at a beautiful restaurant at the foot of the Malvern hills in Worcestershire – I'm not sure I'll ever hear the like.

I left the band soon after that tour and worked on several tours with Finbar. His stage persona is infectious; it is a joy to watch him effortlessly take command of a room. He works hard at his craft, and shows great respect to audience and fellow musicians alike. His pipe playing is exquisite and he has mastered that Traveller free-style of piping, a unique interpretation of our shared Irish music heritage which has been handed down from generation to generation. Finbar's approach to his music makes for a great music lesson, but a magnificent tenet for life: 'We don't need to play the same notes all the time,' he'd say. 'You play with your imagination, and I'll play with mine,' and that's how it should always be.

# A FORMULA 1 BODHRÁN PLAYER

Before every show, we gathered round in a huddle and Finbar would say, 'Right, lads, let's go out there and tell them who we are.' The game is on. We amble out on to the stage and a welcome applause. He sits on his chair, fumbles with the mic stand, gives a slight blow into the mic, a glance around the room and then: 'How youse, I'm Finbar. I come from a small fishing village on the outskirts of Dublin called Ballyfermot.'

A genuine air of relaxation spreads through the entire auditorium as the gig moves up and up with powerful songs, interspersed with tunes, great stories, and jokes as he reaches the final crescendo with the entire house singing, 'When you were sweet, when you were sweet . . . sixteen.' I loved his stories about his mother and father, who were ever present in the air at every single gig. You laughed at the simplest of stories and it was always down to his impeccable timing and delivery.

'I could never understand me mother. At dinner she's there telling you to "Get it into you, son, it'll do you the power of good" . . . and then later on if I was sick, she says, "Get it out of you, son, it will do you the power of good." I was a very confused young fella.'

Among all his instruments, an incredible set of Uilleann pipes gets an introduction, as he explains the various parts and how they work. 'These are the only instruments we can call our own, cause everything else has been robbed on us.' Then with a slight Scottish accent he says, 'Many years ago we gave these to the Scots, and for a laugh we told them to blow into them.' He talks about the great pipers of old, Johnny and Felix Doran: 'Johnny was the Jimi Hendrix of Irish piping.' When Finbar delivers a slow, sweet air on the pipes, his entire body is at play as he weaves in and out of the melody, emotion and passion flowing through his fingers.

When he breaks into a set of reels, that's another story – played at breakneck speed and not for the faint-of-heart accompanist. His brother Paul was once asked by a very serious folk music interviewer why he played so fast and he quickly replied, 'Because I can.'

There was a gig we played at Eddie Jordan's birthday bash in a lovely restaurant on the banks of the Thames, where Eddie invited himself to accompany Finbar for a few tunes on bodhrán. It was his party, after all, and he'll play if he wants to. Finbar leaned over to me and whispered, 'Stay with me, sham. I'll give Eddie some real Formula 1 speed and we'll see how he manages! Watch this.'

'This could be trouble,' I thought.

Finbar begins with the 'Bucks of Oranmore' at moderate speed – moderate for Finn at least – with Eddie sitting comfortably with the rhythm, a satisfied look on his face. 'Right, sham.' Finbar winked and he was gone, ninety miles an hour with Eddie in hot pursuit. A hundred and fifty miles an hour . . . As the tune entered its second lap, Eddie developed some engine trouble and hit a wall. Finbar smiled over at Eddie: 'What's the story, sham? Can you not keep up?' Eddie, a little shook, leant over and said into his ear, 'Furey, ya bollix! Remember who's paying for the gig!'

It was quite a night. After dinner I met my one and only favourite Beatle – though I have to confess to never having owned a Beatles album. Despite it, I did really love the songs and music of George Harrison, and I did own a few of his solo albums: *Concert for Bangladesh*, *All Things Must Pass* and a more recent one, *Cloud Nine*. Eddie kindly introduced me to George and his lovely wife Olivia, and it was a pleasure to hear George talk about how much he enjoyed Irish music. I usually take these introductions in my stride, but this was special.

## SELF-SERVICE CATERING

The gig was everything to Finbar, it was the sole purpose to his day – unless there was a golf course nearby where he could take your money with ease. He seldom ate breakfast, and always insisted on an early start to get to the next town in time for lunch and a snooze before the sound check. It was normal to watch Finbar down a few raw eggs later on during the bus journey or open a tin of salmon and eat it. He explained that back in the day, his father, Ted, travelled Ireland most of his life collecting tunes and songs, and as they were growing up, he taught Finbar and the boys the Traveller ways of the road – always have something in your bag that will see you through the pangs of hunger. Ted and his wife Nora, a Clare woman, instilled in their family a deep respect and understanding of Traveller music and the life. I loved listening to Finn's stories about his mother and father and the ways of the Traveller culture.

Too often, Finbar would arrive into a town to discover that all the eateries were closed till six o'clock. So one day he located a kitchen appliance store and purchased a slow cooker. On his way back to the hotel, he called in to the butcher and supermarket for supplies. Back in the room, he filled the slow cooker, had a snooze and invited all the lads around for dinner before the sound check.

Problem solved – well, at least that problem, anyway. As the tour progressed, other band members took turns to host the dinner. On occasion the odour would permeate throughout the hotel floor: 'Hey, sham, are you cooking curry today? Ya can smell it everywhere!' After a series of complaints, someone had the brainwave to spray Olbas oil on the carpet outside the designated kitchen bedroom – which only attracted more attention.

The slow cooker had its last outing in a hotel on the north-west coast of England – and an outing it was. By that stage they had learned to put the pot on the outside window ledge to alleviate the cooking smells in the room, and to prevent agitated hotel staff from knocking on the door. This new system was working fine until they arrived at a remote seaside town. As before, Finbar filled the pot with a stew mix, switched it on, placed it outside and went off into town for a stroll with the lads. A couple of hours later, they rounded the bend up the hotel driveway, looking forward to a good feed, when they saw the flock of seagulls, hovering and screeching over the cooker, in consternation. Finn managed to retrieve the pot, but the gulls had destroyed it. Its final resting place was in the hotel skip.

# PAN-CELTIC CODDLE

After a futile search for an open restaurant in the Scottish Highlands, Finbar walked into a grocery shop and noticed a small haggis and a few sausages under a glass cloche and had an idea. The Ireland–Scotland rugby match was on TV later that afternoon and he was all set to head back to the room, put his feet up and watch the game in comfort after a nice meal. He returned to his room with the food, half-filled the kettle with water, taped the on/off button to 'on' and inserted the haggis and sausages.

'I was bleedin' starvin'. So I kept topping up the kettle while I watched the build-up to the match. As soon as I thought it was ready, I opened the lid, but the haggis had expanded in the heat and was wedged inside. I tried everything, but no way was it coming out. With all the prodding the haggis burst and practically filled the kettle. The kettle was fecked now, sham, so what could I do? I was starvin', so I sat on the bed with my kettle, and ate a haggis stew while Scotland beat the Irish at the rugby. The next morning I had to go out and find a new kettle.' What a great idea for a folk festival dish – a pan-Celtic coddle.

## SHEILA'S PICKLED ONIONS

Despite his occasional misadventures on the road, food is a constant in Finbar's life. When we would rehearse at the Furey home in Rathfarnham, Finn's wife Sheila spoiled us with her wonderful cooking, with so many of her great recipes handed down from generations of her Scottish ancestry.

I left the house on many occasions with a jar of her delicious pickles. I asked her for the recipe several times but it never happened. When I got in touch for the pickle recipe for this book, she laughed, saying she had forgotten it and had not made them for years. Apparently their daughter Kat also craves those pickles, and was constantly on to Sheila to make them again and again. One day in the local supermarket Sheila bought a jar of pickled onions and hatched a plan. She took them home, transferred the contents to another jar, added a few of her own favourite spices and presented them to Kat, saying nothing at all. 'God, the idea of peeling all those onions, Mike! Poor Kat, I hadn't the heart to tell her.'

# Marie's Scottish shortbread

Marie Peebles, Finbar's mother-in-law, was very particular about her shortbread – and with good reason; it's one of Finn's favourite things to eat. Take note of the oven stages, as there are both changes in temperature and oven position. I might have a slight issue with the margarine here. I am a butter baker, but then my own mum always preferred working with margarine. She maintained it was much better for baking. I'll not argue with either mum.

340g margarine
125g caster sugar
100g cornflour
400g self-raising flour

1. Preheat the oven to 140°C/120°C fan/gas 1.
2. Cream the margarine and sugar together.
3. Stir in the cornflour and flour.
4. Knead together, then roll out until 1cm thick.
5. Lift the dough and place it on a well-greased baking tray, smoothing it out and pressing it right into the corners. Prick with a fork and bake on the middle shelf of the oven for 1¼ hours.
6. Transfer to a lower shelf, reduce the heat to 80°C/60°C fan/gas 1, or as low as it will go, and bake for another hour.
7. Allow the shortbread to cool completely on a wire rack, then carefully cut it to your preferred shape, ensuring the knife goes right through the cake.
8. Carefully remove each piece of shortbread and place in an airtight container. I like to separate each layer with parchment paper.

# A Scottish tablet

A Scottish tablet is like a fudge, though not as smooth; it has a grainy, crumbly texture and is very sweet. It is cooked at a higher temperature than fudge, so take a bit of care. You'll need a sugar thermometer. Otherwise there is a technique to test that the sugar has reached what's called a hard ball stage. You simply take a teaspoon of the very hot liquid and drop it into cold water. As it cools, you can test the mixture to make sure it forms a hard ball. If not, carry on with the boil. Recipes vary from margarine to salted or unsalted butter. Sheila has to hide some of this away in case the boss goes through the entire tablet in one sitting.

125g margarine
150ml milk
900g granulated sugar
1 x 397g tin of condensed milk
1 tsp vanilla extract

1. Melt the margarine in a large pan on a low heat, then add the milk and sugar and heat until the sugar is dissolved, stirring constantly to avoid it sticking to the pan.
2. Carefully stir in the condensed milk and vanilla extract and bring to the boil for 20 minutes at 120°C, stirring constantly. The mixture will start to bubble and take on a dark colour.
3. Remove the pan from the heat and beat vigorously for 5 to 10 minutes, or just use an electric mixer to save your elbow.
4. When it all comes together, place on a baking tray lined with greaseproof paper, pushing it out to the corners.
5. Let it cool completely, then cut into pieces of your preferred size.

*Scottish tablet takes all sorts of easy and tasty variations. For a mocha flavour, add 25g of instant coffee and 25g of cocoa powder; for orange, add the juice and zest of a small orange; for tutti-frutti, add 100g of mixed sliced almonds, raisins, sultanas and/or chopped glacé cherries. These measurements are only a guide. You may wish to add more or less according to your taste.*

# CHAPTER 7

# RONNIE, I HARDLY KNEW YA . . .

*There's a sailor gone to sea only he knows how it feels*
*As he bids a fond farewell to all his kin,*
*As he walks along the shore to his love, he throws a rose.*
*I'll return again in winter or in spring.*
*We had it all. We had the best of times.*
*We had a life that dreams are made of.*
                    – 'We Had It All', *El Amor de Mi Vida* (2006)

In the early 80s, Stockton's Wing were the new kids on the block, and the Dubliners welcomed us as one of their own, throwing a warm arm around our collective shoulders and offering great encouragement and advice. The music of the Dubliners was the soundtrack of our youth. My brother Kieran fashioned his banjo-playing in the style of Barney McKenna, and one of his regular pieces for the All-Star Hanrahan Family Review was an intricate piece called 'Barney's Mozart', so their support meant quite a lot to both of us.

We first met the Dubliners on an Irish festival tour which also included Jim McCann and the Dublin City Ramblers, along with the Furey Brothers and Davy Arthur. Our first show was in Zwolle in southern Holland, and after a successful gig and a very late night some of the group rose very late the following morning, causing us to miss a flight to Cologne for connection on to the second gig in Berlin. Germany was still a divided country, and the Allies maintained control of all traffic to and from Berlin, so it was difficult to reorganise our travel arrangements at such short notice. Concerned organisers eventually hired a private jet to take us down to Cologne. The plush interior and cream leather seats were soon filled with instruments, bags and a motley crew of Irish folkies. It must have been a strange sight indeed. When we arrived at Cologne, we were told there was a further delay to get to Berlin, so we sat around and eventually boarded just as the festival was due to begin. Once in Berlin, we rushed through arrivals and were heading for the tour coach when a few people came us to us and said that the festival had been cancelled and everybody had gone home very disappointed. Someone had made that decision while we were in the air.

At the hotel we met a very dejected festival organiser and Ronnie Drew suggested we all go for a drink, as there was very little else we could do at that stage. It had been a long day, but nothing compared to the long night that unfolded as we drank and sang our way through a few of Berlin's finest Irish bars.

The following week Ronnie invited Stockton's Wing to dinner at his home in Greystones in County Wicklow, prior to a gig we were to play with

American songwriter Jim Page. It was my first time to meet Ronnie's wife, Deirdre, and taste her amazing food. That dinner sealed a friendship that lasted the rest of their days. Later on, both Jim and Ronnie joined us on stage, and that too was the beginning of a collaboration that lasted many years. Over the next fifteen years we met at various gigs, recorded a few songs and stayed in touch as often as possible.

Years later, in 1997, Ronnie invited me out to 'have a look' at a theatre show he was writing with a view to a run at Andrew's Lane in Dublin later that year: 'I just want your advice, Mikie, and I think I need a guitar player as well. You might know someone who can play the odd solo to break it up a little.' While this certainly presented me with a good opportunity, I was acutely aware of my shortcomings on guitar solos. My discipline was strictly rhythm and accompaniment, but the opportunity to work closely with Ronnie Drew was far too exciting a prospect to pass up without at least a decent attempt, so I called out to him to have a look.

He talked me through the script, which included childhood stories, early working years at the Telephone Exchange in Dublin, his move to Franco's Spain, songs and stories from his friend, poet Paddy Kavanagh, and hilarious anecdotes from Stephen Behan and his son Brendan. There were songs from playwright Sean O'Casey, and of course, some of the more popular ballads from the Dubliners archive.

After coffee and gossip with Deirdre, we moved to the front room to run through some of the songs. He started with the beautiful 'Raglan Road', and after the third verse, looked over and nodded at my guitar for the solo – whereupon I immediately lost all power in my left hand. I steadied myself, rattled, and frantically searched the neck of the guitar for any notes even loosely connected with the famous melody of 'Raglan Road'. I couldn't find any. I had a quick glance towards Ronnie; his expression said, 'Oh, mother of Jaysus.'

He graciously agreed to another rehearsal, so I went home mortified but determined to do better. I knew that *Ronnie, I Hardly Knew Ya* as a show was going to be exceptional, and I knew I had to be with him on his journey. I eventually worked out a melodic solo and played it a hundred times a day until my fingers found their fluency. I then went through the other songs and practised, practised, practised. I returned to rehearsals a little shaky from nerves, but sailed through the solo without any fuss. Ronnie sat back and puffed on his trademark Cohiba. 'That was a lovely bit of guitar-playing there, Mikie. We'll be grand.'

I've always said that Ronnie made me a better guitarist. 'Would you g'wan outta that, Mike,' he'd chuckle, slightly embarrassed, but it was all true. Working with Ronnie certainly made me a much more competent musician.

I knew from the outset that I had to improve my guitar playing to match his performance. I had always been either a solo performer or in a group set-up with bands like Stockton's Wing and Finbar Furey. There's a flexibility to playing your own tunes alone, and a comfort in the protection of that big ensemble sound, like being an actor in a large cast. This was a different gig, one voice with one instrument, and it required new skills. Knowing that my playing would be laid bare, I spent hours developing my own distinctive style, striving at all times to complement centre stage, where Ronnie could comfortably deliver the stories, songs, energy and passion of *Ronnie, I Hardly Knew Ya*. I knew every word of the script. Our director, Derek Chapman, offered some great theatrical advice, tips and suggestions on how to interpret the show's emotions through my playing. I had great fun in particular on our verse from 'Finnegan's Wake', as I tried to interpret the crazy scenes of the corpse rising from the dead or a bottle crashing over Tim's head. For 'McAlpine's Fusiliers', Derek suggested that I work in a phrase from 'The Rose of Tralee' on the line 'I come from County Kerry'. It was subtle, so I always loved it when people got that one.

Every evening after sound check I remained on stage alone until doors at seven, working on my technique while Ronnie was backstage doing the very same with the script. We never stopped tweaking and improving the show.

# ELVIS IN THE HOUSE

One night at Andrew's Lane Theatre, the stage manager came into the dressing room just before curtain call to announce that Elvis Costello and Irish guitar hero Anto Drennan were in the house. The more famous Elvis being there had no effect on my nerves, but Anto was a very different story. He's one of our great guitarists, and for me, the leader of the pack. So my hero was going to be sitting out there, checking out my new sound. I was more than a little petrified at the thought of him following my every manoeuvre. Needless to say, he wasn't likely to be doing anything of the kind, but I was too young and nervous to know that. It mattered nought to me that he had been a good friend for a long, long time; the fact is, you don't want to screw up a solo when Anto Drennan is in the house, simple as – forget about Elvis. When I confided in him after that show how shaken I'd been to hear he was there, he looked at me in shock and told me to cop on to myself.

Believe it or not, Ronnie dreaded curtain call as a matter of course, but this was too much. If I thought I was intimidated by Anto, Ronnie was far worse about Elvis. 'Oh my Jaysus, Mikie, did she just say Elvis Costello? Why would she say that just before the gig? What am I goin' to do? I can't remember anything. What's the opening line again? Ah, Jaysus. Why are we even doin' this to ourselves?' Ronnie always got himself into a frenzy before every gig, like a fever-ridden cowboy in a Sunday afternoon movie, so hard did he shake with fear. He'd be in a terrible state, constantly gargling some concoction of honey, lemon and God-knows-what, creating truly stomach-churning noises. These were usually interspersed with growls – 'Aaaaaaaghghgh!' – that reached depths never since ventured by the human voice. I quickly learned that Ronnie Drew warming up for a gig was not for the faint-hearted, so I developed my own routine far away in the corner doing cryptic crosswords and word puzzles. My heart always went out to those experiencing the spectacle for the first time.

'Five minutes, gentlemen.'

In that dark space backstage, you have a few moments to yourself before each gig – strange, nervy moments as the hush descends on a chattering theatre, lights are lowered and the side curtain is drawn open for your entrance. You take in a deep breath, share a warm hug and a 'Good luck, see you on the other side,' then stroll onto a warm, welcoming stage and let the air out. 'Good evening, ladies and gentlemen. My name is Ronnie Drew, and this is my friend, Mike Hanrahan.'

## THAT'S ENTERTAINMENT

Ronnie taught me the true art of entertainment. We presented each performance as if it were an opening night. He taught me to enjoy the applause, take it in and then leave it to rest back in its auditorium: tomorrow was another day, another audience, another challenge. His performance and delivery were astonishing. I embraced his approach, and developed my skills with each passing gig. My role as musician and singer expanded into tour manager, agent, writer and producer, a relationship that lasted for the remaining eleven years of Ronnie's life. Yet whenever he sang 'McAlpine's Fusiliers', I'd be transported back to the living room of our family home in St Michael's Villas and our old Philips valve record player, where I first heard him sing. It was thrilling to snap back into real time and see him only a yard away from me. As much as I had always looked up to him, Ronnie was a very inclusive performer, and we were a good team that travelled very well together, sharing many wonderful experiences, both with music and food – because Ronnie, believe it or not, was a serious foodie.

## HAKE, RATTLE AND ROLL

Ronnie had left Ireland in the late 50s for Seville in southern Spain, where he worked as an English teacher – and 'If you believe that,' he would say, 'you'll believe anything.' While in Spain he developed a deep love and respect for its people, culture, language, music, and of course its cuisine. Ronnie regularly cooked at home, whether it was a breakfast of slowly fried garlic, chopped parsley with fresh chillies finished with a fried egg, or a simple lunch of fresh whiting dusted in seasoned flour and cooked in the pan with real Irish butter and the best Spanish olive oil. He enjoyed cooking, and when the occasion called for a more elaborate presentation, Ronnie stepped up and delivered some excellent dishes. Food was a defining element of the Drew household.

Every visit to Killincarraig Road in Greystones, a picturesque seaside village, started at a table on the edge of the kitchen where Deirdre and Ronnie sat, drinking coffee, perusing newspapers or going through the morning post amid a plume of cigar and cigarette smoke that rose gently to the ever-present cloud that hung just beneath the low ceiling. There was always something to eat – fresh cakes, chocolates or exotic sweets – plenty of chat and even more music industry gossip, which we loved. Cakes were either

baked by daughter Cliodhna, or from the country market at the church hall in nearby Delgany.

But when Ronnie planned a special dinner, it was a major event, and it took on a life of its own. He approached cooking with the same fastidious attention to detail as he did his gigs. He was meticulous, deliberate – and slow. One clove of garlic could take ten minutes to peel and slice, with a technique akin to Paulie's prison-cell cooking scene in *Goodfellas*.

Both Ronnie and Deirdre insisted on local produce: meat from Farrelly's craft butchers, vegetables from the local greengrocer and fish from either the village or Caviston's in Glasthule. In the early days, 'exotic' produce such as red peppers, chillies and asparagus was not readily available locally, so Deirdre would often make the trip into the city to stock the larder for upcoming special occasions. Olive oils and butter were preferred to vegetable or sunflower oil.

Most of Ronnie's recipes were influenced by his early working years in Andalusia, southern Spain, especially his hake with salsa verde. Some might argue while it's not a classic verde, it is green, and has the two major components, fresh parsley and garlic. I would never have recommended taking this point up with Ronnie – although I'd have paid handsomely to hear his reply. Regardless, it was spectacular, or as Anto Drennan put it, 'Jaysus, Ronnie, this is so good I'm going straight home to change all my money into pesetas.'

Ronnie insisted on evenly-cut fillets with no tail ends. A field of parsley would be patiently chopped, garlic cloves prepped as above, onions – 'white ones, not those red excuses for onions' – peeled and diced, asparagus tips carefully shaved and snapped at the perfect spot, clams thrice rinsed and inspected for any deterioration with a tap against the bowl for signs of life. Ingredients were laid out on every available surface, with all kitchen chores suspended for the duration, apart from the boiling of the kettle for a cuppa.

He used La Ina fino sherry or San Patricio fino, a sherry named after Saint Patrick by an Irishman called Garvey, who first produced and exported it to the world from Cádiz back in the day. Fish stock was usually made fresh or taken from the freezer. It's always a good idea to make plenty of stock and freeze it for future occasions.

# Hake with salsa verde
Serves 4

You will need a sauté pan or a deep frying pan, although I have cooked this in an earthenware casserole dish. Start with a high heat to brown the fish, but return it to medium. It can be finished in the oven, of course, but keep an eye on it. You may prefer to use other fish, but it has to be a chunky, meaty variety. Warm your bowls in a very low oven while you cook.

2 tbsp good olive oil or rapeseed oil
50g butter
4 large hake fillets, about 250g each (ask your fishmonger for centre only, no tails)
50g flour, lightly seasoned, for dusting
2 cloves of garlic, crushed (use the back of the knife against a chopping board)
250g fresh parsley, chopped
2 shot glasses of good dry sherry
120ml fish stock
12 asparagus spears, cleaned and ends snapped off
4 large or 8 small Dublin Bay prawns in their shells (peeled are fine, but lack the wow factor)
300g rinsed clams
80g frozen peas
2 lemons, cut into 4 wedges, to serve
Sea salt and freshly ground black pepper
Salad, potatoes or mash, to serve (optional)

1. Heat the oil and butter in the pan over a medium heat.
2. Lightly dust the fish fillets with flour. When the pan is hot, colour the hake to a nice, crisp tan – about 3 to 4 minutes. Remove the fish to a plate and set aside.
3. Add the garlic and cook for 1 minute, followed by two-thirds of the parsley, reserving the rest for later. Stir.
4. Add the sherry and reduce a little, then add the fish stock. Bring to the boil.
5. Return the hake to the pan, followed by the asparagus, prawns and finally the clams and the peas. Cook until the clams open (no need to cover the pan). Add salt and pepper to taste.
6. Transfer to a warm bowl, sprinkle the remaining parsley over the top and serve with a little bowl of lemon wedges. Sometimes I dip the wedges in the parsley for presentation.
7. Serve with a nice crisp salad, crushed potatoes with lemon, or a lovely mash.

# LIMERICK HAM

Ronnie could be a divil, as they say, in restaurants. He loved fish, but never enjoyed the ordeal of negotiating around its complicated bone structure, fun though it was for the rest of us to watch his frustration mount as he tried. He loved it when the chef or server offered to fillet fish at the table. He had rules for meat, too. All beef steaks had to be lean, with no gristle or fat. 'Now I don't like the gristle,' he would explain. 'I'll have the sirloin, but will you ask the chef to cut off any fat. I don't like that at all. I know it says eight ounces so I don't care if it's reduced to four ounces as long as there's no fat, and I'll pay the full price.'

His hotel supper of choice was a simple onion sandwich, insisting on white onions, sliced, whereupon he would demonstrate to the front desk by sliding his right palm across his left. 'And not chopped!' he would stress, one hand chopping vigorously against the other open palm. It was hard not to laugh, particularly in a foreign hotel with a concierge who had little or no grasp of the English language. Such a simple sandwich was often prone to complications, so our German agent solved the problem by adding it to the gig rider.

Coffee, ordered with a little jug of fresh pouring cream, was also mimed, but regardless would arrive with a big dollop of whipped cream lobbed into the coffee.

At home in Ireland, Ronnie would ask the waiter to confirm that the Limerick ham was indeed from Limerick, and not from Tipperary, as ham from that particular county caused him serious indigestion. He'd sit back, delighted with himself, awaiting the reply. Quite often the head chef looked out through the service hatch to see who was asking such a stupid question, only to receive a satisfied salute from Ronnie, beaming with delight. 'Howeyeh, head!'

Another regular was, 'Excuse me, miss, the chicken … is that chicken ding?' Pointing to the chicken Maryland on the menu.

The bemused server would reply, 'No, sir, it's chicken Maryland.'

'Yeah, I know it says that, but is it cooked in the ding-ding machine?' Ronnie wasn't one for shortcuts.

Deirdre and Ronnie loved bacon and cabbage, but Ronnie insisted on the leaner cut, while Deirdre preferred the tastier end. One day she sent him to Farrelly's butchers in Delgany for the bacon and as he drove away, she called the butcher to be sure to give him the fatty end. The butcher replied, 'Deirdre, love, it's like this. When Ronnie buys the bacon, he gets the lean end, and when you're buying, I'll give you the other end – and that's the only way it works for us. Ye will have to sort it out amongst yourselves.'

## BREAKFAST IN BED

On the road, Ronnie was up early every morning, downstairs with his cup of coffee, pouring cream, a Cohiba cigar and a book. He loved reading, especially anything by Flann O'Brien or Paddy Kavanagh. Our daily touring routine began with an early breakfast, then into the bus or car and off to the next town for a good lunch, afternoon nap, sound check and the show. Sometimes Ronnie treated himself to breakfast in bed in the hotel. Inside each door hung a breakfast card displaying your options; you ticked the required items, hung it outside your door for the night porter to collect on his rounds while you enjoyed your night's sleep, and come the morning, your breakfast arrived. Experience taught Ronnie to refine his order sheet by adding a few personal notes for the morning kitchen staff. In addition to the breakfast items, carefully ticked, he wrote on every available blank space: 'knife, fork, spoons, milk, sugar, salt, pepper, pouring cream, butter – please.'

'The amount of times,' he'd explain, 'that you'd be sitting down, excited and ready to tuck into your lovely boiled egg and you notice there's no spoon, or there's no salt, or cream for the coffee or maybe even a bit of butter for the toast, you think, "Oh my Jaysus," 'cause by the time you ring down, the breakfast will be frozen. So I try to avoid any of that.' You could never fault his logic.

## THE DREW BREAKFAST

Ronnie loved to cook breakfast at home. His showstopper was huevos a la flamenca, or flamenco eggs. Flamenco is a rhythmic style of music and dance from Andalusia which Ronnie loved. He sang many Spanish songs, and indeed had the rudiments of flamenco guitar from his early days in

# Huevos a la flamenca
Serves 4

4 tomatoes, skinned and chopped
1 tbsp olive oil or rapeseed oil
4 cloves of garlic, peeled and left whole
8 slices of garlic salami
8 small asparagus tips, cleaned
500g frozen peas
400g tin cannellini beans, drained (optional)
4 medium free-range eggs
Sea salt and freshly ground black pepper

1. This is best done in a deep frying pan. Start by boiling a kettle for the tomatoes, and preheat your oven to 180°C/160°C fan/gas 4.
2. Slice a small cross on the bottom side of each tomato. Fill a large bowl with the water from the boiled kettle and carefully drop the tomatoes into the hot water for 15 seconds. Remove with a slotted spoon and peel with ease. Chop into large pieces.
3. Gently heat the oil, and lightly fry the whole garlic cloves.
4. Add the tomatoes, and a little salt and pepper. Simmer to reduce and thicken into a tomato sauce.
5. Line four heatproof bowls with a layer of salami, followed by asparagus, peas, cannellini beans and finally the tomato sauce.
6. Put the bowls into the oven for 10 minutes.
7. Remove from the oven and make a little well in the centre of each bowlful with the back of a spoon. Crack an egg into the depression. Return to the oven for about 7 minutes, or until the eggs are cooked to your liking.

Spain. Occasionally he would strum the guitar with the traditional flamenco technique, just as part of a dressing-room warm-up. I never had any doubt that he could have mastered the art and become a true *tacaor*.

## IT'S ALL ABOUT TIMING

Ronnie had superb timing when it came to delivering a story, but his musical timing was not so legendary. His great friend and musical director Earl 'Darby' Gill recalled how Ronnie kept missing the entrance to his big song during *Joseph and the Amazing Technicolor Dreamcoat* at the Gaiety Theatre in Dublin. Darby adjusted the orchestra timing to suit Ronnie, assuring him that all would be right on the night. When it came to the big moment, there was a musical kerfuffle, which straightened out after a few bars. After the show Ronnie found Earl, to apologise for 'feckin' it up for everybody'.

Earl replied, 'It's OK, Ronnie, you didn't feck it up at all. You actually came in on the right spot for once. We actually rehearsed half a beat late to suit you, but you got it right for a change, so we got it wrong. Ya bollix.' You simply had no choice but to tune in to his rhythm and be musically vigilant at all times. He certainly kept me on my toes, and I developed what I called 'the Ronnie ear', which served me very well during the course of our wonderful career together.

## THE TAPAS WRAP PARTY

Our first run at Andrew's Lane was a resounding success, receiving extremely positive reviews and sell-out houses. We celebrated the final curtain with a wrap party at a Spanish tapas bar in a pretty sandstone building on D'Olier Street in Dublin. For house parties a tapas presentation can be spectacular, and so much fun to assemble. Ronnie loved the idea of tapas. Small portions of food cooked well, enjoyed in good company with a nice glass of beer or wine – or a cup of tea if that's your fancy. Here are a few recipes from Ronnie, along with a few more I discovered along the way.

## *Patatas al pobre*: Poor man's spuds
Serves 4 to 6

1kg potatoes (the new Wexford
variety is superb)
250ml olive oil
2 onions, peeled and thinly sliced
1 or 2 bay leaves
6 cloves of garlic, roughly crushed
2 red or green peppers, cored and
chopped
A little sea salt

1. Peel and thinly slice the potatoes.
Keep them dry.

2. Heat a frying pan, add about a
quarter of the oil, and fry the
onions over a gentle heat for
20 minutes.
3. Add the bay leaves, garlic, chopped
peppers and salt and cook for
another 10 minutes.
4. Add the rest of the oil, and when
it's hot, add the potatoes. Simmer
until the potatoes are tender.
5. Pour off the oil, but always reserve
for further use as it's full of flavour.
6. Serve in a warmed dish.

## *Gambas al ajillo*: Garlic prawns
Serves about 4

We all know this one from our holidays. There are so many versions, but this
recipe is interesting, as the shells are used for extra flavour.

500g fresh prawns, peeled with shells
reserved
6 cloves of garlic, 4 crushed and
2 sliced
200ml olive oil
2 fresh red chillies, thinly sliced
(deseeded if you like)
1 tsp bicarbonate of soda and a pinch
of salt, mixed
A dash of sherry vinegar
A bunch of fresh parsley, roughly
chopped
Sea salt and freshly ground black
pepper

1. Toss the empty prawn shells with the
crushed garlic, olive oil and chillies
and fry on a medium heat until the
shells are a bright red and the garlic is
cooked. Stir regularly as you go,
so the garlic doesn't burn.
2. Strain into a bowl, pushing the shells
against the strainer to get maximum
flavour into the oil, and return the
strained oil to the pan.
3. Toss the prawns in the bicarb and salt
mixture and add to the pan. Cook for
a minute, then add the sliced garlic
and cook for a couple of minutes.
4. Add the sherry vinegar, salt, pepper
and fresh parsley and serve in a
warmed bowl.

# Monkfish, chorizo and chickpeas
Serves 3 to 4

I have served this on many menus. It can be simply served as a main course on a bed of crushed potatoes, or even better, with a parsnip, potato and sage mash.

A little olive oil
1 small good-quality chorizo sausage, peeled and chopped
1 medium onion, peeled and chopped
1 carrot, diced
1 celery stick, trimmed and chopped
2 cloves of garlic, peeled and chopped
1 bay leaf
1 medium glass of good red wine
2 tsp sherry vinegar
1 x 400g tin of chopped tomatoes, or use fresh peeled ones if you prefer
250g cooked chickpeas
Sugar or honey
2 tbsp chopped fresh oregano or marjoram
1 monkfish tail, cleaned and chopped into rounds
500g baby spinach, washed
Lemon or lime wedges, to serve

1. Warm a little olive oil and cook the chorizo, onion, carrots and celery for about 6 minutes, until tender.
2. Add the garlic and bay leaf and cook for 1 minute.
3. Add the wine and sherry vinegar and reduce.
4. Add the tomatoes and chickpeas, a little sugar or honey and a pinch of the herbs.
5. Add the monkfish and cook on a low heat for about 10 minutes until the fish is cooked through.
6. Add the spinach and stir. Serve in warm bowls – the spinach will wilt on its way to the table.
7. Sprinkle with the rest of the herbs and serve with wedges of lemon or lime.

# DEIRDRE DREW, THE CONTESSA

Deirdre loved family, friends, visitors and a busy house. Ronnie often arrived with strays from his many sojourns and she provided refuge to one and all. Out-of-work actors, musicians, poets and writers all found comfort and friendship readily available at their house. Piper Séamus Ennis once stayed at their house for six months and taught Ronnie about the music of Ireland, leaving him with reams of notes on singers and songs from every county. As we travelled from gig to gig, Ronnie would seek out those characters to share tunes and stories.

Deirdre enjoyed a celebration, a dinner party, a day at the races or a visit to a nice restaurant. She liked all things sweet, and I was privileged to be on her Christmas pudding list. She wrote out the recipe but forgot the instructions, so her wonderful daughter Cliodhna helped to piece it all back together for me. Most of Deirdre's recipes were handed down from her mother, Betty McCartan. Betty was married to Patrick McCartan, whom she first met in America. As a writer and editor of the *Irish Freedom Journal*, Patrick played a crucial role in the development of the new emerging Ireland during the very early years of the twentieth century. On his return to Ireland, he trained as a doctor while setting up the Dungannon Clubs, a precursor to the original Sinn Féin, with one Bulmer Hobson, another central figure in the build-up to the Easter Rising of 1916. Patrick trained many young volunteers of the Irish Republican Brotherhood from his base in Tyrone. He was due to take part in the Rising, but was arrested and sent to prison in England. He later contested by-elections in South Armagh, failed, but later succeeded in Tullamore. In 1918 he was elected to the first Dáil and appointed as a Sinn Féin representative in America until 1921. He was re-elected in Laois/Offaly in 1921 but quickly became disillusioned with politics following the Treaty of 1922, which he reluctantly supported. In 1945 he ran for President of Ireland but failed to get the required vote, and was elected to the Irish Senate in 1948. He served until 1951. Ronnie and his father-in-law Patrick only met a couple of times, but Ronnie had a great respect for the man and his history. I always had a passing interest in Irish history, but hours in the car with Ronnie spurred me on to understand much more about our heritage.

Deirdre studied Archaeology at UCD and was a member of the cast at Dublin's famous Pike Theatre, where she also ran the coffee shop. She met Ronnie in the early 60s and they married soon after.

I am delighted to share Deirdre's recipes, some of which came down from her mother. Her kitchen was always active, full of ingredients, recipes and a few old cookbooks.

# Deirdre's crème caramel
Serves 4

**For the caramel**
170g sugar
2 tbsp water

**For the custard**
150ml milk
275ml cream
5 large eggs
1 shot of whiskey
1 tsp vanilla extract

1. Preheat the oven to 150°C/130°C fan/gas 2.
2. Melt the sugar on a medium heat for 10 to 15 minutes, until it is a dark, runny liquid.
3. Add the water – be careful here, as it will spit.
4. Return to the heat and mix until smooth.
5. Pour three-quarters of the caramel into one large dish or several small dishes.
6. Add the milk and cream to the remaining caramel and bring nearly to the boil. If any lumps of caramel remain, keep stirring until it melts.
7. Whisk the eggs in a large bowl and slowly add the hot liquid, continuing to mix.
8. Stir in the whiskey and vanilla.
9. Pour the mixture into the dish or dishes.
10. Place the dishes in a high-sided roasting tin and carefully pour boiling water into the tin until it rises halfway up the dishes. Cook in the oven for 1¼ hours.

# THE GREAT CODDLE DEBATE

Ronnie and I were invited to perform for the old Irish Labour movement at their headquarters in Beggars Bush in Ballsbridge. The event was billed as the Great Coddle Debate. Speakers espoused the wonders of coddle and argued for or against the dark or the pale – with or without gravy. I think a coddle debate occurs every night in some Dublin household, and Ronnie and Deirdre were no different: they loved coddle and cooked it quite regularly. In 1979 when the Pope came to visit Ireland, his trip was to last three long days. Ronnie and Deirdre were not at all religious but the papal visit stirred their interest, along with that of the entire nation. Deirdre decided to cook enough coddle to last the length of the visit, to allow them to watch it all on television without the distraction of having to cook. You have to love the image of the two of them sitting in their pyjamas with the bowl of coddle and buttered brown bread and a pot of tea as they watched papal events unfold on the telly.

## It's a long, long way from Clare to coddle
Feeds about 4 hungry musicians

A coddle is a Dublin dish made of boiled sausages, bacon and spuds. A chef I worked with, Vickie O'Sullivan, insists on making a cup of concentrated vegetable soup to add just before serving.

500g potatoes, peeled and chopped
2 carrots, diced ('Whaaaaaaat?!' I hear some of you yell . . .)
2 medium onions, peeled and diced
200g bacon, diced
200g good Irish sausages, whole or halved
500ml vegetable or chicken stock (optional – water is fine)
Chopped fresh thyme (optional)
Chopped fresh parsley, to serve (optional)
Sea salt and freshly ground pepper

1. Put half the potatoes and all the other ingredients apart from the herbs into a pan, and bring to the boil. Simmer for 25 minutes. Check for seasoning, and add the thyme, if using.
2. Add the rest of the potatoes and cook until tender, about 20 minutes.
3. Sprinkle with parsley, if using, just before serving.

# A HAZARD-FREE GOLF COURSE

I cannot recall ever falling out with Ronnie. We had a healthy respect for each other. We both went through bouts of depression, and perhaps that comes with the lifestyle of intense touring schedules immediately followed by the stark contrast of the hush and comfortable pace of home life. We often spoke about some of these lows, but the highs were always wonderful and thankfully presented themselves far more often.

In one such quiet moment, I convinced Ronnie to join me in a game of golf, a sport that, like many others, he never really understood. Ronnie's only sport was horse-racing. Games of soccer, hurling, football or anything else played with two feet had no attraction for him whatsoever. He'd ridicule those of us who enjoyed hitting a white ball around a green field, and loathed sports being shown in bars and restaurants – unless it was a bunch of horses running around in circles.

I was a regular golfer who always travelled with a few clubs in the car, ready for action. After Ronnie's first outing on the golf course there was no going back, he was hooked. Within a couple of weeks, I set him up with a bag of clubs, a trolley and a couple of lessons. He quickly developed a fairly decent swing, and played three or four times a week. He was like a new man. I brought him to a few fun celebrity amateur competitions, where we met lots of other musicians, and soon he developed his own group of players who quickly became his golfing friends. We joked about having to get our instruments delivered to gigs as there was no room in the car with all the golf gear. We mapped our tour schedules noting all local golf courses and filled the early part of our days playing golf before the evening gigs. Often we had green fees waived in exchange for photos with captains, vice-captains and various club members. I usually sat these out in the bar and gleefully looked on as he earned us our free round of golf.

Deirdre was delighted with his new hobby, which had given him a new lease of life and friends, including a few great old-timers in the Wicklow Hills. For him it was a welcome escape; Ronnie was such a recognisable public figure, constantly in demand wherever he went, but on the golf course, a Ronnie Drew wrapped in wet gear, hat and shades was invisible to the world. He found peace and quiet from every tee to green. Or at least until he found the golf hazards, water, sand, trees and rough, which always brought out some very colourful language. His voice was then unmistakable as it carried a variety of expletives across the fairways. After one particularly frustrating round, he announced, 'When I win the lotto, Mikie, I am going to build my own golf course: one with no trees, no hills, no water, no rough and definitely no bunkers. No fucking hazards at all, Mikie.' I think it might have been a metaphor for the kind of life he longed for: straight shooting, down the middle, no rough edges, no nonsense, no fuss, no bullshit, no imperilment and no repercussions.

## THE LAWN MOWER WE BORROWED

Beyond cooking, Ronnie's domestic prowess was practically non-existent, and so he preferred to leave the chores to more willing candidates. Deirdre told me she had to plead with him one day to finish cutting the lawn she had started while she went to the shops before they closed. Ronnie dutifully carried out the task with his usual fine attention to detail. When Deirdre returned, he stood at the gate admiring his efforts, saying, 'I finished that for you, love. Who gave us a lend of the lawn mower? I'll drop it back to them.'

'Ronnie,' Deirdre despaired, 'that's *our* lawn mower, love. We've had it for five years. You can put that back in the shed where it belongs.'

I asked her if he even knew where the shed was. 'Just about, Mike.'

## THE FAMILY SWEET TOOTH

Ronnie and Deirdre's daughter, Cliodhna, follows in their culinary footsteps with equal dedication and passion. Whenever we meet, our conversation centres mainly on food, with the music barely in a supporting role. Both of us particularly like the food of Yotam Ottolenghi and often exchange recipes. We first met many years ago at the famous Windmill Lane recording studios, then home of U2, where Cliodhna ran reception when Stockton's Wing was in, recording *Light in the Western Sky*. Now that I think of it, we played at her wedding. She runs a very successful acting agency representing many young actors, including her brother Phelim, an accomplished Abbey actor who has appeared in numerous films and stage shows. I called to her house recently to talk about this book, and when I arrived into her kitchen, she presented me with reams of notes – a treasure chest of recipes from Deirdre, Ronnie and her grandmother Betty. She also shares their sweet tooth.

# Cliodhna Drew's lemon posset

Serves 4

250g caster sugar
900ml cream
Juice of 3 lemons

1. Gently dissolve the sugar in the cream over a low heat, stirring all the time.
2. Bring to the boil for 3 minutes. Add the lemon juice.
3. Strain into glasses and cool in the fridge.

## GONE OUR SAD CAPTAIN

Ronnie was a dedicated hypochondriac and his many perceived illnesses were a constant source of amusement to myself and Deirdre. We exchanged weekly reports on his latest aches and ailments. One day in 2006, Deirdre simply said, 'I think he's right this time, Mike.' There was a profound sadness in her voice. It was devastating news. Little did any of us know that Deirdre herself would leave us within months of that announcement. In 2007, while Ronnie was enjoying a short but very welcome respite from his treatment, Deirdre was diagnosed and soon moved on after a very short illness. It was a terribly sad time for all of us who knew and loved this incredibly beautiful, spirited, gentle, generous woman who filled our lives with such joy.

Towards the end we were booked to play a gig at the Guinness Hop Store for St Patrick's Day. Ronnie was quite ill in the weeks leading up to the gig, but he insisted on performing. The show was a sad event, as he struggled with his memory, searching for lyrics, his fingers not connecting with the guitar because of the peripheral neuropathy associated with his cancer treatment. It all caused him great distress. A few days later he called and said he needed to do another gig. It was to be his final gig, the last audience, the last show. It was at Ballymaloe House, where I had already started a new career as a professional cook. Eleanor Shanley and Frankie Lane joined us for what turned out to be an incredible gig. We finished the show with a very emotional rendition of 'We Had It All'. In August 2008, Ronnie moved on after a very tough illness. To lose a friend is hard but to lose two, well . . . But good people leave good memories, and in Ronnie and Deirdre's case, they left us an ocean.

# CHAPTER 8

---

# LEGENDS

# LOMBARD STREET

Behind the successes of the likes of Ronnie Drew, Liam Clancy, Finbar Furey, Paddy Reilly, Johnny McAvoy and Jim McCann were equally talented men and women who put it all together from music offices around Ireland, but one in particular is special to me. On Lombard Street, near the junction of Pearse Street and Westland Row, stands a four-storey building (now called Westland Studios) that housed managers, agents, publishers, public relations and record companies, with a state-of-the-art ground floor studio. It was owned by Tom Costelloe and run by his wonderful daughter Deirdre, and was sometimes referred to as the Tin Pan Alley of Irish music, producing countless hit singles and albums. There was a constant hum of business within its walls. It was there I was told as a very young musician that 'show business' has two words: 'One has only four letters, but the longer one is the word you really need to understand.' It took years for that advice to sink in.

Deirdre offered late-night sessions for a fraction of the cost to young economically challenged bands, so we spent many long nights working there, emerging to the early-morning sunshine just a stroll from the Dockers pub for breakfast pints and some local dockland banter. The studio would eventually acquire a decent catering facility, but in those early days, our 3 a.m. lunch break consisted of coffee with a ham, cheese and coleslaw sandwich, or a sliced loaf toasted on a two-bar heater in the control room. Dem were de days.

A few floors up, the managers schemed and agents spent hours calling venues to fill the diaries. Most of us musicians were convinced that the agents stood a good distance from a wall map, throwing darts to determine the location of each gig. It seemed the only plausible explanation for a weekend of gigs that had you criss-crossing the four corners of Ireland. One of those agents was a young guy called Louis Walsh, who at one stage applied to be our manager. We turned him down, of course. How could we have known?

# BIG JIM

Jim Hand had his management office on the second floor. He left Drogheda in the early sixties to sell cars in Cavan before moving down to Dublin, where he met young promoters Oliver Barry and Jim Aiken to begin an illustrious career in music, working at first with the George O'Reilly organisation. Hand created his first number-one hit with Dermot O'Brien singing 'The Merry Ploughboy'. Other successes followed, with Paddy Cole and the Capital Showband, the Tremolos, Johnny Logan, Brendan Grace, and of course the Fureys and Davy Arthur with 'The Green Fields of France', which Jim Hand had first heard on a Stockton's Wing album. For years he jibed us with, 'Have ye any more of those hit songs to give away, lads?'

Jim is rightly credited for reinvigorating the Dubliners' career with the 1987 release of *25 Years Celebration*, a collaboration with many of the younger Irish artists including ourselves, and the Pogues with the iconic 'Irish Rover'. Jim became our manager in the latter half of the 80s, and was the one who convinced director Jim Sheridan to give us a part in *The Field*. He soon handed most of the responsibilities to his young son Brian, whom we quickly nicknamed 'Nearly Jim'.

# A ROAST

As lifetime honorary president of the Music Industry Golf Society (MIGS), Jim was tasked with delivering a speech at each prize-giving. In truth, it was a roast. As he went for the microphone, music heads of all kinds could be seen scurrying away, leaping behind pillars or hiding in the shadows of colleagues – anything to avoid his searchlight gaze. He moved seamlessly from one victim to the next, only flirting with acceptable banter, hardly catching his breath as he highlighted one's failure to chart, another's misdemeanours – any and all break-ups, fights, court battles, embarrassing stories, or hint of a rumour, all were fair game. When it was over, those of us who escaped the onslaught exhaled a large sigh of relief.

His great friend Brian Molloy bore the brunt of many a roasting. Brian was an accomplished businessman, but was quite shy and reserved in company. He was the first real manager we had, and in the summer of 1980 he decided to spend some time with us at a folk festival in Nyon on the shores of Lake Geneva, Switzerland. Brian had never been to a folk festival before, and arrived in a spectacular white suit, tie and shades, looking very managerial. Afro-Caribbean band Osibisa were rocking out a powerful rhythmic set for a huge dancing crowd, who were pulling all sorts of erotic poses under a cloud of weed. As we negotiated our way backstage, Brian pulled at my shirt. 'God, some of these people are in a right state, Mike! Look at your wan over there dancing – oh my God, she has no clothes on at all!'

After our gig we decided to give Brian the full festival experience, by plying him with everything on offer until the last of his inhibitions melted away around midnight as he climbed onto a table to finish a dance routine. With his balance wavering, he soon fell face down into the muddied ground. The white suit had been tamed. We eventually found our way back to the hotel, but Brian had little time to ready himself for the morning flight home. We heard later that his wife was none too pleased with us and Brian consequently refused any further invitations to party. At the next MIGS gathering, however, Jim Hand fairly coloured the story of Brian and the not-too-sparkling white suit.

Jim practically lived in an Indian restaurant on Camden Street, which was often referred to as his office. He loved his grub and cooking gadgets, and according to his son Brian, he was one of the first in the country to own a microwave when they hit the Irish shelves. 'Unfortunately,' said Brian, 'Da never read the instructions, and his first meal was a pot of fresh mussels from his beloved Clogherhead. He filled the pot with water and placed it in the oven, then pressed the button. I'll say no more.'

## DOWN UNDER

As part of the great Irish music family, we meet in all sorts of places in all sorts of circumstances, the world over. We have travelled hours on tour buses, met at festivals, corporate gigs, charity golf outings, did TV shows and fund-raising events. But the most wonderful gathering of all was on tour down under in Australia and New Zealand as part of the Guinness Celebration of Irish Music, organised by exuberant British actor and concert promoter Jon Nichols.

We played on three of those tours and shared some great times with the Dubliners, Brendan Grace, Frances Black, Davy Spillane, Artie McGlynn, Nollaig Casey, Christy Moore, Paddy Reilly, Maura O'Connell, Kieran Goss, Barleycorn, Mary Black, Niall Tóibín, Dolores Keane, Máire Ní Chathasaigh and Jim McCann. Friendships develop during intensive touring as you move from city to city, taking in the culture, staying in nice hotels and dining on really good local food. On one occasion myself and a favourite piper of mine, Liam Óg O'Flynn, who made his set of pipes sound like an orchestra in full flow, decided to try Japanese food for the first time. We found a restaurant around the corner from our Sebel Townhouse hotel in King's Cross, Sydney, where we struggled to order, to put it mildly – we had no Japanese and our hosts had zero English. The food seemed very cheap compared to the price of a bottle of wine. Within minutes, our starter and main courses arrived together, each piece barely visible in its own tiny dish. 'I think we have this all wrong, Mike,' says Liam. We called over the waiter and we were soon surrounded by the entire family trying to understand our hand gestures. After much miming and tummy-rubbing, the table was cleared, a fondue-style burner placed between us, and a large pan full of raw fish and vegetables presented for our inspection. The waiter replaced the glass lid and then pointed to twenty-five minutes on his watch. 'Aaaahhhhh, yes . . . more wine, please.' The food was stunning and a wonderful friendship was sealed over that pot of stewing fish.

# LEGENDS OF IRISH FOLK: THE CONCERT

Brian Hand grew up surrounded by all these great entertainers, and listened to the many stories from his dad and heard many tales from our tours down under. He had an idea and so, *Legends of Irish Folk* was born. It caught the public imagination, and there is no doubt Jim would have been very proud of his son's imagination, foresight and achievement in bringing it all together. I was given the role of musical director and enlisted the help of my friend Pat 'Fitzy' Fitzpatrick on piano, along with ex-Stockton's Wing fiddle maestro Maurice Lennon, to contribute their many talents.

My job was simple: to create an easy ensemble sound, sympathetic to each artist, allowing them to weave their way through the songs and stories. My dad always believed that natural talent plays the sweetest air. That to me is the creative energy and the essence of folk music: very free, extremely personal and in the moment. I am not at all academically minded, while Fitzy knew his crotchets and quavers, a highly educated musician who moved easily between genres, from orchestras to jazz bands, to musicals, to great rock bands like Katmandu, Something Happens and Aslan. Surprisingly, he knew very little about folk music prior to the Legends, so he was delighted to come on board. I took great pride telling friends that I was his MD, and had every intention of ensuring he stayed well within the confines of the three chords of folk; no demented seventh chords would be allowed anywhere near our stage.

We were great friends and fellow cynics who thrived on a connection that kept us tight right up to his untimely death at sixty-one from cancer. His wife Rebecca kindly invited me to present the eulogy. I focused on Fitzy, the guy who meant so much to our local Mounttown community. As I finished speaking, I thought I heard his voice scream, 'Right, lads. Let's folk this joint! Folk on, man!' with a reversed peace sign to the sky.

## SO LONELY ROUND DE FIELDS

The *Legends* concert opened with Paddy Reilly. He was the right man to start, always guaranteed to come in on time. A twenty-five-minute slot was just that; not twenty-four or twenty-six. We joked that if his set was threatening to go over, he'd probably stop mid-chorus to make it home on time. Pre-gig, Paddy worked himself into a frenzy of nerves, spending an hour or so alone in his dressing room, dreading the curtain call. Yet you never sensed that during his performance, which was steady and tight, as his beautifully pitched, penetrating voice reached every seat in the house. The audience responded in kind, filling the room with a rousing chorus of 'Low
Lie the Fields of Athenry'.

Paddy was also a dedicated student and a fan of opera, which goes some way towards explaining his impressive delivery. While on tour he loved to visit

the Met in New York or La Scala in Milan. I once studied bel canto singing with Frank Merriman in Dublin, where I rediscovered my voice, and as a bonus fell in love with opera. Most arias are, after all, beautiful simple folk songs. 'There is a voice within each one of us,' Frank used to say. 'We are all born with perfect pitch and only become bad singers as a result of obstacles that are placed in our path as we grow older. Did you ever hear a child scream out of tune? No, because no such child exists. Your voice is always there, you just need to let it flow.' Always loved those words.

So, like Paddy, I have a deep appreciation for the likes of Jussi Björling, Enrico Caruso and Maria Callas. I visited La Scala once when I was in Milan with Stockton's Wing, recording a TV promo for Italia '90. In the lobby, I heard beautiful music coming from an open door into the auditorium and I asked the porter if I could see the theatre. He said no, as the orchestra was rehearsing, but I persevered, explaining I was a folk musician over from Ireland for one night only, and listed off the names of all my favourite tenors. He left for a few minutes, then returned and motioned for me to follow in silence. We went up a flight of stairs and into a very plush booth. In his broken English, the porter whispered that I had a few minutes, smiled and left. I sank into a comfortable chair, surveyed the theatre and its beautiful decor, and peered down into the pit of musicians who were tuning, followed by silence as the conductor issued instructions. The music started – I closed my eyes to the sounds of *Carmen* as it sprang to life and filled the room, and for that moment, I understood the concept of heaven.

Whenever and wherever I'd meet Paddy Reilly over the years, conversation would invariably lead to opera, though our other crossover was a little closer to home, as our respective management teams shared rooms at Lombard Street. In the 80s he found a new home in America, where he opened a bar in Manhattan with his friend Steve Duggan.

We met in Boston one time and Paddy brought me to a restaurant for a feed of New England crabs with Old Bay seasoning, a classic spice mix for seafood from Maryland. It's a blend of paprika, celery salt, cayenne, dry mustard, mace, bay leaf and cinnamon, all ground up together into a powder and smeared all over the crab. Seafood heaven. I was so taken by it that as soon as I got home, I researched the recipe – though now, of course, it's available all over in fancy grocers and on the American shelf of some supermarkets.

## WELL, GOODBYE, MUIRSHEEN DURKIN

Johnny McEvoy's songs were all miniature novels: sometimes action thrillers, sometimes love stories and the odd tale of tragedy. At our first sound check for *Legends*, I was amazed that I remembered every word of 'The Boston Burglar' and 'The Black Velvet Band'. An easy musician to work with, Johnny was definite and strict on his musical arrangements but, typical of ballad-singers, tended to waver a little on rhythm. Ronnie Drew was renowned for missing the beat, so I was well schooled in that regard, and able to adjust to Johnny's time-keeping. His sensitivity to the lyrics, the music and the mood of the room, however, was constant throughout the performance. He brought the entire audience along for the journey as they sang every word, and you'd almost feel you were at home by the open fire, such was the ease of his performance.

While Johnny's show was practically flawless, he would often come off stage bothered by a strange chord or the odd movement of a song – forever the perfectionist. In recent years he has spoken openly about his depression, which came as a surprise to many. He was one of the first musicians that I can recall who shone a light on that darkness. His honesty endeared him to many, and certainly helped develop a better understanding of the bleakness and despair that people feel while living with depression. He made the path a little easier for others to walk upon.

## RONNIE, THE CAPTAIN AND HIS CREW

Ronnie Drew finished the first half of that show and gave it everything. Knowing he only had twenty-five minutes, Ronnie rattled off as many stories and songs as he could in quick time. He was a musician's musician, and that gig was like home to him. I have dedicated Chapter 7 to this Legend because he may have been the greatest I ever met.

## JIM McCANN

Our MC for the evening was Jim McCann, a very accomplished singer with a string of hit singles to his name and a career that dated back to 1965, when he joined ballad group The Ludlows to record their first hit single, 'The Butcher Boy'. The following year they created history as the first Irish folk group to reach number one with 'The Sea Around Us'. The Ludlows would go on to represent Ireland in the Eurovision Song Contest on two occasions.

Jim then branched out as a solo performer and secured his own television special, *The McCann Man*, which showcased his versatility as a singer. He loved singing Leonard Cohen and Bob Dylan, and even appeared alongside Luke Kelly in the stage musical *Joseph and the Amazing Technicolor Dreamcoat. The McCann Man* also gave us that moving Luke Kelly version of Phil Coulter's ballad 'Scorn Not His Simplicity'. Jim later joined the Dubliners in '74 to replace Ronnie, who left to pursue a solo career and spend more time with his family. In 1979 Ronnie returned to the Dubliners and Jim resumed his solo career, releasing several albums and hit songs, including 'Grace'. He returned once more to the Dubliners in 2002 for a short stint, but remained their regular guest for the rest of his days.

He was once managed by Brian Molloy over at Lombard, so we toured Europe and Australia together on occasion. He was great company – except on an aeroplane. For people who travel so much, fear of flying is surprisingly common among musicians. Ronnie Drew's airport anxiety spells required delicate management, but Jim's fear sank to a different level of dread.

Then there was the two of them combined. Nothing could have prepared me for my first trip to Australia: I was in the middle seat, Jim McCann to the left and Ronnie Drew to the right. Never again. I was chatting to one of the lads in the next aisle when the flight attendant began her safety presentation. Ronnie started blessing himself and becoming very fidgety, making all sorts of grunting noises, while Jim suddenly froze in his seat, holding white-knuckled to the armrests, his entire upper body tensed. Then he started to shake. As the captain announced our take-off and the engines roared, Jim shifted his grip to my left arm and squeezed like a python around its prey. His eyebrows rose, his teeth clenched, and soon his entire body was trembling. I was sure my wrist was being severed, such was the intensity of his grip, and a severe pain shot through to my shoulder and spread right down to my toes. When we levelled off, the captain finally announced he was switching off the seat belt sign, and Jim relaxed his grip. 'Sorry about that, Mike. Jaysus, I hate that part of it!' he said, and started reading a magazine. I slowly drew my arm in and marvelled at the bruising. Ronnie was also back to his jovial self, as my arm went into spasm. On the second leg of the flight, I found a spare seat far away from Dread Row.

Throughout his musical career, Jim McCann's vocal was sublime, lyrical, sweet, delicate and full of emotion. He played beautiful guitar and his introductions were legendary. Unfortunately, a few years before the *Legends* gig, Jim had lost the use of his vocal cords to throat cancer, but he courageously reinvented himself as a photographer and writer.

Inviting Jim to MC for *Legends* was a great call by Brian Hand, for although his voice was very weak, our wonderful sound engineer Tom O'Brien took care of it seamlessly, with no adverse effect on either Jim's ailing vocal cords or, more importantly, his confidence. The ultimate professional, he never missed a stop to our dressing room to wish us well. His opening remarks at all the *Legends* gigs went, 'Good evening, ladies and gentlemen, and welcome. Before I go any further, I'd like to introduce the band. Mike,' he'd say, turning to me, 'this is Maurice on fiddle, and this is Pat on piano. Maurice, this is Mike . . . ' He gave a polished performance every night, and joined us on guitar for the finale.

## THE INTERVAL AND THE PHANTOM RIDER

A welcome feature of every *Legends* gig was the excellent green room food service. Promoter Pat Egan always takes great care of his performers, so it was no surprise when we arrived at the Gaiety Theatre for our first concert to find a beautiful array of food spread out across the green room table. There were all sorts of sandwiches, salads, fruits, biscuits, drinks and freshly brewed coffee. We tucked in and had already done a fair bit of damage when the door swung open, and in rushed a frantic-looking stage manager. He fixed his gaze on the destruction, and his expression darkened. His language followed suit: 'What the fuck are ye doing, lads? That's not your food at all! You can't eat that! Oh, my Jaysus, that's terrible, oh God, that's for the fuckin' panto crew rehearsing upstairs! Jaysus, they'll go mad!' We left the room fairly lively, offering our apologies, but that just drew more abuse. The food was quickly replaced from our own rider and the panto crew only laughed when we went to apologise, but I can still see the look of horror on the face of that stage manager, and hear his extraordinary abusive vocabulary ringing in my ears.

## THE GLADIATORS

After intermission, the second half of the gig was a roller coaster. Finbar Furey and Liam Clancy were like two gladiators putting it up to each other. They alternated slots each night, and we wondered whether as they handed over the baton it was more a case of 'Good luck' or 'All yours, follow that!'

Each had a tremendous story to tell, with careers spanning decades in two of the most iconic groups in world folk music, and although diametrically opposed in image and content, the Clancys with their well-groomed, scripted stage personas against the Fureys' and Davy Arthur's streetwise image and frantic tunes – they were both powerhouses of talent and craft who produced some of the most beautiful ballads in Irish folk music. Not too many musicians have Bob Dylan or Billy Connolly citing them as main influences. With so much to contribute to the show each night, the schedule was thrown out the window as each sang well beyond curfew – but no one complained, not even the theatre management.

## LIAM CLANCY AND THE POWER OF THE SPOKEN WORD

Liam ambled out onto the stage, tipped his cap to the band, and found his way to centre stage. He stood there for a second to draw a hush from the audience, smiled, and from that moment the space was his and his alone, where he enthralled, wooed and caressed the hearts of the entire audience, drifting effortlessly from songs to poetry to storytelling. We heard about

Bob Dylan, Joan Baez, the heady days of Greenwich Village. We sang along to 'The Dutchman' and finished with a rousing rendition of 'Those Were the Days'.

In Stockton's Wing, we had our own private nickname for Liam: 'the power of the spoken word'. It came from a party in a hotel room at Milwaukee Irish Fest many years before. There was a lot of drink taken, and it was well into the night in a very noisy room when Liam decided to play a slow air on the concertina and recite the poem 'A Lament for Thomas McDonagh' by Francis Ledwidge. He called for silence, which took a few attempts, his voice rising in volume with each appeal. The room eventually hushed at the words 'He shall not hear the bittern cry in the wild sky', over the low drone from his concertina. It seemed to last a lifetime, but no one broke the silence as he weaved his way through the words and then into a beautiful air, 'The Yellow Bittern', later the title of a film about his life. As the concertina faded, he turned to us and whispered, 'The power of the spoken word, lads, the power of the spoken word.'

## ACAPULCO A CAPELLA

We had a power cut one night at the Legends as Finn had just begun 'The Green Fields of France'. The crowd heckled, and Finbar rose from his chair, moved to the front of the stage, hushed the crowd and continued a capella (or acapulco, as a friend of mine used to say). At the chorus, he urged everyone to join in and the room erupted. He directed a silence for the final verse, you could hear a pin drop, and then the swell again into the finishing chorus. Finbar applauded the crowd, turned to the band, winked, and sat back on his chair, a very satisfied man. A legend.

## THE PARTING GLASS

A finale was called, and Brian Hand captured it on camera. The very best of our music together on one stage, all egos relaxed, the audience enthralled as the Legends offered their goodbye for the evening: 'Come fill to me the parting glass, goodnight and joy be with you all.'

# CHAPTER 9

---

# VAGABONDS

We always called them 'Nigels'. They were the managers, agents and record company reps who expressed fervent admiration for your every word and deed. It was an enthusiasm that usually lasted for the duration of your success. Our first record-company runner was an over-zealous individual called Nigel, whose ego-caressing compliments were spewed out at every possible opportunity, to the point where we had to sit him down and tell him to calm down, because we didn't believe a word he was saying. He was practically redundant for the rest of the trip.

In the early to mid-80s Dublin was awash with A&R scouts eager to find the next U2. Many of the major record companies had only years earlier passed on Bono and the boys, much to their eternal regret and shame, so there was a determination not to make the same mistake again. For a few years, it seemed Dublin had been declared rock band central. Swarms of execs combed the nightclubs, music bars and rehearsal studios to sign the next big thing. Some of the bands had minor success, but many unfortunately either ended up in the bottom drawer or morphed into another version of themselves, only to be ruthlessly cast aside again by the suits in London. As a result, rehearsal rooms were awash with musicians writing or recording their demos for consideration. It became an inside joke that you were either working or 'wroiting', pronounced with a very posh Dublin 4 accent – everyone who was anyone was at it. Litton Lane rehearsal studios on Bachelors Walk was the hive of this creative activity.

The Wing used Litton as a rehearsal space for the live show, which had developed into somewhat of an extravaganza with the addition of a very specialised state-of-the-art pyrotechnic lighting show. Someone suggested we add a few fancy dance moves, so we hired a choreographer in to put us through our paces – did I just admit to that? Our manager then suggested we focus on our health and strength, so we all signed up with fitness queen Carolyn Brown, who ran a gym on the top floor of Litton. We were frequent visitors all right, but Carolyn insisted that while we were the worst bunch of guys she ever trained, we were by far the funniest, as we laughed and joked our way through the circuits, spending most of our time checking out the treadmill talent. She was probably right. To complete our new image, we had a dress designer in to fit us out with the latest fashion, which had its moments. Unfortunately, some of that very expensive clobber couldn't hold up to the demands of crowded venues like Woodies in Castleisland, where thousands packed into a sweat cavern. Our newly designed stage gear soon wilted for want of a rinse or a rub of an iron, particularly a cream cotton Paul Costelloe suit I had that looked anything but fetching after a run of consecutive two-hour sweat fests.

Aslan signed to our management team, along with Cactus World News and Flo McSweeney's Toy with Rhythm. It was a great place to be, always among friends. Many bands came and went during those Hurricane Nigel years, but some survived, like Something Happens, Light a Big Fire and the Radiators, to produce great music, and of course Aslan, who are still knocking it out of the park.

The 80s Dublin music scene was like a small village, and Litton was one of its little coffee shops where we all met to talk music, play music and make plans.

My go-to gig in Dublin was Belfast band Katmandu at the Baggot Inn, which featured my pal Fitzy on keys, Trevor Hutchinson on bass and Peter McKinney on drums, with the inimitable Marty Lundy on vocals. Katmandu pushed the barriers of entertainment, with Marty often finishing the final chorus from a stool in the front bar of the Baggot Inn, next door to its main venue. He was a star performer.

# LESLIE DOWDALL, YOU ARE MY SISTER

One band stood slightly apart from many at the time. In Tua Nua were signed to U2's Mother label, and had a really interesting fusion sound of rock, pop with elements of traditional Irish music. It was Horslips meets Simple Minds, but delivered with a powerful vocal from Leslie Dowdall, a stunning, very stylish young singer with lots of attitude and confidence, but most of all, a voice so distinctive and full of personality that it caught the attention of everyone. Whatever about the band, it was widely anticipated that she was destined for greatness in the music business. In Tua Nua toured extensively with U2, Simple Minds, and even got to sing with Bob Dylan on his appearance at Slane Castle. I knew Leslie through various music events, and we had a particularly great day at the Bob-Geldof-inspired Self Aid concert in Dublin, where we played to over 25,000 people in the RDS. We were billed back to back with In Tua Nua, which gave us a few memorable hours together backstage.

They had a few hit singles and were soon flown to LA to record 'The Big One', that breakthrough album we all hoped for in those heady days. By then they had signed to Virgin, released two successful albums and enjoyed minor

success in the British charts. While recording that third album in LA, the band split. Leslie returned home devastated by the experience. She drifted away from the scene and started working as a waitress in several restaurants. I remember meeting her one day at Captain America's on Grafton Street, and her attitude was a resigned, 'I have to pay the rent, Mike.'

A year later she collapsed at her house on Baggot Street and was rushed to hospital, to be diagnosed with renal cancer. After months of intensive treatment and surgery, she lost a kidney but an inner strength and determination helped her survive the trauma and return to full health. She often recalls reciting a daily mantra as she walked the hospital corridors with her IV unit: 'Let's get through this, just let's get through this, Leslie.' She did just that.

She returned to songwriting and went knocking on doors looking for a record deal. She convinced promoter Denis Desmond to fund a new album: *No Guilt, No Guile* was released, charted and gave us that brilliant hit song 'Wonderful Thing'. Hot Press voted her Female Vocalist of the Year.

We now perform together as a duo whenever the opportunity arises. I love the gig with Leslie, as it takes me beyond my music comfort zone, sometimes way out into the unknown. Our songs have a basic structure that allows us to move to wherever the atmosphere of the room dictates. It is very special and rewarding to sit out on that creative edge; we like to keep it that way, slightly off-track.

Some of the venues we've played have been equally off-track. A few years ago, we arrived very early for a gig at an old and deserted theatre. The sound crew, management or any manner of staff were nowhere to be seen. After we banged on the door for a few minutes, an elderly lady appeared.

'What do ye want?'

'We're playing here tonight.'

'Oh, I see. Well, there won't be anyone here for another couple of hours, but ye might as well come in from the cold. I'm only here to do a bit of cleaning. I'll call Patricia and let her know ye have arrived. I'll put on the lights and ye can make yer way to the dressing room – it's right behind the stage to your right. Would ye like a cuppa?'

We made our way down a spiral staircase through a creaking door into an ice-cold room. Wind whistled from a cracked window pane. We sat on a wooden bench to survey the scene before us. A three-legged metal coatstand stood lonesome in the corner with a faded white collarless shirt dangling from a wire hanger, almost human as it swayed in the draught. Strewn across one section of the floor were hundreds of raffle tickets, along with a couple of cracked mugs, a pair of old leather boots and a man's cap. On the counter, where once sat the pride of local thespia donning their alter egos, two used make-up tubes and a few brushes lay beside an empty tissue box. Wedged into the corner was a two-foot square metallic fridge with the words 'Red Bull' fading on its rusted glass panelled door. We looked at each other and started to smile.

'Not like the old days, Mike,' Leslie managed through the laughter.

'No sign of Nigel anywhere. Maybe that's what's left of him on the hanger.'

'But can you imagine all the *craic* that went on in here?'

We painted a picture of this room in its heyday, all hustle and bustle, full of lovely people rushing around, showering us with compliments and niceties with a yaw and an oh-my-word as they gestured and finger-clicked the rookies to rearrange the already well-arranged flower arrangements. Crisp linen on the tables, full of goodies, fresh fruit, cheese and fancy biscuits, plates with towers of perfectly cut gourmet sandwiches, bottles of sparking water, fridges bulging with expensive wines, beers and tonic waters – then the cloud of Brut that suddenly choked the air prior to curtain call.

Yet we climbed back up that spiral stairwell to one of the most amazing gigs of our careers, to be reminded that music is the only reason we went there in the first place. Some venues have a certain energy that sets them apart. I like to think it's the ghosts of entertainment past urging you on from the cracks and crevices of venues like the Meeting Place, the Baggot Inn, McGonagle's, Sir Henry's in Cork, Dolan's in Limerick, and that wonderful old National Stadium in Dublin.

If I were to choose a personal favourite venue for myself and Leslie, then I can look no further than an old schoolhouse tucked away in the Wicklow Hills. Many years ago, actor Pat Nolan decided to take over the old Conary Community Hall just outside Avoca in Wicklow. His dream was to bring theatre to the people, and he certainly made it come true. He presented all sorts of plays, pageants, kids' theatre, live music and poetry to a very supportive audience, who arrived, some with their own cushions, to enjoy the show and spend the interval catching up on gossip over a cuppa and some chocolate biscuits. When the curtain came down, they'd announce upcoming local events and head across to the pub to close out the day. At one particular gig we had to clear the stage after sound check to allow the parish priest to set up and say Mass for the locals. After he'd finished, they had their tea while we reset for the show. It was a community hall in all its glory.

Leslie lives in Glenmalure in Wicklow, so a rehearsal with her is like a day out for me. I leave Dublin early in the morning for the journey south, winding my way through the mountains to her wooden cottage tucked away in the hillside. We'll spend an hour catching up on news and gossip, talk food and music before playing a single note. Then we crank up the volume and send our songs out through the open windows to the animals who roam freely in the glen below. There's a great freedom in that space, and perhaps that is where our magic begins. It's certainly a far cry from the buzzing hive of Litton Lane, but somewhere along the road we stopped trying to take over the music world, to concentrate instead on making the one we have a more pleasurable place in which to dwell, whether by making food or making music.

# Tea-smoked salmon
Serves 6

On one beautiful afternoon in the Wicklow sun I treated some of Leslie's neighbours to one of my favourite dishes, a home-smoked salmon, one which draws on our beautiful local fish, and our cosy national obsession with tea. It's a little fussy to set up, but it's delicious, and well worth the extra effort.

   You'll need a food thermometer, tin foil, and a wok with a grill insert or a deep grill pan.

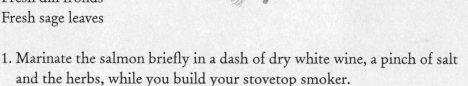

750g piece of salmon
2 tbsp goji berry, ginger or lemon tea
2 tbsp rice
2 tbsp brown sugar
Lemon or lime wedges, to serve

**For the marinade**
Dry white wine
Sea salt
Fresh dill fronds
Fresh sage leaves

1. Marinate the salmon briefly in a dash of dry white wine, a pinch of salt and the herbs, while you build your stovetop smoker.
2. Place the tea, rice and sugar on a sheet of tin foil on the bottom of the wok or pan. Place the circular grill insert on top, like a miniature barbecue. Cover the grill insert with another sheet of tin foil. Prick holes in the top sheet of foil, then place the pan over the hob on a low heat and allow to smoke.
3. Once it's smoking, lay the salmon on top of the pricked foil and cover tightly with the lid. If you have no lid, use another layer of foil tightly packed to prevent any smoke escaping.
4. After 8 to 10 minutes, lift off the top foil layer. Ensure the salmon has cooked beyond 55°C.
5. Serve with wedges of lemon and/or lime, and if you have the time rustle up a fresh cucumber relish and a few tasty salads.

# Leslie's Thai green curry from scratch
Serves 6 to 8

Like most of my music friends, Leslie likes to cook and she usually treats
me to a feast after a day of music. If her husband Enrique is around, then the
theme is normally Spanish, but occasionally she drifts back to her beloved
Thai green curry, which is probably the best I have ever tasted. Ingredients are
a-plenty in the Wicklow Hills. It is a bountiful garden of fresh produce, with a
wonderful selection of cheeses, honey, beer and, in recent years, very tasty wine,
supplemented with spoils from the Macreddin Village Food Market, which
showcases the work and passion of so many great local producers.

1 tbsp rapeseed oil
2 tbsp Thai green curry paste (see page 184)
1 onion, thinly sliced
6 chicken breasts, skinned and cut into strips
1 x 400ml tin of coconut milk
2 lime leaves (optional)
2 tbsp Thai fish sauce
1 tbsp caster sugar
1 yellow pepper, cored and thinly sliced
A handful of shiitake mushrooms
Sea salt and freshly ground black pepper
Thai jasmine rice and fresh coriander leaves (optional), to serve

1. Heat the oil in a wok over a high heat until smoking. Add the green curry
   paste and the onion, and stir-fry for 1–2 minutes.
2. Add the chicken and stir to coat. Continue to stir-fry for 1–2 minutes, or
   until the chicken has browned on all sides.
3. Add the coconut milk, lime leaves (if using), fish sauce and sugar, and stir
   well.
4. Bring the mixture to the boil, then reduce the heat until simmering. Add
   the peppers and mushrooms, and continue to simmer for 8 minutes, or
   until the sauce has thickened.
5. Serve with a sprinkle of coriander leaves, if liked, and Thai jasmine rice.

# Leslie's homemade green Thai curry paste

Most Thai curry pastes are pretty standard, but I have picked up a few tips along the way from Leslie and other enthusiasts. While not at all necessary, the roasting of the shallots, garlic and ginger or galangal adds an extra layer of flavour to Leslie's recipe.

You can of course buy good-quality curry paste from the supermarket shelves, but there's something about creating your own that makes this dish special. Some recipes use galangal, which is a root from the ginger family and often used in Asian cooking. For red curry paste you can use red chillies and some paprika for colour. This keeps well in the fridge.

4 shallots, peeled
1 thumb of fresh ginger or galangal, thinly sliced
1 bulb of garlic, top sliced off
A couple of glugs of olive oil
Sea salt
2 tsp each of ground cumin, coriander and turmeric
1 bunch of fresh coriander, stems and leaves
4 green chillies, deseeded and chopped
I lemongrass stalk, finely chopped
1 lime, juice and zest
6 kaffir lime leaves, roughly crunched
2 tsp Thai fish sauce

1. Optional, but worth the effort for extra flavour. Wrap the shallots, ginger or galangal and garlic, with a little oil and a pinch of salt, in tin foil and roast in a preheated oven at 170°C/150°C fan/gas 3 for 20 minutes.
2. Cool, then squeeze the garlic from its soft skin into a food processor and add all the other ingredients. Pulse to your preferred consistency. It will hold for about 5 or 6 days in the fridge.

# PAUL ASHFORD

*Monday saw you walking down the avenue of dreams,*
*Your head in your heart, that's the way it seemed.*
*Tuesday you were chosen, a hero of your age.*
*As you stood there on the threshold you had it made.*
*What's a week in the life of a fallin' idol? No one knows.*
*What's a week in the life of a fallen idol? It comes and goes.*
– 'A Week in the Life (of a Fallen Idol)', *Someone Like You* (1994)

My great friend Paul Ashford began his career in the early 60s as a bass guitarist with various beat groups in and around Bray in County Wicklow. As teenagers, Paul and his best pal Fran O'Toole left a group called the Chosen Few to join Dickie Rock and the Miami Showband. Paul lived the life of a superstar for a few years, until he left the Miami Showband in the early 70s to join Emmet Spiceland, and later, Stepaside.

In July 1975, the Miami Showband were stopped at a checkpoint in County Down. Fran O'Toole, Brian McCoy and Tony Geraghty were murdered in the massacre that followed. Des McAlea and bassist Stephen Travers survived the attack. The murders of Fran, Tony and Brian had a profound effect on Paul, the Irish music industry and the entire country. We were all shocked at the killing of innocent musicians whose only purpose was to entertain those communities caught in the Troubles. Many years later, in 2006, Stephen Travers asked Paul to help organise a concert at Vicar Street to raise funds for a permanent memorial to the band at Parnell Square in Dublin, beside the old National Ballroom, right across the street from the Garden of Remembrance.

Paul asked me to join the team, and in July we filled the venue for a host of musicians to pay their respects, including Brendan Bowyer, Ronnie Drew, Ronan Collins, Tina Reynolds, Brendan O'Brien, Johnny Fean, the Conquerors, Jimmy Magee, Fr Brian Darcy, the Indians and countless others who showed up for the gig. I had the unenviable task of stage manager, but I treasure every minute of that very special night. A couple of years later, both myself and Paul stood proudly with Stephen, Des and members of the O'Toole, Geraghty and McCoy families as Bertie Ahern unveiled the memorial entitled 'Let's Dance' to an audience of musicians, singers and fans.

Jerry Lee Lewis lived in our community in Dún Laoghaire for a short while, and his wife Kerry celebrated her sixtieth birthday at our local pub, McCormack's. The pickup band was Paul on bass and his friend Robbie

Brennan on drums. Jerry Lee loved the two guys so much, he brought them on a tour, and when it was over, they both slipped with ease back into life at home.

A record company then hired Paul to manage a young girl band, and after a few weeks he surprised everyone when he arrived back in the pub dressed in a sheepskin jacket, flashy suit, shiny leather shoes and with a head full of confidence. He had a new office in the city that came with a secretary, a state-of-the-art stereo system and a fancy new phone. Ten months later, after spending over £250,000 recording songs that were rejected by the head office in London, Paul was dropped from the team. In the pub a week later, he got some roasting from his friend, music agent and cynic Aidan Hand. 'You're a failure, sham! Useless! You robbed a fortune from that poor record company over in London and you've no shame at all. You call yourself a businessman – some businessman you turned out to be, Ashford.'

Paul stood there until Aido ran out of steam. 'Aido, you're supposed to be the smart one,' he replied. 'Think about this: you say I'm a failure, that I'm no businessman, but the way I see it, the record company is down about £300,000 at this stage, all right? I reckon with the new clobber and my new stereo, I'm up about £20,000. So, who's the businessman now?' That was vintage Ashconomics.

## DEAR LORD, IT'S SHAY HEALY

Shay began as a cameraman for RTÉ, filming those controversial finger-licking images of the TV's first celebrity chef Monica Sheridan that we all enjoyed back home in St Michael's Villas, and he has remained at the cutting edge of our entertainment industry for decades.

We were regular enough on his wonderful TV programme, *Nighthawks*, which scattered the Irish broadcasting rule book to the wind. Guests and audience were situated in a very relaxed café/bar environment. Cans of beer helped to relax certain interviewees, who oftentimes revealed a few hidden nuggets of information. Shay was never found wanting when it came to knowing how to extract information from those of the political persuasion. Former justice minister Sean Doherty once famously claimed on the show that he was fired by Charles J. Haughey over alleged phone-tapping revelations. Shay went straight for the jugular: 'So you took the rap for Charlie Haughey. Do you feel let down?' 'I do,' Doherty replied, before carrying on and going deeper. Shay had no idea the extent of the scoop landed at his door until the ex-minister called him aside later to point it out to him. It transpired to be the beginning of the end for Haughey – and a huge boost for *Nighthawks'* viewing figures.

Shay is a great man for advice, and on the golf course I once confided in him that I was in trouble. My career was at an all-time low, I had left the band, got married and bought a house all in the same year, but I had no money coming in and very few prospects in sight. 'What should I do, Shay?' I pleaded.

'Mike, I've been up and down more times than I care to remember: winning Eurovision, broke, making documentaries, broke, doing TV shows, broke. I'm surprised Deedee has put up with me all this time, but she has. My best advice is to do what I do. When I get out of bed every morning, I kneel down, bless myself, hold my hands together and say a little prayer: "Dear Lord, Hustle, hustle, hustle. Amen."'

I laughed so hard as he strolled off down the fairway, delighted with himself. I'm sure it had been decades since he'd last fallen to his knees in prayer, if ever, but the lesson was brilliant – and very Shay Healy. I often think of his little prayer whenever those niggling doubts come back to gnaw at me.

# HAPPY BIRTHDAY, SHAY

Shay celebrated his seventieth birthday at the Sugar Club in Dublin, and I was invited to sing a song. The running order had me up after Paul Brady, and I cringed. I thanked Shay for the vote of confidence and he laughed and assured me I'd be fine. Brady went down a storm, as expected, and my insides began to cave in, a feeling I'd not known for some years. As the crowd bellowed for more Paul Brady, guitarist Jimmy Smyth announced, 'OK, folks, another friend of Shay's would like to sing a song now. Please welcome Mikie Hanrahan.' There was light applause and I relaxed a little. Something made me think of my dad, and his offbeat sense of humour. I started in.

'Thank you, I'm delighted to be here to honour the great man. You know, I've been performing all of my life – on big stages, on small stages – I've played with so many people over the years, but tonight here at the Sugar Club I've realised a dream. I'm here to sing for my great friend Shay Healy, and can hardly believe that Paul Brady was my support act. It don't get much better than that, folks. Give him a good hand now. Thanks, Paul, you certainly got them going.'

To my relief, the theatre reverberated in laughter and applause. Shay came up to me afterwards.

'Jaysus, Hanrahan, you're some huar of a man.'

'Didn't I only learn it from the master?' I replied.

At my own sixtieth birthday party, Shay walked through the door and made straight for the stage to say hello.

'Fair play to you, Shay, thanks for coming.'

'I couldn't miss your party, Mike. So, what time am I on?'

# SHARON SHANNON AND THE GARDEN OF VEGAN

Sharon has often spoken about the influence of Stockton's Wing on her early music growing up, and it is always lovely to hear that, especially when it's from a musician you admire so much. We obviously share a Clare connection, as she grew up on a farm in Bealacana, a townland straddling the borders of Ruan and Corofin in County Clare, but we have much more in common than that. Our respective families are steeped in traditional Irish music, all taught music by the maestro Frank Custy in the village school house at Toonagh. We also hold deep and treasured links to the music and history of the Kilfenora Céilí Band, we have played and sung many a tune together and enjoy exploring all sorts of creative possibilities. We share a love of animals, and in recent years have explored the world of good, sustainable food – albeit in very different ways. Sharon is vegan, and passionately promotes awareness of the plight of animals in factory farms.

Back when I was a vegetarian, I could never understand how vegans could live on nuts, leaves and lentils. Sharon recently explained it all: 'You can veganise all your regular and favourite dishes. You can make casseroles, roasts, stews, shepherd's pie, cheeseburgers – using vegan cheese, of course – Thai curries, Indian curries, bolognese, sushi . . . soups, especially Asian-style spicy soups like tom yum, coconut curry soups or Russian borscht. You can imitate the fanciest of posh cuisine, vegan style, or create amazing recipes with the likes of tofu—' Everything had been going so well. I'd nearly crossed over, until tofu was mentioned. The texture is all wrong for my palate. Sharon wasn't daunted. 'OK, you don't have to eat tofu. You can make incredible dishes with a little bit of imagination, and there are thousands of recipes available on the net, right at your fingertips, like amazing raw-food salads. I love avocado, sun-dried tomatoes, nuts, seeds, lentils, chickpeas, edamame beans, kidney beans, black beans, and my favourite of all, sprouted seeds, which are seriously good for you . . .'

She considers the vegan movement to be a peaceful rebellion against the exploitation of animals and the destruction of the planet. A little time in her company and you realise that for her it is a very measured and considered lifestyle choice.

Ecologically, veganism certainly makes sense, as we need to consider our carbon footprint in order to protect the planet for future generations. Greenhouse gas emissions from the large livestock and poultry farms are seriously harming our environment, and there is no doubt that grain used to sustain our appetite for meat could be easily redirected to combat much of our world's hunger. Animal agriculture can be directly linked to the devastation of our oceans, rivers and forests, locally and globally.

I once witnessed the destruction of a river's entire ecosystem as a direct result of chemical poisoning. The beautiful river Kiltha, an important salmon-spawning tributary, flows alongside Pat Shortt's bar in Castlemartyr, meandering to its confluence with the river Dower before it rests at Youghal Bay. Early one morning in the middle of August, as I crossed the bridge to head for the kitchen, I noticed a few locals walking up and down the riverside. Something was wrong. What we witnessed there was truly shocking, and so sad. Thousands of fish – brown trout, brook lampreys, salmon fry, parr, sticklebacks and countless other species – were floating downstream, some still gasping, choking for the want of air, all the rest were dead. Somewhere upstream had been contaminated, causing oxygen depletion; the life was literally taken from the river. Six kilometres of life, destroyed in a matter of hours. After much agitation and some help from a local journalist, there was speculation about a food-related production facility, but sadly, and predictably, we never got much further.

So it's easy for me to understand the vegan dedication to environmental issues, and I try to include some vegan recipes in my home cooking as a step in the right direction we might all consider. The arguments are compelling. Sharon is equally compelling, and she makes a point to 'create the demand':

'If you're passing by an ice-cream parlour and know full well that they won't have vegan ice-cream – ASK ANYWAY.' A few years ago, she put it all into action and set up the 'Garden of Vegan' catering bus, which is spotted at various music and food festivals selling her proper vegan nosh to the multitudes. If you're lucky there might be a tune thrown in for good measure.

*Oh mamma, take a look out on your fields.*
*Can you see them tearing down your trees?*
*What can it all mean?*
*Oh mamma, is there nothing you can do?*
*You tell me that your fighting days are through*
*There must be something you can do.*

*It must have been heaven when you smiled.*
*It must have been heaven when you smiled.*
　　　　　　– 'When You Smiled', *What You Know* (2002)

# Beetroot and ginger summer salad
Serves 4

Over the years I have been asked many times to cook a vegan dish, and though bookshelves are heaving with vegan recipes, this is my go-to favourite. It has a lot going on and its colours are spectacular.

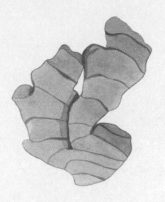

1 bunch of whole beets, mixed colours if possible
2 tbsp oil
1 clove of garlic, crushed
1 thumb of ginger, grated
1 tbsp cider vinegar
1 tbsp pomegranate molasses
Chopped mixed fresh herbs (such as rosemary, sage, thyme, marjoram)
1kg baby spinach leaves, washed and de-stalked
Toasted walnuts
Sea salt and freshly ground black pepper

1. Preheat the oven to 180°C/160°C fan/gas 4.
2. Put the beets into a roasting tray, cover with tin foil and roast for 1 hour. Check with a skewer for tenderness. Continue to cook for longer if necessary. Remove from the oven and discard the foil.
3. Make the dressing: put the oil, garlic, ginger, vinegar, pomegranate molasses and chopped herbs into a jar and shake to mix. Test for seasoning and balance and adjust accordingly.
4. Peel the cooked, cooled beets, then slice or chop them and toss with a little of the dressing, holding some dressing back to serve.
5. Fill a bowl with spinach, add the beets and top with walnuts. Sprinkle a little more dressing on top and serve.

*Variation: Beetroot with baby leeks is also delicious. Cut 1 or 2 cleaned, trimmed baby leeks to about 5cm in length. Poach them in water with fresh herbs (rosemary, thyme, bay, etc.) until soft but not falling apart, then drain and add to the chopped beetroot before adding the dressing.*

# CHAPTER 10

# BALLYMALOE COOKERY SCHOOL

*Take me away, where we can stay*
*So far away from the blue.*
    – 'From the Blue', *What You Know* (2002)

# YOUGHAL, EAST CORK, 2018

The phone alarm rattles me from sleep and I rise, sun blazing through a skylight. The room is like a sauna, and of course I forgot to pull the blind. Outside I see the spire of the Collegiate Church, where I had played the night before with my great friend, balladeer Roy Buckley. The church has hosted many gigs in its 820-year history, but last night it was our turn to fill its chambers with songs. Beside it stands the home of Sir Walter Raleigh, who lorded it over the town, using the vast port for his comings and goings. Locally, his achievements typically receive a mixed blessing, but one review in the pub after the gig ran, 'Lads. While he may have brought the spuds to Ireland, like, and all that tobacco, like, I want ye to think about this now. Right: are you with me? Both [pronounced 'boat'] have left their own indelible mark on this lovely little country of ours, y'know: the fags and the spuds . . . I'm only sayin', like!'

I've come back for a few days, researching my four-year stint from September 2009 to October 2013, on the East Cork food trail. I met many old friends to reminisce, and as Dad would say, 'I made a great gather': my car is full of goodies – herbs, fruit, organic veg, crazy homemade sauces, a cutting from a 250-year-old dying damson tree given to me by a self-styled food professor living out in the boondocks of Cloyne – and Roy's partner Olga kindly presented me with my first starter culture for vinegar.

## IN THE BEGINNING

I head cross-country and eventually turn right up the driveway past vibrant fields of gold rapeseed to Ballymaloe House. I find Rory Allen in an outhouse apartment, a wrench in one hand and a piece of copper piping in the other. 'It never changes, Mike, there's always something to do here. This old lady certainly keeps me on my toes.' As we sit on the porch eating lunch with the kitchen staff, his sister Yasmin helps their mother, a frail Mrs Allen, slowly to the kitchen door. I wonder if she is keeping up her daily routine to taste the soup. It would be the last time I would meet this truly inspirational woman.

## EARTH MOTHER

Myrtle Allen was educated in England, but when war broke out her parents brought her home to Ireland to finish her schooling at New Town school in Waterford. The school at that time was in serious financial difficulty, and local farmer Wilson Strangman stepped in to help in its recovery. Strangman ran a very successful vegetable business out of Kinoith estate, now the home of Ballymaloe Cookery School. Myrtle recalls that one night during lights out a few of the girls were chatting and asked her if she had yet met the dashing young student, Ivan Allen. Perhaps she had her eye on him from early on. Strangman later invited Ivan to work on the estate as farm manager.

 Ivan and Myrtle met again at a party in Jim Simpson's Ballymaloe House, and their relationship flourished from that moment. When the Simpsons later decided to sell, Jim asked Ivan to drive him to the auction in Cork. Many local farmers attended but refused to offer up any bids, and the house was removed from sale. Ivan spoke with Wilson Strangman, and together they put in a bid well beyond the asking price, which was welcomed by a relieved Simpson family.

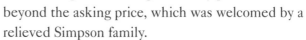

 Ivan and Myrtle married, worked the farm and reared a family. Myrtle began writing a regular cookery column for the *Irish Farmers Journal*. When the kids slowly began leaving the nest, she convinced Ivan to open a restaurant offering Irish country house cuisine. Many people thought she had lost all sense of reason setting up in the middle of nowhere, but they did it. In the early years, with the help of two friends, Myrtle cooked on an old Aga, while Ivan commandeered front of house and Joe Cronin ran the bar. My favourite archive video footage shows a very busy Myrtle rushing around the kitchen in her bare feet. Can you imagine the furore that would cause these days?

Produce was supplied to the restaurant by her own farm, neighbouring farmers, local craft butchers and Ballycotton fisherman Joby McNamara. Myrtle and Ivan created the original field-to-fork-to-mouth model, providing plenty of local employment down through the years. It is difficult to measure the influence they both had on the Irish food landscape, but it was prodigious. Years ago, when I was researching old Irish recipes for Pat Shortt's bar, I called over to her for some advice. It was a beautiful summer's day as she sat there in the shade, a newspaper spread across her knees as she topped and tailed freshly picked gooseberries for the evening menu. She offered me some wonderful ideas for my kitchen project, even though she could never remember my name, referring to me only as 'the lovely musician'. She always came to any sessions or gigs I played in the house, and I had the honour of serving her food on a few occasions at Shortt's, which she always seemed to enjoy.

# RORY

As a young man, Rory Allen migrated to study horticulture and agriculture in New Zealand and returned in '74 to help out on the busy farm, which then held over 100 Jersey cows, free-range pigs and cattle, everything from potatoes to sugar beets, barley, tomatoes, garlic, herbs and onions for home sale and export to the UK. Later on, following a period of international economic turmoil, Rory convinced his father to downsize and consolidate the family business by concentrating on the house and gardens. You are more likely to see Rory in muddied dungarees mending the old pipe system, digging holes, or driving an old banger from shed to field than in a tuxedo waiting to greet you at the entrance door like his dad used to do. He leaves all of that and the general running of affairs to his lovely wife, Hazel. He has long had an interest in music, and still Rory entertains guests in the drawing room, playing the guitar and singing the songs of Percy French, the Dubliners and the Clancy Brothers, adding a few tall tales in between, in a very quaint old Irish parlour fashion. Back in the day he would organise an annual festival, inviting many musicians to come and play in the drawing room.

## MY INTRODUCTION

Eleanor Shanley invited me to perform with her for one of those shows, and it was my entrée to the Ballymaloe world. During the week, we performed in the cookery school for Myrtle's daughter-in-law, Darina Allen, and her students, and after a beautiful lunch we toured the gardens, greenhouse and kitchens with a non-stop, passionate commentary from a very animated Darina. I was smitten, stunned into the sudden realisation that I had stumbled upon a special place. I had a feeling that afternoon that I might return.

Later that evening I spoke with Rory about how I had reached a crossroads in my life, and he suggested I come down and do the course. 'Sure, what have you got to lose, lad? You would love it, and you'd learn so much about food that will stay with you forever. It might be the best thing you could do for yourself.'

## DECISIONS, DECISIONS, DECISIONS

I returned home to Donna excited about food and the prospect of a new challenge. The previous two years had been tough on both of us. After twelve years on the board of IMRO, the Irish Music Rights Organisation, six as its chairman, I had resigned on a matter of principle. However painful it was, I knew it was the right thing to do. We also had devastating news with Ronnie's terminal cancer diagnosis, and as a couple we had faced our toughest challenge of all with the dim reality of a life without children. Although heartbroken, we had the inner strength to re-energise and try to move on with our lives. Fertility treatment is a very intense and highly charged emotional journey that offers no escape routes as you reach that point where reality is a stark, difficult, palpable fact, with acknowledgement being the only painful step available to you. There was no tangible support system in place for couples in our predicament, although things have changed for the better in recent years. We managed it together and were coming to terms with a future far different from how we had dreamed. Donna always liked the idea of travel and exploration, and decided on a solo trip to help her put the pieces all back together. Ballymaloe sounded like a good option for me. The healing had truly begun.

## BACK TO SCHOOL

So, in early September 2007, I arrived at Ballymaloe Cookery School, alone, full of trepidation, but very excited about this new venture. I was given directions to my cottage in Ballycotton, and told to return the following morning at 8 a.m. for a welcome tour with the other students. Students! *Moi* . . . a student. My word, imagine that – at my age.

I found my cottage on the outskirts of the village, turned the key and surveyed my new home. An open fire – always a good start – a sitting room, dining area and the smallest kitchen I had ever seen, even smaller than my mum's scullery, but I felt very comfortable right at that moment. I sat in silence to take it all in. A new leaf, a new life. I strolled down to the village and found the Blackbird pub, called a pint of Guinness and the barman soon enquired if I was visiting.

'No,' I said. 'I'm here doing a course over at the cookery school.'

'Oh, good man. You're very welcome. My name is Chris. You should enjoy that course – it's a great place, everyone enjoys it.'

A few musicians arrived with guitars, keyboards and a double bass and set up by the front window. The music was so good, I stayed to listen to the wonderful songs of guitarist Seany Kelleher. I returned later to the cottage, and as

I settled by the fire the front door opened and a young woman walked through – Camilla, my new housemate.

Camilla Stoddart edited food books for a large London publishing house, where she worked with the great Claudia Roden, Nigel Slater and Gary Rhodes. Impressive stuff. Here we were two complete strangers whose lives and cultures were at odds, yet we managed very well together. She had a very grand British accent, was very precise in her language, rarely swore, had impeccable manners and in her own way was quite vulnerable and extremely gentle. By contrast, I came from a working-class family, spoke with a broad Clare drawl interspersed with very colourful language, street-wise and very protective of my own vulnerability. We developed a great friendship, and offered each other lots of support throughout the course and beyond.

The following day we were joined by Lara McKee, a beautiful young English fitness student who excelled in water sports, mountaineering, running, tennis, skiing, boarding and God only knows what else. The two women were very studious and academically competitive, whereas I had no interest in the school books at all and had a negative retention span. I knew that success on the course hinged purely on my practical abilities, so I cooked quite a lot during my time there to hone my skills. Both of them tried very hard to help me along with my studies, holding quiz sessions that regularly exposed the limits of my concentration, so I tended to sneak out to the pub while they studied. Each evening they both neatly filed away their recipe sheets as mine developed into a mound by the kitchen table.

Despite the size of the cottage, there was food everywhere: hard cheeses sat on the windowsill eagerly awaiting daily salt feeds; cottage and goat's cheeses hung dripping from every available hook into the sink; sourdoughs bubbled throughout the house; a variety of jams and sauces from our foraging sat in every odd jar and pot we could fill. Each evening we sat together to eat and work through the following day's menu for class. At weekends, I'd bring them to see the sights of East Cork and West Waterford, and we enjoyed great nights at the Blackbird or over at the Ballymaloe House sessions with Rory.

## MY FIRST DAY

On our first morning at the school, myself and Camilla met Caroline Hennessy, a journalist and food blogger, and Mary O'Farrell, who ran a pub outside Mitchelstown, and we all sat down in a room full of very young students. Just then Darina rushed into the room. 'Good morning, everyone, welcome to Ballymaloe.'

We were taken on a tour of the farm and gardens, where I saw my first almond tree, then a fig tree. We saw peach, kiwi, elderflower, raspberry, gooseberry, myrtleberry and loganberry bushes. Each step brought something new, and over the following years I would delight at their moment of seasonal glory, along with the wild strawberries, hellebores, calendula, nasturtiums, primroses and my dad's favourite, fuchsias, when they each burst into life. The herb garden grew all types of parsley, thyme, tarragon, bay, coriander and sage. As we visited the beautiful shell house, and the largest greenhouse I had ever seen, I was reminded of my first tour here only months before, and I knew I had made the right decision.

## THE GAP YEAR

Back in the demo room I counted sixty-five students, mainly teenagers and twenty- or thirty-somethings. I felt a little uneasy, and extremely old. Darina gave a brief road map of the course, talked a little about food politics, food ethics, sustainability – and a lot about the rules and regulations, which was directed exclusively to the younger crew, whose lodgings were literally in Darina's back yard. We were given our welcome pack, and asked to introduce ourselves with a few small words. 'Hi, I'm John, but my friends call me JC. I'm from Dublin, and I'm on a gap year.' 'Hi, I'm Peach. I'm from England, and I'm on a gap year.' 'Hi, I'm Margaux from England, and I'm on a gap year.' 'Hi, I'm India, I'm from England, I'm on a gap year.' 'Hi, my name is Caroline, I am a food writer and blogger, and I'm here to learn how to cook better.' 'Hi, I'm Mary. I run a business and need to up-skill.' It was my turn. 'Hi, I'm Mike, I'm from Clare and I'm also on a gap year . . .' The entire room went into convulsions. I had made sixty-four new friends who knew nothing about me except that I was old – very old. It had started as a joke, but it was true in a way: I was on one of those gap years.

# Sloe gin
Makes approx. 1 litre

Our first task as students? To make some hooch. Camilla provided the recipe, and all three of us went off picking sloes. Back at home with our haul, we sat piercing the sour sloe berries, the fruit of the blackthorn tree. The blackthorn appears in centuries of Irish folklore, and its name is derived from the old Celtic word for 'strife'. Its thorns are said to protect the tree from unwelcome cutters. Folklore also suggests the best time to pick sloes is on the full moon, when the moon fairies leave the tree to pay homage to their goddess. Perhaps that's why a glass of sloe gin could bring you to the moon and back.

500g ripe sloes, pierced with a needle
250g granulated sugar
1 litre gin

1. Mix all the ingredients in a 2-litre Kilner jar, close the lid tightly, and store in a dark, cool place.
2. Every few days, turn the jar upside down.
3. After 3 months, strain the gin through a sieve and be merry.

## THE PUB

We settled into the course, and time out in Ballycotton proved a great respite from the intensity of the kitchens. In the evenings, I made my way to the Blackbird pub, occasionally accompanied by Camilla and Lara. Chris, the owner, was a charming man and always up for conversation. It was busy, and the clientele included lots of fishermen, the lifeboat crew and all the local chefs, plus students for drinks and celebrations. It sold alcohol, crisps, peanuts – and new gourmet ready-meals from Cully and Sully, two local guys who within a few years sold the business for a fortune to a big American company. Hard to believe that it had its first outing in the Blackbird, a simple choice of shepherd's pie or fish pie. Each was wrapped in pastry, and served in an earthenware dish together with a fork and a serviette for the comfort of hungry students and the Ballycotton fishing community.

## SEANY KELLEHER

No one knew who I was in Ballycotton, and it was liberating. They knew nothing about me at the school, and for a while I had no past – just living in the present with no sight towards the future. That type of environment helped me begin to create a new life. I slowly threw away some of the shackles and protective armour that I'd built up when I left the Wing and in the tough years that followed, and allowed people through, listened to their life stories, their heartaches and joys. I treasured each and every moment spent in their company. All those new friends, great teachers, fishermen, farmers, gardeners, but I especially loved my new music soulmate, guitarist Seany K and all his great buddies, whom I'd met down the Blackbird that first night. After Chris discovered my true identity, he suggested I join the lads for a few songs, and I played with them every week after that.

# PEACH

Away from the comfort zone of the musicians down at the Blackbird, at school I gathered an entirely different set of new friends.

It wasn't as easy as you might think. Even then, the younger students seemed to spend all their free time staring into mobile phones, either laughing or screeching out in horror. So often during what seemed to me like a very interesting conversation, a beep would send them rummaging through pockets or bags for their phones. That was it, conversation over, leaving me to continue talking to the wind while they thumbed away. One of these students, Florence 'Peaches' Petri, apologised one day for drifting to the beep, and suggested I join in on the fun and sign up for Facebook. 'Ah Jaysus, no, that's not my style at all, Peach.'

The following day, we sat in the lobby after school and she logged in all my details. Within minutes, there I was. Welcome to Facebook, Mike Hanrahan. Peach smiled. 'Now you have to become friends with all of us. Look! There's JC and Margaux. Just click on that and you'll be friends.' Wow, how easy to make friends, I thought. Isn't life getting very odd.

I couldn't log back into my account for some reason, though, and after several attempts that afternoon, I abandoned the notion of a life on Facebook. The following day Peach discovered she'd logged my email as 'nifo@mikehanrahan.com'. I kept that log-in for years. Peach became my connection to a much younger generation at the school and her friendship and kindness assured me a bridge to an extremely large generation gap. She included me in all the fun, and when it got all too young for me, I simply slipped away and picked it all up the following day. She was an inspiration in so many ways.

She never missed a Sunday music session at the Blackbird. I was under the impression that she only came for the music, until she admitted one day through a flood of tears that she was in love with one of the young musicians and far too afraid to say anything for fear of rejection. Poor Peaches, she was distraught, so I mustered up as much paternal advice as I could, and begged her to stay away from musicians. 'They're no good, Peach, I should know.' My words withered away of course; for years she has worked at a very successful music agency in London, and is constantly surrounded by musicians. So much for my advice!

Myself and Peach were partnered in the kitchen very early in the course. Her infectious, zany personality reached in and found a Mike

Hanrahan who had been marked absent for many years. I never laughed or clowned around so much as I did when we were paired for kitchen duties. Nothing was sacred, even the tried-and-tested recipe itself. With absolutely no previous cooking experience, she chose to see the recipe only as a rough guide. 'I used to help Mum baking, but I ate more than I made, Mike.'

She obviously didn't pay any more attention in her mum's kitchen than she did to the recipes. 'Mike, is this a colander?' she asked one day, holding up a strainer. 'Almost,' I replied.

Each day brought its own Peach moment.

'Mike, there's a terrible smell of burning somewhere.'

'Yes, Peach. Take a look at your pot of cream there on the hob.'

'Mike, my bread! Ha ha ha . . . it's smouldering, there's smoke coming up from the dough.'

'Yeah, I think you'll find the setting a bit high there, Peach.'

It was action all the way. Most of the flour she used found its way to the floor or all over her apron. Chocolate was there to be eaten, so only what she could spare made it onto the cake. We were constantly being monitored by teachers, and at one stage I was taken aside and asked if everything was OK – would I prefer another partner? Certainly not, she was a breath of fresh air, and I was enjoying every moment of it.

We managed to get through most of the recipes on time, but it was in presentation that we met the creative Peach. I doubt if Ballymaloe had ever seen such colour and extravagance as her daily artistic presentations, which were often eagerly awaited by the students and some of the more liberally minded teachers. Auntie Florrie's orange cake was turned out almost like a hat bound for Ascot. Even crème brûlée came with a spectacular flourish. The recipe called for basic sugarcraft; we had learned in a demo to pour caramelised sugar over the back of an oiled soup ladle to make a sparkling caramel decoration. To Peach, it presented an opportunity for modern art. Sugarcraft is aptly named, as it requires time and experience, of which we had very little.

After several attempts and plenty of exasperated 'Ah, Mike's', she had what looked like a guitar. She then set about shaping a caramelised sugar peach. Meanwhile, a small mound of caramelised pots, spoons and knives was taking over our work station. When she was ready, she planted the peach and the odd-looking guitar onto the brûlée, placed the ramekin on a white serving plate and crushed the excess caramel all around. Like all

her creations, her sculpture had its own backstory. Peach proudly stood by her plate and told the teacher a very long story about a young English girl called Peach who was feeling very sad but it all ended happy ever after as she jumped in her peach-shaped carriage with Mike, her Prince Charming, heading for a big celebration, the Sunday session at the Blackbird. When asked about the crushed sugar, she replied, 'Oh, that's the rest of the students following on to the pub.' I don't think they'd ever seen or heard the like, but she should probably be writing children's fantasy books, such is her imagination. She is without doubt the kind of daughter I would have loved and cherished.

# Peach brûlée
Serves 4 hungry people

500ml double cream
1 tsp vanilla extract, or ½ a vanilla pod
80g caster sugar
6 egg yolks
2 peaches, boiled until soft in a sugar syrup of equal parts water and sugar,
    then stoned and peeled (you can use tinned peaches if you wish. About
    2 slices per person. If you like, you can slice the peaches and gently
    caramelise them in a little butter, sugar and lemon until they colour
    slightly)
Light brown sugar, for topping

1. Put the cream and vanilla into a saucepan and gently heat to the 'shiver'
   stage, as Darina used to call it – starting to move but not boiling.
2. Whisk the caster sugar and the egg yolks, and gently add the heated cream,
   whisking all the time.
3. Strain the custard through a very fine sieve.
4. Put the peach slices into the 4 ramekins and pour the custard on top until
   almost full. Leave a little room at the top of each ramekin.
5. To create a water bath or bain-marie, half-fill a regular deep roasting tray
   with hot water, enough that the ramekins will be half-submerged. Place the
   ramekins in the bath and rest a sheet of baking parchment gently on top.
6. Bake for 30 minutes, until the custard is set, then allow to cool. Store in the
   fridge until ready to serve.
7. To serve, place the ramekins on a baking tray and sprinkle each one with
   light brown sugar. Heat under a preheated grill until the sugar melts. You
   could use a blowtorch, but make sure you have the kitchen to yourself.
8. Let the sugar cool to form a hard crust.

# CAROLINE HENNESSY

Caroline was a successful journalist at RTÉ, wrote for food magazine *Intermezzo*, and had created the Bibliocook blog. She had come to the course to expand her knowledge, and had rented a house with her husband Scott Baigent. Scott dreamed of brewing his own craft beer, and in 2010 the Eight Degrees Brewing Company was established at the foot of the Galtee Mountains from a small one-bed cottage shared by Caroline, Scott, baby Hannah and business partner Cam Wallace. The following Easter we were introduced to Howling Gale Ale. The cottage has been extended now, and the brewery has its own place and a strong standing in the world of craft beer, having won countless awards. It's one of my favourite craft beers, and is widely available in pubs and off-licences. The name comes from Ireland's longitude – eight degrees west – and, as it happens, from the perfect serving temperature in °C for the beer. And as Caroline so rightly says, 'After a few bottles, people also start leaning at eight degrees.'

We stayed in touch after the course, enjoying a few at our Irish craft beer and cheese tasting events at Pat Shortt's bar, where we matched their stout with my favourite Crozier blue cheese from Tipperary. It's hard to keep up with her, as these days Caroline continues to juggle between family life with two beautiful daughters, updating her blog at Bibliocook, writing for the *Examiner*, broadcasting for *Culture File* on Lyric FM, while working at Eight Degrees. She is secretary of the Irish Food Writers' Guild, and a couple of years ago published her first book, *Sláinte: The Complete Book on Irish Craft Beer*. Her encouragement throughout my culinary career has been invaluable, and I salute her immense contribution to Irish food. I was delighted when she kindly passed on this recipe – these brownies really pack a punch.

# Caroline's double-chocolate Knockmealdown Irish Stout brownies

Makes 30 brownies

100g plain flour
50g cocoa
¼ tsp salt
½ tsp baking powder
150g dark chocolate
175g butter
200g caster sugar
2 eggs
½ tsp vanilla extract
250ml Knockmealdown Irish Stout
Warm Salted Caramel Ale Sauce (page 208) and vanilla ice cream, to serve

1. Preheat the oven to 180°C/160°C fan/gas 4. Line a rectangular 2 x 25 x 30cm Swiss roll tin with greaseproof paper.
2. Sift the flour, cocoa, salt and baking powder together in a bowl and set to one side.
3. Gently melt the chocolate and butter together in a large heavy-based saucepan over a low heat. Take it off the cooker and add the sugar, whisking until smooth.
4. Allow to cool slightly, then whisk in the eggs, vanilla, porter and, finally, the sifted dry ingredients until just blended.
5. Pour into the prepared tin – this is a very runny mixture – and bake in the preheated oven for 18–20 minutes, until set and a skewer inserted into the middle comes out clean. Because of the amount of liquid used, you don't need to underbake these brownies.
6. Cool in the tin, then cut into 30 pieces and store – if you have any left – in an airtight tin. These get more delectably moist the longer you keep them. Serve with a scoop of good vanilla ice cream and some warm Salted Caramel Ale Sauce (see page 208) for a superb dessert.

*Caroline adds a very useful tip: if these brownies are staying at home, in all their delicious richness, I use 100g of flour. If, however, I'm making them for an event or tasting, I increase the flour to 125g so that they don't fall apart en route.*

# Salted caramel ale sauce

Caroline suggested to try it with stout or porter as well, so long as you avoid anything that's going to taste too hoppy when it is reduced.

330ml Eight Degrees beer
30g butter
100g muscovado sugar
¼–½ tsp flaky sea salt
250ml cream
1 tsp vanilla extract

1. Bring the beer to the boil in a heavy saucepan over a medium heat and cook until reduced by two-thirds, to approximately 110ml. Depending on the size of your saucepan, this can take from 10 to 15 minutes.
2. Add the butter, sugar and salt. Stir until everything has melted, then whisk in the cream and vanilla off the heat. Bring back to the boil and cook, bubbling rapidly and stirring regularly, for another 6–8 minutes, until it has thickened.
3. Serve warm.

# MARY O'FARRELL

Another of my crew was Mary O'Farrell, whose pub in North Cork served drink and Sunday roasts. She was tired of the mundane offering and wanted to step it up a few gears, so decided on the course at Ballymaloe.

We both treasure our memories of that time. 'I still can't get over how quickly a smell or a taste can transport me back to my days in Ballymaloe. The sugary smell of Aunty Florence's baking orange sponge, the distinctive nutty taste and smell of malted wheat flakes, slowly toasting on my granary bread. You could never get yours to rise as well as mine, Mike!' Yeah, right, Mary.

One of Mary's favourite food memories is our fresh fish goujons. 'Mike, these make me dream of sea air and endlessly squawking sea gulls. Darina Allen demonstrated the goujons recipe to us on a Friday, just in time for my show-off lunch. It was a Sunday, the morning after the night before in the local, which was rocking with music by yourself and Seany, and I wasn't the only one who had been bit by the bar. I left them all in bed, headed off to Mass and then on to a cliff walk. So what did I see, but a fishing boat just about to anchor at the pier in Ballycotton. The kind fisherman gave me a cod, fresh off the boat, a five-kilo cod with all its sea juices and no bag. Off down the village holding it out in front of me by the tail and they all coming out of the next Mass. What a sight!

'A fine lunch we had of lightly spiced goujons of fresh cod, homemade tartare, minty mushy peas and chips, followed by a few tunes on the guitar. You can guess where that led us to – back to the bar. So much for staying over the weekend to study for our final exams.'

# Galty Valley hake fritters with seaweed salt
Serves 4

Mary's energy knows no bounds, as she has since developed her pub and catering business as she'd hoped. The real jewel in her crown is her Galty Valley customised mobile catering, which services both private and public events. Her slogan says it all: 'My kitchen, your place', as she brings the best of ingredients to your venue and cooks to order. She still goes to the coast to pick up fresh fish for the food truck, and whenever their noticeboard reads 'Fresh fish from Kinsale', there's a crowd under the hatch within minutes for the fresh hake fritters, complemented with a beer from her favourite local brewery, Eight Degrees.

150g plain white flour, and extra for dusting
50g cornflour
330ml Eight Degrees Bohemian Pilsner
Vegetable oil for frying
800g fresh hake, skinned and cut into fingers
Sea salt and freshly ground black pepper

## For the seaweed salt
1 sheet of nori seaweed (available from most large supermarkets or Asian grocers)
3 tsp sea salt flakes

## For the lemon mayo
1 lemon
4 heaped tbsp good-quality or homemade mayo

1. For the seaweed salt, pulse the sheet of nori in a food processor a few times and add to the flakes of sea salt.
2. For the lemon mayo, zest the lemon and add it to the mayo, along with the juice of half the lemon. Cut the other half into wedges and use for garnish.
3. For the batter, mix the flour and cornflour in a very large bowl. Make a well in the centre and gradually whisk in the pilsner.
4. Heat the vegetable oil for frying to 180°C.
5. Dust each piece of fish in seasoned flour and shake off the excess.
6. Dip into the batter one at a time, shake off the excess, then slowly put them into the hot oil.
7. Cook for 2 minutes, until golden, then remove and drain on kitchen paper. Season straight away with the seaweed salt.
8. Serve immediately with the lemon mayo and a fresh lemon wedge.

*Mary's tip: For best results, make the batter just before you cook the fish, and only use the Eight Degrees Pilsner, as it gives it a unique flavour.*

## THE PUDDING CONUNDRUM

During the course, local producers came to the school to talk about their products, and share their views on sustainability, agriculture and protection of the environment. Many wanted to reignite interest in the old ways of preserving foodstuffs, something Darina constantly encouraged during the course, urging us to follow each season and use the food that nature delivers. One particular butcher spoke passionately about the dying art of making black and white pudding. As kids growing up in Ennis, we often called in to the back of Abbey Street to watch neighbour and farrier Frank Malone shoe his horses. That entire backstreet was a hive of animal activity, with a piggery and several butchers' yards as well as a few abattoirs. I often stayed to watch the butchers make the black pudding. Times have certainly changed since my after-school rambles.

Because of costs, coupled with the stringent rules now governing the use of fresh blood in the production of black pudding, many artisan producers are forced to import a dry product from Holland and Spain, which is manufactured under strict EU rules – but for many, its traceability remains in question. It's an odd system that causes much grief to some of our producers. The Food Safety Authority, which is diligent and exceptionally good at policing good food management, is quite clear in its rules: it is legal to use fresh blood once the conditions are hygienically in line with the law. Personally, I try to search for the homemade product.

White pudding, on the other hand, is normally made from pork, suet and barley. We have some excellent varieties in Ireland. In Scotland, they make a red pudding using beef, bacon, suet, spices and rusk, and it's often served with chips. I tasted it once, but a pudding is a pudding for me, either black or white. I worked in a restaurant where head chef Vinny Kelly experimented with boudin noir, which is a rich French sausage, but contains lots of great flavours. In Spain you get the powerful morcilla, which I served at the Artisan Parlour, thanks to my great friend Alvaro, who once gave me his mother's incredible soup recipe with brown lentils and black pudding.

## SCHOOL'S OUT

There is no doubt that three months away at the Ballymaloe Cookery School could qualify as an out-of-body experience. You live, sleep and breathe while floating around in a culinary bubble in a galaxy far away from the real world, developing a relationship with a group of complete strangers from all walks of life, creeds, cultures and characters. You share stories, laughter, sorrow and joy. It is a very intense environment that brings its success, failure, frustration and elation. I embraced the entire operation, the learning, the music, the food – and especially my new friends.

Having lived more or less exclusively in a world of music for most of my life, I found it so invigorating to be in a place where I had no past, just the present. I also acquired a new skillset and knowledge, which was such a boost to my confidence. It was certainly difficult to come down from the high – although the final-week exams somewhat tempered the mood. On top of it all was the emotional cloud of our impending departure that hung over the entire school.

My main focus that week was the practical exams, which went exceptionally well, especially my starter dish of homemade goat's cheese, which received rave reviews from the powers that be. As a student, I fell in love with the art of cheese-making, particularly goat's cheese. The wonderful Jane Murphy from Ardsallagh gave her time freely to talk me through the techniques during a visit to the school, and thereafter on the phone or at her stall at the Midleton Farmers' Market. At that time, she had over a hundred goats – and each had a name. She played classical music to calm the herd while they were being milked. When I finished at Ballymaloe I was offered a further six months' study at Gubbeen to learn more about cheese and preserving food, but finances ruled that I needed to get back home to find some work: the holiday was over.

# THE HALL OF FAME

I was so proud to have my goat's cheese recipe included in Darina's 2009 book, *Forgotten Skills of Cooking*. Goat's cheese can be made at home once the equipment is super-clean and you're very precise on temperatures. I prefer using raw goat's milk, as it gives a much richer, creamier flavour, but you can use shop-bought regular or organic pasteurised milk, which is readily available. You can easily get the starter culture online – Flora Danica, a 'mesophilic starter', but you can also use an existing cheese as a culture instead. (Another option is making your own starter, but this requires a little study and practice – if you're in love with the art of cheese-making, though, a world of wonder awaits!)

The basics for cheese-making can be bought at your local kitchen shop or online. In the case of the rennet and starter culture, a little goes a long way; the equipment can be washed and re-used. You'll need a thermometer, perforated cheese moulds or muslin, and a starter culture if not using existing cheese.

## Homemade goat's cheese

2 litres goat's milk (raw milk if you can get it)
1 tsp starter culture
1 drop of liquid rennet
Cheese moulds or muslin
A rack and/or basin

1. Heat the milk in a stainless-steel saucepan to 70°C.
2. Turn off the heat and allow to cool to 26°C.
3. Gently stir in the starter culture and leave for 1 hour.
4. Stir in the rennet. Cover and leave for up 24 hours, until the curds have formed.
5. If using moulds, fill each with the mix and place on a rack over a basin. Leave to drain for 24 hours. Turn and drain for another 24 hours. I prefer to use muslin: fill it with cheese, tie a knot and suspend over a basin in the sink to allow it to drain for 24 to 36 hours, depending on how wet or dry you like your cheese. The whey that's left in the basin can have lots of other good uses instead of simply pouring it down the drain: it's used in baking, fermenting, lemonades, soaking grains, and farmers feed it to their animals. I have read that it is recommended as a natural hair product, and makes for a good facial, though I have yet to explore that one.
6. If not using moulds, you can shape the cheese by hand, then wrap it in cheese paper or put into a container. Best eaten fresh, but it will stay in the fridge for about 5 to 6 days. Add some of your favourite herbs if you wish. St Tola in County Clare roll one of their products in food-grade ash and it both looks and tastes great. Some people add salt, but I don't think it needs any.

# END OF THE RUN

*I'm dreaming down that old dirt road.*
*I'm dreaming now of home sweet home,*
*Rolling hills on a wild western shore.*
*Take me home, lonesome road.*
— 'Lonesome Road', *Someone Like You* (1994)

I left kitchen academia in the lap of the gods. I sat there and answered as best I could. Perhaps those grinds from Lara and Camilla on the definitions of mother and daughter sauces along with all the rest were in fact embedded in my brain, waiting for their moment to emerge onto the exam paper.

I will never know what it was that did the trick, but a few weeks later I received my certificate with a distinction, so maybe I owe the two girls a pint for their persistence. I was now well equipped with new skills, a deeper understanding of food, some wonderful friends and a far better person for the Ballymaloe experience.

Returning to Dublin was very strange at first, and it took me a good while to settle back into the routine of home and community, like I'd come back from a long tour. That sudden change of pace takes its toll as you try to readjust and recharge, but this particular return was more intense than before. However, I was now back in real time, and I had no choice but to think about my next move.

# CHAPTER 11

# LEARNING

# CURVE

## McCORMACK'S HEAD CHEF?

Now hooked on food, I felt had to delve further. However, it was thirty years since my last job interview, and I had no CV – just a music biog, which was of no use at all to me or my potential employers. So I went in search of work. My first job was in private catering with Leslie Tomelty, a former Ballymaloe student and the wife of my old Stockton's Wing roommate Peter Keenan. She was an excellent cook who taught me so much in a very short space of time. We cooked for many of the big houses in Ballsbridge and at fancy wedding venues in the Wicklow Hills, and every gig was different. I also worked for my good friends Didi and Dan Kennedy, who had catered our own wedding. Some of their events were major productions. Walking into a Dan and Didi gig was like entering a film set. The kitchen might be in a large garden marquee or in an outhouse. From early morning, cater hire companies dropped off hundreds of plates, cutlery, bowls all neatly wrapped and stacked, hobs were rolled into position, large slender cylinders of gas connected, fridges set and stocked, water boilers filled and set to simmer, countless chopping boards, knives and utensils strategically placed around the site, and then the fresh ingredients arrived, checked in for quality, and finally the team assembled for the pep talk, or prep talk as I prefer to call it. Dan the Man built the kitchens on site: he was the engine, the sparks, the problem-solver, and Didi was coolness personified as she went about presenting the most amazing spreads – and enormous ones too.

Instead of prepping forty lobster, langoustines or crabs, you were put in a corner with 300 – and each one had to be perfect. You found a work patch and let no one dare enter, it was yours for that particular chore. Large pans

bubbling with salted water, systematically filled with the fish, cooled in a tub of iced water and oh, how your hand numbed as you stirred. Prawns had to be carefully peeled, deveined with each tail left intact, crab meat separated into brown and white, but those lobsters, they certainly got their revenge as you tried to extract the meat from their very prickly shells. One particular starter was a slice of lobster tail, with a sautéed king prawn, a crab mayo, some lemon and greens, all carefully assembled and placed on mobile food service racks. They looked beautiful on the plate but there were hundreds of them. I never wanted to see another lobster after that particular shift. The team worked together as one unit at service and after the last dessert passed through the curtain we celebrated with a few glasses of wine and a very jovial recap of the day's work, with never a bad word spoken. Well, Dan and Didi had their moments, but nothing unusual for a husband and wife working together in such an intense environment. They were a powerful team.

In the midst of this, I saw an ad for Caviston's, the famous south Dublin gourmet grocer family, who were opening a new place in Greystones after the success of their expanded business and fish restaurant in Sandycove, and decided to call. My interview was odd, to say the least. I had to cook sample dishes for the two young owners at their house, while answering questions on my hopes and dreams for their new business. I landed the job and the proud title of 'head chef'. Three months at cooking school, and here I was about to manage a section of a well-funded start-up for a very well-respected foodie institution. I really should have known better, but I was just as excited as my two rookie owners.

I was given several suppliers' books and asked to compare the prices; rosters had to be written; menus created; and a brand-new kitchen organised. For a start, I had never seen a supplier's book, nor created commercial menus. I had no idea how to make a kitchen or its service efficient. I simply had no idea at all.

After six weeks of struggling, sleepless nights and hours of deliberation, I called the owners to tell them I was not head chef material by any stretch. I wasn't even a chef, if I was honest; I was a rookie cook who knew nothing about the business of ordering, stock control or menu-writing. It was very hard to admit my inadequacies, but it certainly was the right thing to do. I excused myself from the role, and set about finding a job somewhere down on the lower rungs of the kitchen ladder.

# McCORMACK'S BURNS UNIT

I called my good friend, Dún Laoghaire publican Paddy McCormack, for some advice. I've known Paddy and his family since 1984, when they refurbished the family pub and introduced south Dublin to its first ever gastro pub experience. It was the place to be, and still is for the likes of me and its many regulars. Our local is a very popular and extremely busy eatery, and Paddy suggested a trial run in the kitchen might do me no harm at all. If it worked out, he promised to show me the ropes, and if not, we'd move on. 'I think what you've done is amazing – a bit crazy, but very brave. There's no one I know who has taken on such a career change at your age,' he said. 'I think this could work, y'know. For both of us.'

I spent eighteen months in that kitchen, working initially with long-time chef Big John, who was far more concerned with my health and safety than the food I was putting out during the first few weeks there – and for good reason. I spent at least one day a week for the first two months at St Michael's Hospital A&E. I'd say they thought I was a resident. One morning I was rushing around so fast that I hit my head on the industrial microwave oven door. That required stitches. My last major burn was so bad I had to stay out of work for four days. The night it happened, I was on fryer duty, cooking chips and goujons, when I left a plate on top of the grill. I picked it up without a thought and – I could hear the sizzle. The place was packed with diners, so I got the burn kit out and cold water flowing. I insisted on staying, even though my right hand was starting to bubble slightly, and then a lot. John pleaded with me to go home, but I said I couldn't leave him a man down, so he relented and put me on salads and garnish. My gloved right hand was placed in a bucket of ice as I garnished with my left. I finished out my shift and went home. Donna took one look and said, 'A&E for you first thing in the morning. That is a very serious burn.' She was right.

On my return to work, John sat me down. 'Are you really sure you want to do this? I don't think you're cut out for this, myself. Imagine if you couldn't play guitar again because you damaged your hand cooking feckin' goujons! Seriously, Mike.'

Fair point but I said I was not beaten just yet.

'Right, Mike,' he replied. 'I think you're mad to be at this, I really do. At your age, most chefs have had enough of this shit and only want to get out of the game, find a handy number and retire gracefully. This kitchen is an animal. There is no hiding place. But, I know you won't listen to me, and you really want to carry on. So, I'll make a deal with you. I will teach you as much as I can, but first, for crying out loud, will you slow the fuck down in the kitchen? Take your time, and pay attention to the dangers that surround you. Everything will happen in its own good time. Organise yourself and your station first. Develop a system that suits you. I personally think you're crazy, but I'll help you out for sure.' A mighty man.

I was put to chopping-board duty from early morning, and prepped the entire menu over the following weeks, keeping well away from some of the danger zones. Within a few months I was moved to lunch service, then designated the salad counter. Working for a spell on cold food meant I could give up my A&E membership card, and Paddy allowed me carte blanche, all within a certain budget of course, to develop the salad bar presentation. I created a mini Ottolenghi-style salad bar, which was an instant hit. I was a real fan of Ottolenghi, having attended one of his London courses soon after I finished at Ballymaloe. His food is incredible and I wanted everyone to taste the wonders of his creations. That period was a huge boost to my confidence.

A few months later I was back to the heat on carvery lunch, soon choosing my own presentation, and it was there I began to embrace the challenge. I had finally learned the basics and was prepared to do what had been beyond me at Caviston's. I was free to order any product I required, but always under the watchful eye of our wonderful accountant and stocktaker Derry Smith. Everything he taught me about stock control was put to great use in later years.

Paddy never stopped advising me on customer care and staff relations, which also stood me in good stead for the future. During my time there, he took extra care to explain how he managed it all. All customer concerns were met head-on, and dealt with in a very direct and honest way, an approach I have used throughout my food career. He dealt with staff issues the very same way. He regularly proved that great theory that there are three sides to every story: your side, my side and, somewhere sitting in the middle, the truth. He never lost the cool: he listened, paused and then tried to reason.

Paddy ran a very tight ship, and was adamant that all health and safety rules be followed. He trusted his chefs, and gave us freedom to express ourselves at lunch and evening specials, which allowed people the opportunity to try new recipes and get creative. The main menu was to be cooked as directed, and he never liked to hear any customer asking if a certain chef was on duty. His drive was to develop a team that worked equally and efficiently together, to produce a consistently good experience. There were no stars in McCormack's. His staff reciprocated with absolute commitment to the job.

I had a wonderful experience there, and moved through the ranks until I eventually got to work the pass, first on a quiet Monday night and then for the weekend frenzies and a back-breaking Sunday lunch, followed by a crazy evening service. In the beginning 'the pass' is every chef's nightmare. It's the spot in the kitchen where everything comes together from the various stations: starters, mains, garnish and final presentation check before going to the table. It's the front line between floor and kitchen, where nerves are frayed in the tense heat of battle – with several orders on the go, timing is essential. The team at Mac's taught me how to keep a cool head as the machine pinged out its never-ending ream of order dockets. Those shifts were truly hectic – tough, but fulfilling.

I finally achieved my purpose at McCormack's when I understood first-hand how the kitchen engine turns. So, by August 2009, I needed a fresh challenge. It was time to move on. I had a constant hankering to return to Ballymaloe that had been with me since the day I finished college. Then one day, I received an email from the school seeking trainee teachers. For days, I thought of nothing else and instinctively, I felt I had to return. Donna supported the idea, so I called and spoke with Darina at length about the job and she invited me down.

I said my goodbyes to McCormack's, which remains my beloved local pub and venue for most family occasions. I called Rory Allen, and he offered me a chalet at the rear of Ballymaloe House to get me started until I found somewhere more permanent to stay. It looked like I was on my way back to East Cork.

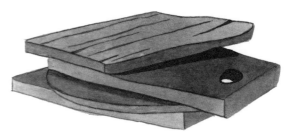

# BACK TO WORK AT BALLYMALOE

*I've been missing you, wishing I was back again,*
*Here I am and I'm feeling so alone,*
*Wishing I was back again in Avondale.*
     – 'Avondale', *Full Flight* (1986)

It was late in the evening when I arrived at Ballymaloe House and found my way out to the chalet. I sat with a cup of tea and a sandwich on the veranda. It was so quiet out there, far away from the world, under a beautiful clear autumn sky, the rustle of the trees interrupted by the odd faint sound of a car in the distant night. In the next field a herd of cattle settled down for the evening. 'Here I am again,' I thought, 'I wonder what lies ahead.' I suddenly felt totally alone in the world, but quite at ease. I had been there for a good while when I heard a little robin chirp nearby, and then he chirped a little more. He made his way onto the decking and stared at me for quite a long time, moving over and back, always keeping a safe distance. He was obviously hungry and as he eventually ate my breadcrumbs, I realised I was not alone at all.

The following morning, I climbed the stairs to my first 8 a.m. conference on daily routines, staff briefings, orders of work, student concerns, teachers' queries and the day's recipes. I arrived at my 'office' in Kitchen Two, along with my two fellow teachers and our eighteen students, who were eagerly standing by at their workstations, fully equipped and ready for a morning of chaos that somehow always produced a beautiful communal lunch. There were four working kitchens at the school, serving sixty-five students. Each week a teacher was assigned six students, and our responsibility was to help them through the daily recipes stage by stage, focusing on the development of their skills and techniques from prep to cooking, to seasoning and finally presentation.

You soon discover that a teacher's life is very different to that of the students. Apart from the obvious teaching responsibilities, the hours are much longer and the workload is extremely demanding all the time. In the early weeks I relied heavily on my fellow staff members to steer me in the right direction on the recipes and techniques. They were so patient and kind as they answered countless questions, keeping a constant eye on my progress and interaction with the students, always at the ready to jump in and offer help and advice.

Kitchen 2 was run by Mamie, who had an encyclopedic knowledge of recipes, and, most importantly, of the techniques to bring any disaster back from the brink. She gave me a loan of her bible on recipe rescues, and that was such a revelation. She often boasted that she could save almost anything, and I believe her on that count. She certainly saved me from a few near disasters in my early weeks teaching, regularly calling me aside to whisper guidance on a particular student's technique.

Though the moods of the staff could waver, students were generally very easy to work with and caused very little bother. When they finished the morning cook, we rated their efforts, taking notes on their progress. All stations were then wiped clean and equipment returned to its rightful positions, although pots, pans and cutlery often strayed. Teachers served lunch with the help of whichever of the students were rostered, cleaned up, then reset the dining-room tables for the following day. A quick bite of food was followed by a rush to a very intense and busy demo kitchen prep area, where we joined the back-up team for Darina, her brother and business partner Rory O'Connell, or Rachel Allen, who were the main attraction, out front, demonstrating the following day's recipes to the students.

Over at the demo kitchen, my prep was constantly monitored to ensure that when presented, those giving the lecture would not be distracted by a shabby prep tray. Each ingredient was exactly as described in the recipe: a 3cm piece of red pepper could not be 3.5cm. It was that precise, and rightly so. Darina was so exact and on top of her game, we often joked that she could probably tell you how many extra grains of sugar you presented to her. In that regard, some of the senior staff often saved me from many an après-show dressing-down. They also pointed out various idiosyncrasies of each demo leader; some liked particular presentation plates, others preferred certain utensils; some liked banter, others got on with the task – and all that knowledge made it easier to be a more efficient member of the team.

It was backstage at the demo kitchen that I learned so much about the art of cooking from the senior squad. In the early days I struggled with a couple of teaching techniques, so Rory suggested a few sessions on the quieter Tuesday afternoons. These one-to-ones honed my capabilities and truly bolstered my confidence with the students. Rory has since become something of a reluctant TV star, with several cooking series in the can, both solo and a few classics with his older sister Darina. His first book *Master It* was a national bestseller – and to think he'd been reluctant to write it! He truly is a master chef.

In the beginning, for some unknown reason, one of the demo team confined me to wash-up, which was a nightmare, not for the washing-up, but because I missed all of the following day's techniques relying on notes and tips from the other teachers. After I complained I was moved closer to the action, much to the annoyance of my mother superior. In time I slowly worked my way through the ranks to be out there on the main stage, in the thick of it. It was the closest thing to a live gig, with everyone on their toes, adrenalin pumping. When the demo finally ended, we served the students some food, cleaned down the stations, bagged a few leftover snacks and headed for home. I was rarely back before 8 p.m. A quick bite of food, a recap on the day's notes, a phone call to Donna and sleep. Well . . . I sometimes managed to hit the pub for a quiet pint, which was only fifty yards from my front door. Purely medicinal, of course.

# ROSE COTTAGE

At that stage I had moved from the chalet at Ballymaloe House to the beautiful Rose Cottage, a tiny, quaint old building in the middle of Ballycotton village. One bedroom, an open attic and a living room with a little kitchenette in the corner. There I made yogurts, breads, preserves, and cooked all types of fresh fish provided by my seafaring neighbour, Darragh, who often called me over to choose a fish from his day's catch, spread out on newspapers across his kitchen table. 'Take your pick there, Mike.' How I loved that table: fresh ling, cod, maybe the odd stray sea bass and beautiful prawns. Stunning.

The television served as a shelf, as the reception was dependent on clear weather conditions, which were almost non-existent during a Ballycotton winter, but I had my CD player with lots of great music to fill the silence. Heat was eventually distributed around by a very quirky wood-burning stove that reacted badly to the strong easterly winds – if you blinked, the room was engulfed in black smoke in seconds. Someone suggested I create a natural draught by opening the front door as I set the fire, which was perfect, except for when it rained. It had a personality all of its own, and I loved it. I was surrounded by wonderful neighbours, three very individual pubs and a close, welcoming community. Monday and Tuesday nights were often spent at Mike and Brid O'Shea's Schooner Bar, where the weekend sports were discussed and news stories parsed with a few of the locals. On Friday afternoons, whenever I could, I would leave early for Dublin and return for the Sunday music session at the Blackbird with Sean Kelleher and the crew. A few yards further back on Main Street is Seany McGrath's pub. They used to say Sean was grumpy, but I loved his sarcastic wit and divil-may-care attitude to life. One Sunday morning a regular arrived with three newspapers, and sat there for hours, flicking through each segment and some of the magazines. When he'd finished, he placed the newspapers in a pile and left. When he returned the following Wednesday night, Sean walked to his table and presented him with the heap of papers, saying, 'You can take away all your shite with you tonight, we don't offer a refuse service here, we sell drink!'

## MY KITCHEN SOULMATE

Sorcha Moynihan had a degree in economics and maths, and was halfway through a degree in pharmacy when she decided to opt out and go to Ballymaloe. She'd lived on its recipes most of her life, as her mum was an avid fan who regularly attended the short courses. When Sorcha completed the cookery course, she went back to Cork City to work at various restaurants, but Ballymaloe kept calling and she returned to work as a trainee teacher on the same day I started there. Although she was many years younger than me, we were soulmates from the very beginning, two rookies nervous in our new environment who promised to look out for each other at every turn. We certainly did that as we moved through the ranks and eventually out onto that demo stage. She's now a senior member of staff at Ballymaloe and is much-loved by her students. Ballymaloe can be a high-octane environment, so we were lucky to have each other, along with a few more members of staff as a tight little family unit.

Recently I arranged to meet her back at the school, and as we strolled through the various gardens with her beautiful young daughter Erin, she said something very special: 'Mike, no matter what the school gave us, which was a lot, we gave so much in return. We should never forget that.' I heard echoes of Sammy Davis Jr. and his two-way street ringing in my ear.

## CHEESE ROOM

There is a permanent cheese room at the school now, but a few years ago myself and Emer Fitzgerald, a very experienced member of staff, went on an intensive cheese course to help us set up the school's first cheese room. Part of that course necessarily focused on the new and stringent health and safety rules that govern cheese-making. While we were busy sourcing equipment, Darina whitewashed the walls to give the room a country-kitchen effect in keeping with its surrounding environment, but with no regard whatsoever for the rules. However, much as I agree with Darina's take on the sometimes crazy world of food regulations, myself and Emer knew we had to dig in on this one. We had a battle on our hands to persuade her to remove the whitewash, but she eventually caved in, and the cheese room opened its doors to the first batches of yogurt, semi-hard and soft cheeses, much to the delight of the students and staff. I still recall the excitement at the arrival of our first cheese vat, the ladles, the pots and shelves, and these days it's a thriving hub of activity.

## THE SPICE BOYS

When I was a student at Ballymaloe, I often walked to the village of Shannagarry to visit Arun Kapil at his tiny basement unit in the Stephen Pearce Pottery. Arun was an ex-London rocker who left it all behind to sell fresh, imported spices to a burgeoning East Cork food community. I still have some of his early complementary recipes that came with every purchase. He loved to share his encyclopedic knowledge of spices and talk passionately about his plans to sell his spice blends right across the world. His dream was realised from that small space in the bowels of the Design Centre as he patiently developed the business. At first, he sold at all the local farmers' markets, then to the local restaurants, and today his company Green Saffron sells its products from many supermarket shelves and fills the spice trays of top chefs in Dublin, London, New York and Sydney. He regularly visited Ballymaloe while I was teaching there, and I was first assistant for any of his guest demos. It was rock and roll with all the pots and pans, and we became known as the 'Spice Boys'. Ouch! Not at all cool.

## MEETING SOME HEROES

During that year I worked on three twelve-week courses, countless short courses and got to cook with some of my true food heroes, including Skye Gyngell and Yotam Ottolenghi, who came to demonstrate their recipes and cooking styles. Camilla Stoddart, my old roommate, had presented me with a trip to Leith's college in London a few years previously to enjoy a course with Yotam Ottolenghi and Sami Tamimi. Back in Ballymaloe, I found Yotam wandering through the gardens and he recognised me immediately, saying, 'Hey! You're the musician!' Later on I introduced him to Ballycotton and a pint of the black stuff. Working on his demo team was a thrill, but to tell the truth, I was already a total Otto groupie. I talked him up so much, there was no way they could have left me out of his demo squad. I must have cooked every recipe from his first book; it was his mix of spices, his food matching, combining all those odd ingredients that really impressed me, and it was the first time I'd been a groupie since I discovered Irish Celtic rock band Horslips when I was a teenager. They were the first band I heard stretch Irish music beyond its comfort zone, and I tracked their rising star in a Horslips scrapbook, saved all press cuttings and bought all the albums. I suppose I saw Yotam in the same light, taking Middle Eastern cuisine and giving it a western palette, stretching the norms of food way beyond its comfort zone – a food troubadour.

Skye Gyngell's books are always close at hand; the mix of ingredients and her no-nonsense approach to good food has taught me that simplicity is the real challenge as you to try and achieve perfection. Skye insists on carefully chosen, healthy, tasty ingredients; a prep cupboard filled with scented oils, spices and herbs; and always using whatever the season yields. Simplicity is a difficult discipline, but certainly suits the domestic kitchen. Her approach reminds me of the old Nashville producer who wanted a simple lick to enhance a song, but his young pretender guitarist wouldn't listen. He overplayed his notes and the producer said, 'Son, no need for all those notes. Play it simple. Let your guitar say something nice, and if you got nothing to say, then say nothing at all.'

I was on gazpacho duty for Skye when she visited Ballymaloe, and midway through lunch prep, she called to our kitchen to taste our food. She congratulated me, saying she could not have made it any better. With that, I ran around the kitchen hollering, doing multiple laps of honour. When she discovered I was a professional musician, she was a little startled. She stood back, and asked that million-dollar question: 'Why on earth did you choose the kitchen?'

'I don't know,' I replied. 'I doubt if I ever will know, but today Skye Gyngell likes my gazpacho, and that's about as good as it gets!' She laughed, shook her head and wished me well.

## THE FUN AND LAUGHTER

It was of course thrilling to have famous bakers, chocolatiers and chefs from around the globe as well as our great Irish producers come to talk passionately to Ballymaloe staff and students. Yet this wasn't why I had gone back. I was never going to attend college, so this was the best way I thought possible to improve my craft and hone my skills. Despite the long hours and exhaustion, I loved my job at the school. There were many evenings I never really wanted to leave the place in case I missed a chance to better my skills. If there was a late reception to be organised, my hand was usually raised.

A huge part of the appeal for me was working with the students. I felt a special kinship with students who valued this kind of learning – those who, like me, were considering a career change, but also others who were upskilling, and those who just wanted to learn. For some it was a major financial commitment, and I could understand what that entailed. And of course, what I'd learned in music and rediscovered as a 'mature' student was that I loved being around younger people. I loved their energy. As hard as we worked at Ballymaloe, and as serious as our goals often were, there was a good amount of *craic* to be had behind the scenes.

Ballycotton is a small place and the Blackbird was student central, and in such a close community you get a chance to build a rapport, whether in the pub over a pint, at a session, or on the bus for a school outing to local producers. The real connection, though, was working with them in the kitchens from early morning to dusk as they developed their skills and improved as the weeks passed by. That's where the laughter, the frustration, the tears and elation all came to the surface.

One particular day, a student started wailing uncontrollably at lunchtime. At first, we thought she had cut herself or had a bad fall, only to discover that she had lost her family heirloom gold wedding band. We searched everywhere. Sorcha was outside at the hen buckets, gloved and filtering through the morning waste, our boss Florrie and the entire crew was searching drawers, pots, pans, shelves, the weigh-up, the wash-up and out across the yard, but no sign of the ring anywhere. The kitchen was in a state of upheaval, and the poor student was inconsolable. Meanwhile, across the hall at lunch, a fresh loaf of brown soda bread was being sliced open – and out popped the missing ring.

We were all flagged at the start of each course on the various dictary needs of students – vegetarians, vegans, lactose intolerance, various allergies and of course coeliacs. While serving lunch one day the secretary came into the kitchen to say that one of the students forgot to mention that she was a coeliac, so to please keep a watch out for her. With that, one of the teachers jumped up into a Van Halen pose, pumping the air with his fist singing, 'She's a coeliac, coeliac, she's on the floor!'

Many students had previous cooking experience, and some of those had notions. One or two were bold enough to challenge Darina – enjoyable spats with only one winner guaranteed. What I loved most was to watch the progress of those who could not cook at all. To see them develop over the course into very competent and confident cooks was without doubt the greatest joy as a teacher. It was the journey that made a student stand out, no matter what the reason. I remember one vegetarian student who found it difficult during the early days to deal with any meat dishes at all. We all worked with her and when asked to present her proposed exam menu she announced that her main course would include a medium rare steak. She was guaranteed top marks for the progress she'd made.

As the months passed, I became acutely aware that my skills had improved dramatically, and, more importantly, that my confidence had improved beyond recognition. I left the school at the right time, although I came back to cover staff absences for the following three years. I had to move on to the next stage of my career, and I had been developing an idea for young kids at school, but that fell through when the investor got cold feet very close to launch date. That was a blow. Pat Shortt then invited me over for a pint to talk about his annual music festival. He was hoping Stockton's Wing might reunite for the event.

# CHAPTER 12

---

# PAT SHORTT'S BAR

*So, if you have been born to be a rambler,*
*You've taken to that highway for a home,*
*Never let that world fall around you*
*And never fall around the world you own.*
　　　　　　　　– 'No Worries', *Celtic Roots Revival* (1988)

# MY BUDDY SHORTT

As well as being a great comedian and powerful actor, Pat Shortt is also an extremely accomplished musician, his first instrument being saxophone, though he can certainly hold a tune on piano, clarinet, concert flute and tin whistle. I first met Pat back in the early eighties at a few Jon Kenny comedy shows, where he was the sound engineer and often accompanied Jon on the songs. His sax solos were outstanding. As time went on, he developed this very funny on-stage character, a vulnerable sidekick. It was no surprise to any of us who knew him when they formed the duo that was D'Unbelievables.

In 2008 Pat bought a pub by the river Kiltha in Castlemartyr. Each year the pub hosted a music festival, and in 2011 he invited Stockton's Wing down to perform a very rare reunion concert. The gig was a success, and I was delighted to have spent it with a bus-load of Donna's family, who came down from Dublin for a mighty weekend.

Pat phoned a few days later wondering if I knew anyone who might be interested in the head chef position at the pub, and I was immediately interested in the job. My time at the school was drawing to its natural conclusion and I needed a new challenge. I had never really managed my own kitchen, so here was my opportunity. I called over to check out the menu and the prospects. The kitchen offered very basic food, mainly freezer to fryer to plate, with the rest pre-packed and stacked in the fridge with very few fresh products on its shelves. It was a good size, though, and everything was in working order – although the oven had a pre-war look about it, and I was soon to discover that it had only two settings: on and off. The menu was handed out in one of those dark wine-coloured, hard plastic A4 wallet books, reminiscent of old hotel service.

But I saw potential there, with a real opportunity to create my own menu and dedicate my energies to ensuring its success. Donna and I spoke about it, knowing it meant an extension of my time away from home, and that alone would require serious commitment from both of us. I never truly realised the depth of support I was asking of Donna that day, but without her encouragement, support and love – not to mention the sacrifice she made while I spread my culinary wings in the first place – I wouldn't have experienced some of the best years of my working life. They were exciting, creative, fulfilling, and of course, with the Shortt factor, a little zany. I accepted Pat's offer, and my only regret was leaving the beautiful Rose Cottage in Ballycotton for a modern, lifeless apartment in Castlemartyr.

In the early weeks of my tenure, business was poor, with very little footfall. We really needed to promote Shortt's as a destination for food, drink and music. It was also my first real food gig out there under the spotlight, and despite a few differences, it had plenty in common with a music gig. If you drop your guard and start performing below par, your audience will spot it immediately. I knew only too well that whatever standard I set from the beginning had to be maintained consistently. I was lucky to have a great team: a young chef from Cloyne, Liam Gilmartin, and a young Polish woman, Maya Breschi, whom I convinced to leave front of house to join me in the kitchen. I taught her from day one, convinced her to go to college and today she is an excellent chef. I am so proud of her achievements. We had a well-motivated bar staff and a superb kitchen crew, who often went to work with the great Finbar Furey's words ringing in their ears: 'Let's go out there and tell them who we are.'

## FAR FROM BOURGUIGNON

I used those early days to find my feet, get to know the area and meet some of our regular customers. My first dish would be the tried-and-tested beef bourguignon, but to my surprise I had very few takers on its first 'lunch special' outing. I was truly baffled, as it's the perfect comfort food – ideal, I thought, for the hungry traveller. One of the locals, Justin Barry, overheard me discussing it with the bar manager, and he called me aside with a wink
and nod of the head. 'We don't go in for too much of that fancy stuff round here, Mike. I'm not trying to tell you your business at all like, but 'tis far from that Bourguignon we were reared – or you, for that matter, I'd say.' He pronounced 'Bourguignon' with a very posh Cork city Montenotte accent, but regardless, he was right, of course. 'Why not call it what it is – a beef stew – and see how ya get on? They might go for that, like.' The 'beef stew' sold out the next day, and myself and Justin became great friends during my time in East Cork.

One morning I decided to replace the wine in the stew with a pint of Beamish, a local stout from the city, and called it Beamish Braised Beef. It was the first of many recipes with a local association, and the customers really bought into the concept. Cork people claim that Beamish is the oldest brewed porter in Ireland. Whether that's true or not, it is a beautiful drink; slightly bitter, but it drinks very well and is wonderful with a pot of beef and vegetables. We served countless bowls at wedding parties, family celebrations, to tourists as well as to the local farmers and travelling businessmen whose tractors and Audis sat side by side in an incongruous display of style and glorious beauty in the rear car park by the beautiful river Kiltha.

## LATE LATE

During that first month Pat appeared on *The Late Late Show* on RTÉ, and though he was asked about the pub, he just brushed it aside. In truth, he had lost interest in the project, and it was obvious when he referred to it as his 'small pub in East Cork', on one of the biggest TV shows in the country. I was livid that he had spurned such a great PR opportunity for the pub, and

I called him the following morning to vent my frustration. We chatted for a long, long time, one of the best conversations we had – timely and a real game changer. He had indeed lost interest and also figured I would only be hanging around for a few months anyway before moving on to better things. There and then, we reconfirmed our commitment to making the pub work. We spent a few days planning, and it was heartening for everyone to witness Pat's new-found enthusiasm. When he's in gear, everyone involved is brought along in the maelstrom. We never missed another PR opportunity again, chasing every angle available on TV, local radio, the papers, Facebook, Twitter – no boundaries.

We set to refreshing the pub itself. Pat designed a new lighting system. Tired and faded wall hangings were replaced with modern art, and the dartboard and Sky Sports were taken away. That move alone was controversial, but diners could never have competed with the volume of noise from the sports fans. Drab place settings with purple pocket cutlery sets were replaced with clipboards and new menus printed up daily. A welcoming open fire burned bright in the hearth every day. Outside, the yard was cleared, benches added for outdoor seating, and fresh floral arrangements hung from every windowsill. Unbelievably, the food was finishing at 3 p.m. each day, so we stretched that out to 8 or 9 p.m. six days a week, with a 6 p.m. finish on Sundays.

## CRITICS ARE LIKE . . .

Pat's close friend Tim Magee, a food specialist who wrote a column for *Gloss* magazine, offered to come down and meet me, taste my food and give me a little advice. His company, Host PR, represented some major players in the hospitality sector. I was delighted, although slightly nervous. On the day he arrived I had prepared small portions of selected dishes and presented them one by one, then sat back in the safety of the kitchen to await his verdict. I was never one for critics, having been schooled in an Irish music business where Brendan Behan's belief that 'critics are like eunuchs in a harem' was the widely accepted view. Many of the music critics luxuriated in their notoriety, and saw no reason to educate themselves on the drive, inspiration or background of the projects they were about to destroy with their lead pencils. We tried not to take them too seriously, but it never cost me a thought to challenge a critic publicly if I disagreed with their approach or writing.

So it has taken me quite a while to get my head around the 'food critic', most of whom I am delighted to say are quite knowledgeable, and very fair, but certainly wield a lot of power, much more so than their music business counterparts. The arrival of a food critic at a restaurant can cause absolute consternation. One manager I worked for sent the entire building into a flurry at the sight of a critic sitting at a corner table, quietly taking in the atmosphere and decor. He rushed into the kitchen, shouting, 'We need to pull out all the stops now!' Off he went in a flap, unnerving the rest of the crew and probably some of our regular customers too. And there I was, thinking aloud, that all customers are potential food critics and we treat them all equally . . .

'Oh, not now, Mike. For fuck's sake, this is really important,' came his reply.

There is one other 'critical' difference between stage and kitchen which has caused me great difficulty: handling the heckler. In the cauldron of a lively crowd at a gig, the heckler is hell-bent on taking you down a peg or two. His or her quips – sometimes funny, sometimes rude – can, if left unchecked, take the room by storm. But the performer is expected to retort and take away the heckler's moment of glory; fail, and the heckler feels like it's his or her name that should be on the ticket stub. It's a fine line, but through years of experience you develop a technique and a confidence to serve most occasions – it can be a lot of fun sometimes to trade blows and the audience always love a good banter.

I learned from the master heckler-slayer, Ronnie Drew, who trounced many a heckler far too eager for the challenge. Truth is they would have had better luck running the bulls at Pamplona. I cannot recall anyone ever getting the better of his sharp wit, and he hardly ever resorted to bad language – well, hardly ever.

In a restaurant, though, 'hecklers' have the upper hand. If a customer challenges you, even if they're rude, you're expected to just take it – and perhaps even offer a little softener, like a free dessert, or an apology. Fair enough if the food or service is bad, that's one thing, but oftentimes it's a question of a perfectly cooked dish not being what the customer expected or people being inherently awkward. Either way, if the customer is rude about it, they should be fair game, but that's not how it goes, and on many occasions I had to literally bite my lip. Ronnie Drew would have set another standard in chef whites.

# THE MAN MENU

So, Tim arrived and sat with me for a short time discussing my dreams, and he spoke about the many great local producers. Though a food critic, I knew he was not here to write a critique but instead to offer me some advice to help myself and his buddy Pat to get the show on the road. I trusted Tim on first meeting, and his support was steadfast throughout my years at Shortt's. Pat's idea to bring him on board so early was inspired.

He talked through each dish: chowder, amazing; thumbs-up for a pan-fried plaice with red pepper butter; soup, OK; steak, succulent and well cooked; veggie fritters with a little chilli jam were just awesome; a few desserts were pretty good, too. All in all, he loved the food. So far so good. He then read down through the menu line by line, rubbed his hands, sat up right and looked straight into my eyes.

'Right, Mike, I'm not going to bullshit you. This menu is all wrong. Not so much the food – your food is wonderful. It's superb cooking – those fritters were yum. I get the passion, I get the flavours, but the menu reads terribly. It's written by a man, exclusively for men. Any woman who reads this will look for the door, or worse, she'll read it from the window and keep walking. This menu should be your invitation to bring them into this beautiful pub but you most definitely will not succeed with this version – not a hope.'

Silence.

'You need to start thinking about your potential customer base: consider families. Here's a question – who do you think makes most of the dining choices in a family? Not me, not you. It's the ladies and the kids. Have you shown this to Donna yet? And tell me: when was the last time you chose a restaurant? I can guarantee you Donna would not be that excited about this menu: pan-fried fish, fried chips, goujons, fried fritters, cream of mushroom soup . . . come on. It sounds heavy, fried, fattening. It sounds like any old pub menu, and it's not. You're a creative songwriter – be creative and write the song here on this page from starters to desserts. You're using some of the best ingredients around and I applaud you for that but I'm not reading about it. You have a goat's cheese salad – tell us about it! Invite us in. I promise you, I'll come back to you again next week and the week after that for as long as you need me. Your potential here is great. I love your food. Call me anytime, kid.' I think Tim is the only younger guy I've ever allowed to call me kid – it's the way he says it.

His lesson seems quite simple now, but back then it was like a bolt of lightning. I rewrote the menu, much to his approval – my 'Ardsallagh goat's cheese salad with black pudding, slivers of roast red pepper on a bed of organic leaves with house dressing' read far better than 'goat's cheese salad with pudding and peppers'. 'Fresh catch of the day, cooked in the pan with a herb butter, hand-cut chips and rocket salad' replaced 'fish and chips'. It was seasonal, fresh, local, organic, and it was Shortt's own. We set about fine-tuning certain dishes like the humble burger, and created our own sauces to accompany the steaks, and an array of herb butters for the fish; we made ketchups, salad dressings and homemade jellies. Our desserts were hearty and homey, like seasonal fresh fruit crumbles and our number 1 hit, bread and butter pudding.

## THE LOCAL PRODUCERS

East Cork has an abundance of great produce, so, inspired by the new menu and reinvigorated surroundings, I set about the task of sourcing as many ingredients as possible from local producers, and crediting them on the menu. It turned out that the village itself was a veritable Aladdin's cave of foodie goodies, and I was sitting right in the midst of it all. Right opposite the pub stood the village greengrocer and food hall, run by Sean and Dorothy Walsh and their hard-working family. A haven of foodstuffs, it had rows and rows of seasonal fruit, vegetables, nuts, fresh herbs, spices, beautiful cakes and breads, sweet and savoury home baking, and a deli full of freshly made salads, boiled hams and sandwich fillings. Dorothy made her own chutneys and jams, which stood beside a vast selection of exotic oils and vinegars and a complete stock of dried fruits and chocolates. Many of the local restaurants, hotels and the Ballymaloe Cookery School came to stock their larder from the storeroom at the rear of the shop. Over time we developed a great business relationship and a strong bond. Dorothy often remarked that she should just give me my own set of keys, to get supplies on Sunday mornings when the shop was closed and our stocks in the pub were depleted. It wasn't for nothing – I often called them early on Sunday mornings in a flurry, but they never failed to come down to the village and sort me out.

Fifty yards up the street was one of the last of East Cork's craft butchers. Ned Clifford and his daughter Eileen greeted me suspiciously at first, as I was, surprisingly, the first chef from the pub to call looking for meat. They soon supplied most of our meat, and as they had an abattoir behind the shop, all the produce was local and traceable. I learned much from Ned and his sidekick Denis, whose great expression, 'Yerra, Mike, pressure is only for tyres,' became my mantra.

Ned's wife Ann ran their pub across the street. She was a staunch Cork GAA supporter and an ex-county player, always up for some good hurling banter, which kept many of us amused during the hurling season. Every Saturday afternoon Eileen phoned to see if my stock was OK, and she, like the Walshes, would open the shop for a Sunday-morning refill, even after some late-night Saturdays in the city. I've never experienced that type of service anywhere else I have worked. It was a village looking after itself, and everyone helped each other out.

# THE LONESOME BOATMAN

Situated between the butcher and greengrocer was the local chipper. Alan, the owner, certainly knew his spuds: each variety was seasonal, tested again and again until the proper temperature was established to produce the perfect chip. In the beginning I was determined to make my own, but it proved time-consuming, so I asked him to supply me with his freshly cut chips. He agreed, on condition that I convince my fish supplier to provide him with fresh cod and haddock, as our fish was developing a great reputation. The deal was sealed, and the village had two of the best fish and chips on offer in all of East Cork and beyond.

I christened my fisherman Trevor 'The Lonesome Boatman' McNamara. One of my favourite suppliers, he was knowledgeable on all marine issues, a good friend and energetic businessman. After eight years as a naval officer, he retired and returned as a qualified mechanical fitter, but was soon back in the family fishing business that he'd first entered at the age of fifteen. His dad Joby had started fishing at thirteen, and was one of the first to supply Myrtle Allen all those years ago when she opened the Ballymaloe Country House Restaurant. Along with his daughter Niamh, Joby still supplies the house and the cookery school.

Their fish is so fresh, it deserves the best – and the simplest – treatment to really show it off.

# Swimming with the fishes: fish à la nage
Serves 4

Fish à la nage is a fancy term for fish poached in a lovely flavoursome broth. It is one of my favourite ways to serve fish, all goodness and not a heavy sauce in sight. The secret is to use a good broth, and you can develop the dish to suit your own tastes. If you like shellfish, just add them with your fresh fish, though I find mussels too strong for the delicate flavours of the broth. Clams are beautiful with a chunky hake or halibut, and salmon is always wonderful à la nage. You'll need a wide pot with a tight-fitting lid.

1 tbsp rapeseed oil
1 knob of unsalted butter
1 onion, peeled and finely diced
1 knob of ginger, shaved or cut very thin
2 celery sticks, peeled and finely diced
2 carrots, finely diced
½ a medium leek, white part only, finely diced (optional)
½ a glass of good white wine
1 tsp white wine vinegar
½ a fennel bulb, very thinly sliced
Fresh herbs of your choice, finely chopped (I like dill and tarragon)
4 medium darnes of salmon, hake or cod, skin removed
500ml good fish stock (I have made this with veg and chicken, but try to get a good fish stock)
Fresh parsley and dill, plus 2 chive stems, finely chopped
1 lemon
Sea salt and freshly ground black pepper

1. Heat the oil in a sauté or other deep pan, add the butter and onion, and fry gently for 5 minutes.
2. Add the ginger, celery, carrots, and leek if using. Stir to coat, and fry gently for 3 minutes.
3. Add the wine and vinegar and reduce to almost dry.
4. Add the fennel and 1 tablespoon of the herbs, then place the salmon in the pan and pour in enough stock to halfway cover the fish. Season to taste.
5. Cover the pan and cook on a medium heat for 8 to 10 minutes, or until the salmon is almost cooked through. If you have a temperature gauge, anything above 60°C is good.
6. Serve in warmed bowls. Lift the salmon pieces into the bowl and then ladle the broth all around. Garnish with the rest of the herbs and place the chives in an x across the top. Add a wedge of lemon in the centre.

*Tips:*
- *Ask the fishmonger to skin the salmon for you.*
- *You could cut the salmon into little chunks and this would cut down your cooking time to about 5 minutes.*
- *For extra flavour, garnish with some lightly fried sage leaves and/or capers.*
- *You could even whip up a nice salsa verde and put a dollop on top, with the sage and capers all around. Now it's swimming in the Olympics.*

Trevor fishes his seventeen-foot punt out of Ballycotton Bay, although like so many other Irish fishermen, his days on the water will soon be a recreational pursuit. In Ballycotton the evidence of a decimated industry is stark. The once-thriving pier now holds very few punts, and the village rock face towering overhead shows faded signs of a bygone commercial fishing hub. In past years the bay has seen a proliferation of a seal population that destroyed all the fishing nets in their search of food, and this has resulted in some fishermen being forced further out to and beyond the thirty-mile-plus zone. Many are faced with the stark economic choice to invest in larger seafaring vessels or retire. Unfortunately, the latter is proving to be the only viable solution for so many. Those that remain in the bay only fish for lobster and crab. That stock cannot last forever, and without a stronger voice lobbying for the men and women of the sea, it's hard to understand how things will change for the better.

Trevor supplied all my fish at Shortt's, and our daily menu was only printed as his van left the yard. We grilled, baked, poached or pan-cooked quality fish daily, and the product was consistently outstanding. He had such a respect for and knowledge of the sea and its treasures. He introduced me to hake, plaice, scallops, large John Dory and those beautiful little Dories, mullet, turbot, all varieties of sole, wild mussels and my favourite, the beautiful rock cod that feeds on the brown kelp that grows in by the black rocks and gives it its distinctive bronze colour, which also acts as a natural camouflage as it hunts its prey along the bay. Trevor's mum, Frances, often sent me pots of her dressed crab or shrimp. At one stage Trevor hot-smoked his salmon in an old oak whiskey barrel, which was extremely popular in our summer salads. He's regularly found at farmers' markets, with a permanent stall at Mahon in Cork and the Milk Market in Limerick.

# A fish chowder
Serves 4

Our chowder received rave reviews, and got a silver in the Business and Finance Food Awards. We were all delighted with the award, our very first food medal. I never use shellfish in my chowders; I like a good fish mix of salmon, cod, hake and naturally smoked haddock. Try not to use the orange excuse for smoked haddock that's readily available, as the nearest it gets to smoke is probably traffic fumes. It's worth seeking out the genuine variety, and most fish shops stock the real deal. The secret to a really good chowder is very simple: use fresh fish.

1 tbsp rapeseed oil
4 strips of streaky bacon, chopped
25g butter
1 leek, finely chopped
1 glass of white wine
2 tsp white wine vinegar
1 tbsp plain flour (or gluten-free flour)
1 tsp smoked paprika
1 blade of mace or pinch of nutmeg
250ml good fish stock
4 small potatoes, peeled and diced
2 carrots, diced (optional)
250ml full-fat milk
1 tbsp chopped fresh parsley
A pinch of cayenne pepper
600g fish mix (chunks of salmon, hake, cod, etc.)
Sea salt and freshly ground black pepper
Brown bread and butter, to serve

1. Heat the oil and gently cook the bacon. Do not burn.
2. Add the butter and leek. Cover with baking parchment and allow to cook on a low heat for about 4 minutes.
3. Add the wine and vinegar and reduce to almost nothing.
4. Stir in the flour, paprika and mace or nutmeg, and mix in the stock.
5. Add the potatoes, carrots and milk and cook for 15 minutes, stirring regularly. Add a little extra milk if it's too thick.
6. Add a little parsley and cayenne. Season. Because the potatoes absorb much, you will need a little extra salt. Taste before you salt.
7. Your chowder base is ready. It will hold for a couple of days. When required, simply add the fish mix and cook for 3 to 5 minutes. Serve with nice brown bread and real butter.

## D'UNBELIEVABLE BURGER

I developed a recipe for a burger and decided to call it D'Unbelievable burger in honour of Pat's very successful comedy show *D'Unbelievables*. He sent me a worried glance.

'Jaysus, Mike, you'd better be right there. You could be setting yourself up for all sorts.'

He was right, of course, but I had spent a few weeks on the burger and believed it could stand up to its title. There was one secret ingredient though: Pat Coffey's homemade Worcestershire sauce.

## PAT THE ALCHEMIST

Pat Coffey arrived at my kitchen door one Saturday morning with an apple box full of mixed organic leaves and a small bottle of homemade Worcestershire sauce. Within minutes of tasting and talking food I paid him, and he returned every week after that with his selection box, which always contained a few surprises. In between the rocket, mustard, mizuna and lamb's lettuce I'd find a variety of fresh herbs, onions and seasonal vegetables. On occasion I might find a couple of random artichokes, apples, courgettes, peppers, beans, the odd stray chilli and maybe a few fresh eggs thrown in for good measure. Always the same price, and we never worked from an order sheet.

Pat, a Cork man, learned his trade in the fanciful Killiney Castle Hotel, in its day a very fine dining establishment on the Dublin coast. At the height of his career, illness forced him to hang up his chef whites. After months of care and lots of thought, he decided to pursue his passion for old-fashioned sauces, which had consumed much of his spare time as a young chef in the Castle kitchen. At his Yellow House cottage on the outskirts of Cloyne in East Cork you will now find him busy at work in his alchemist's lair, pots bubbling and wooden barrels fermenting.

His concoctions are on the go from morning through to moonlight and beyond, as he patiently takes his ingredients through months or even years bubbling away under his watchful eye. Whether it is his hot chilli, chilli with almonds, Schezuan sauce, blackberry vinegar, raspberry vinegar, elderberry cordial, barbecue, Yemeni zhug or the Worcestershire, each has a depth of flavour seldom found on high-street shelves.

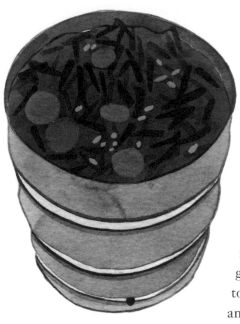

On a recent visit, Pat gave me the grand tour and partially explained his Worcestershire sauce, a potent mix which includes chilli, malt and cider vinegar, molasses, tamarind, garlic, mustard seeds, cloves, cinnamon, onions, and anchovies. There are many more ingredients, but that was as much as he was giving up to me. When I enquired about the rest he said, 'Ah, sure that would be telling, Mike.' All ingredients are transferred to a food grade stainless-steel beer keg and left to macerate for a full year, then strained and poured into oak barrels for another year before they are ready for bottling and the market – although that may be extended to increase its depth of flavour. The sauce at each stage has its own powerful distinctive taste.

He has a vast library of old cookbooks, some of which I thumb through, stopping at various old recipes, which I get to photograph for my own collection. He then presents me with a seven-year-old Pontac sauce, often used in gravies or as an accompaniment to game. It's an elderberry and vinegar mix first created in a high-end London restaurant over 300 years ago, and became prevalent in the kitchens of the aristocracy. I see a recipe for a zhug, and it reminds me of our summer salads when his tasty Yemeni pesto made several successful appearances. Zhug is a mix of garlic, green chilli, olive oil, fresh coriander, ground coriander, ground cumin, cardamom, cloves and seasoning.

Pat's garden, at first glance, has the appearance of an unused farm haggard – until you roam around and discover his world of bloom and beauty. 'These are Chinese prickly ash bushes. I'll

be the first in Ireland to produce Schezuan peppercorns, Mike. No doubt I'll find some old sauce recipe for the first harvest.' I have no doubt he will do just that. The ash leaves are bright and sturdy and stand comfortably in among the indigenous plants, a metaphor for how Pat sees the world he hopes for, and the food he cooks.

The apple trees are a rare Irish breed received from the Irish Seed Savers Association, which is the brainchild of ex-Stockton's Wing bodhrán player Tommy Hayes and his wife Anita. They operate in East Clare and are well worth checking out on the internet or in person if you're travelling through the beautiful East Clare countryside. Pat makes a stock of cider from Tommy's apple trees. Beside the mini-orchard stands the polytunnel, full of organic leaves, herbs, beans, peppers and a very healthy bunch of Hatch chillies. All around, the hens roam freely, clucking away in total comfort.

We spoke for a long time about the kitchen and food provenance. 'As chefs we never really get a chance to properly develop products or recipes. Rushing from one service to the next, it's nearly impossible to find the amount of time required to properly concentrate on that development side of the business. Here I get to spend time testing and improving each recipe, especially the old ones, so I regard myself as very lucky to be able to do that and respect all the good things we grow and consume.' We both agree that while many chefs quite rightly travel the haute couture route, we should never lose sight of the simple things in food, or longstanding traditions. Sometimes the oldest fiddle plays the sweetest tune.

# The D'Unbelievable burger
Makes 6 burgers

When I added the Worcestershire sauce to the burger mix, something magical happened to the flavour. The alchemist's touch created a hit single for Pat Shortt's menu. Use good quality-mince, about 80 per cent lean. Keep a little mustard on the side for cooking.

2 tsp rapeseed oil, plus extra for frying
½ Spanish onion, peeled and roughly chopped
1 clove of garlic, crushed
2 tsp Worcestershire sauce
1 tsp chopped fresh herbs (rosemary, thyme, sage)
2 tsp homemade tomato ketchup
2 tsp Dijon mustard
½ tsp mustard powder
1 small egg, whipped (you may only need half)
600g good-quality beef mince
Sea salt and freshly ground black pepper
Burger buns, to serve
Cheddar, to serve

1. Heat the oil and fry the onion on a very low heat until soft, then add the garlic and Worcestershire sauce and simmer for a couple of minutes. Add the herbs and remove from the heat. Transfer to a cold bowl and set aside.
2. When completely cold add the ketchup and 1 teaspoon of mustard, and liquidise.
3. Add the mince then add just a little of the egg and mix well. Add more egg if you think it is required, but we don't want a very wet burger. VERY IMPORTANT: fry a small piece in the pan to test for seasoning. When you are happy, shape the burgers to your preferred size and store.
4. Tim's top tip: lightly coat the burger with Dijon mustard before frying. It acts as a seal, and helps to retain the moisture. Let it cook slowly, don't turn it every minute, and for crying out loud, don't press down on the burger, as the juice just runs out and all you get is a very dry lump of meat. Serve on a bun, with a nice, strong, melting cheddar.

# WAN TEU, WAN TEU

Pat and I were invited to demo the D'Unbelievable burger at the Midleton Food Festival. There were famous chefs in the line-up that day, all quite professional in their approach and presentation. Pat suggested we take a slightly alternative route: culinary comedy counterpoint. We brought three musician friends along, dressed them in kitchen whites and sat them on a riser in the corner, while we variously prepped food, talked through the burger recipe – and had the piss taken mercilessly by our fearless leader as he ran through a full-fledged slapstick routine. It was pandemonium, and then Pat shouted into his ailing headset.

'Wan teu . . . wan teu? Good, it's still working. Now, ladies and gentlemen, I think it's a good time for the bingo.'

As we neared the end, the audience was guffawing at the high jinks on stage and the burgers were sizzling away on the grill. I've never laughed so much in a kitchen – and can you imagine, we were never invited back again!

# MAZDA

One morning, Pat arrived at the pub dressed in an oversized tweed coat fastened with a rope, some odd class of a rain hat, a stick and a pair of wellington boots. He announced that along with our neighbour, farmer John Smith, he was off to the mart in Dungarvan to buy a heifer for the pub. The idea was that she be reared, slaughtered and butchered locally, and served up in the pub – all very much in keeping with the food ethos of the place.

We filmed his departure and awaited his return. He arrived back very late and the worse for wear after stopping off at various hostelries along the way, including a detour to a farmer friend of John's up in the mountains outside Killagh, where they drank whiskey from china mugs. I was there since with Pat, and the man's measures were way beyond legal. Through the stupor Pat announced that the addition to the team at Shortt's was to be called Mazda, and would stay over at John's farm for the year. When asked why he called her Mazda, he explained that her tag number was 323, and Mazda 323 was his dad's old car. Over the following months he filmed the heifer's life on the farm and posted videos on YouTube, until one particular video went viral. A horsemeat scandal had gripped the nation; it had been discovered that many beefburger products were in fact being made with some horsemeat, and in some instances 100 per cent horsemeat. Pat was over at the farm feeding Mazda when he switched on the video camera and began. 'Today, I'd like to explain the difference between horse cows and heifers – that's cows with no sign of a horse about them at all at all. If you look closely, John, I'm almost sure that it's impossible to put a saddle on that fella.' He cups his hand to his mouth, shouting in to Mazda, 'Hi ho, Silver! Look, John, they don't even recognise horse language. Dem are not horse cows. Dese are heifer cows.' All of thirty seconds had a quarter of a million hits within days.

The following year Ned Clifford did the honours in the abattoir, hung it for a few weeks, then jointed the meat and stored it. For a while, we really were self-sufficient in the beef department, and we tried to do better by our whiskey than the aul china mug.

# Whiskey syllabub
Serves 4

Syllabub works well with the addition of the zest and juice of an orange, and is beautiful served with poached fruit.

Zest and juice of 1 lemon
1 shot of honey
I shot of whiskey
250ml double cream

1. Put the lemon zest, juice, honey and whiskey into a bowl. Mix, then cover and leave in the fridge for a few hours – a day would be better.
2. Gradually whisk in the cream until the mixture thickens. Don't overdo it. Get it to your preferred consistency.
3. Pour into individual glasses and leave to set in the fridge for an hour or two.
4. Serve with Marie Peebles' shortbread fingers (see page 141).

## THE WORLD'S DUMBEST CRIMINALS

Crime was almost non-existent in the village, so we were shocked one morning as we entered the bar to see broken glass on the floor. We searched around the pub but there was no sign of a break-in. We went to study the CCTV and were treated, appropriately enough, to one of the greatest comedy routines of all time.

Two guys wearing hoodies appeared round the back of the pub trying to smash the window, but they could not break the outside glaze. They searched around the yard and found several unlocked beer kegs. 'Bobbie and Clyde' rolled the kegs up to the gate, which was well secured. They then attempted to lift a keg over a six-foot wall, pushing with great effort until one of them lost his grip and the keg went tumbling back down the yard. They tried again and again, to no avail. Clearly exhausted, they took time out for a well-earned rest. One sat in the smoking room by the river, rolling a cigarette. Out of breath and overheated from his efforts, he removed his hoodie, exposing his face to the overhanging camera. His partner was bent over and huffing and puffing by the kitchen door – and promptly whipped off his hoodie and rubbed his head, looking skyward, straight into the kitchen-door camera. Oblivious, they resumed their work and eventually managed to lift all three kegs over the wall, rolled them across the main road and were out of sight. When we checked the front cameras, we watched as they entered a house across the street. Our manager, Mikie John, recognised them straight away. 'Those two langers are from the city. They've been living there for the past few weeks. Weren't they just drinking here last night?'

The following day the police went around to the house and discovered the lads sitting around with their feet on the kegs, smoking cigarettes and watching a movie. To add insult to injury, all the kegs were out of date by months and had been awaiting collection from the brewery. A week later they came and threw a few words of abuse at Mikie John, but that was the last we ever saw of them. They did a little time for their crime, though.

## THE FESTIVAL

Very early on at Shortt's I witnessed what can only be described as the world's dumbest musician perform a full set without playing or singing a single note. He had keyboards with an elaborate backing track, drum machines, electric guitar and vocal mic. As soon as he started up, I saw that the machines were doing everything, including the singing. His guitar chords were, well, nothing I had ever seen – and his solos were so funny, Jeff Beck could not muster such dexterity as he ran his fingers up and down the fretboard. I challenged him afterwards and he just winked at me and said, 'Shur, everyone is doing it, like! What's the problem, like?' in a sweeping Cork lilt. That lilt was the closest he had come to music all night. Needless to say, we never saw him again.

The Kiltha River Music Festival came to town for the August Bank Holiday weekend. It all began on the Tuesday before, with the arrival of the marquee. Stanchions were hoisted one by one, the rat-tat-tat of metal on metal, followed by the canopy, section by section, then the stage, sound and lighting were installed. Pat transported the bar prop from the Killinaskully TV film set all the way from Limerick to Cork in a horsebox. The beer and food started to arrive midweek, as the excitement spread throughout the village. One or two from the village council used the opportunity to flash their badges with letters of complaint or threats of cancellation if the bunting wasn't high enough or noise pollution levels not adhered to. Thankfully the village never listened to them at all and we got on with our preparations.

Initially I found it very odd greeting many of my old musician friends in chef whites, but we fed and watered them very well and they played amazing music in return. Sometimes I'd slip back into the live music; one very special year, I opened the show with a solo set, followed by the sublime voice of Lisa Hannigan. She made way for Briana Corrigan from The Beautiful South, and then Justin Curry from Del Amitri played a blinding solo set on acoustic guitar with a bagful of his hits. Over the years we had Michael Flatley, Philip Donnelly, Eleanor Shanley, John Spillane, De Dannan, Stockton's Wing, Matt Molloy, Arty McGlynn and many more. All day and all night the pub would be full of music, with huge crowds, including holidaying families who often stayed well beyond the 9 p.m. threshold for children – it's such a silly law, and to be honest, if it had been around when I was a kid, I would have missed so many of my heroes perform at sessions. We did make some effort, but often not enough. One night we were well beyond closing time, with the bar still hopping and all ages enjoying a superb music session. 'Jaysus!' Mikie John roared over the music at Pat. 'It's two o'clock, lad. If the guards arrive, we're fecked!'

'Ah sure, it'll be grand,' replied Pat. Just then he noticed three little kids playing away to their hearts' content. 'Jaysus! We will be rightly fecked if they come in and see the kids as well!'

# PA'S PIZZA AND PADDLE

While touring with D'Unbelievables, Pat stopped at Truffles restaurant in Sligo for a pizza. The owner, Bernadette O'Shea, who became highly regarded in Irish culinary circles, had just written her first book, *Pizza Defined*. Bernadette, unknown to Pat, was a close friend of his sister Ann's, so she called over to say hello, and Pat ended up with a copy of the book. It soon became his pizza bible.

Over the years he developed his own special pizza, which he serves up at home as often as twice a week. I called to the house for a demonstration, so much had he gone on about how great it was. His son Lughaidh was emphatic that it was the best on offer from Pat's kitchen. I watched him in action that day, and I have to admit I learned a few classy tips and we had a laugh along the way.

He insists on the exact measure of flour, but is flexible on oil and honey – and very flexible on utensils, as you will see.

### THE PIZZA STONE

A friend suggested that Pat go to a tile centre or home-supply shop and ask for a sample terracotta stone tile, which he did. The stone is the best way to get a crispy base, and though it can be done without one, if you're planning to cook pizza regularly, I suggest you get to the hardware store. Tell them Pat sent you.

### THE PADDLE

This is where it gets very Pat Shortt. He purchased a piece of aluminium sheet metal and cut out a rectangle. On one side, he bent a two-inch strip to stand perpendicular to the main plate. For the handle, he attached a two-foot length of 2 x 2 white deal timber to that strip, using three metal screws. He now had his homemade pizza paddle. 'It's a versatile instrument,' he demonstrates, as he slides an imaginary pizza into and out of the oven. 'It takes the pizza from the oven as you can see, but if I drop the pizza on the floor, well, this is a great man to scoop it up – fairly lively, mind – and land it on the counter before any of the kids notice a thing.'

### THE PAINT SCRAPER

'This is a great yoke altogether, less than 2 euros in the shop. A great man to clear the surface of all sticky excess dough. Later on, I'll use it to cut the portions, and sure if I'm ever stuck while prepping the wall for a lick of paint, you know yourself . . .'

# Pa's pizza base

Makes 6 thick or 8 thin 25cm pizza bases

14g fresh or fast-action yeast
2 tbsp honey
500g strong white or 00 grade flour
¾ tsp sea salt
A few glugs of olive oil
A little extra flour for dusting

**For his equipment**
1 heatproof jug
1 sieve
2 bowls
1 wooden spoon
Mixer with dough hooks (optional)
A clean worktop
Cling film
1 paint scraper
1 sharp knife
1 pastry brush
1 pizza stone or tray
1 pizza paddle (optional but fun)

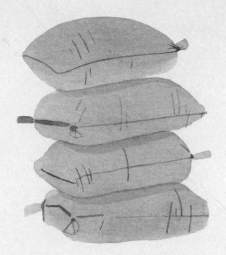

1. Pour 150ml boiling water and 200ml cold water into a jug.
2. Add the yeast, stir, then add the honey. Leave aside. After 10 minutes, it'll have the appearance of an all-white pint of Guinness with a lovely creamy head. Five minutes later, the yeast is ready.
3. Meanwhile, sieve the flour and salt into a bowl.
4. Make a well in the flour. Add the glugs of olive oil and the yeast liquid.
5. Mix gently with a wooden spoon, bringing the mix to a manageable ball.
6. Transfer to a mixer, using the dough hooks, and turn on medium speed for 5 to 7 minutes. You may need to add a dust of flour, as the mix is a little sticky. Before you finish, turn it up to full speed to bring all the dough together, for about 30 seconds.
   OR
   Transfer the dough to a floured surface, and do it by hand – which is my favoured method – gently working the dough for at least 10 minutes.

Pizza Pat says, 'Slide your fingers underneath the dough. Turn it, pull it apart and bring it back together. Stretch the dough by holding both ends, and slap it onto the surface. Bring it together again, and repeat this for 5 or 6 minutes, always with a gentle touch. Forget about kneading the dough too much, OK?' After 5 minutes, transfer to an oiled bowl and cover tightly with cling film. Leave to stand for about an hour in a warm part of the kitchen or until it has at least doubled in size. Pizza Pat says, 'I have often left it there, gone into town or the office, and it's there when I return, just the finest.'

7. The kitchen temperature normally measures in at 20 degrees. After an hour or two in the kitchen, it has doubled in size, Pat knocks back the dough with a punch or two.

8. Cut the dough into 8 equal chunks, and weigh each one – you should get eight 120g pieces of dough.

9. Now shape the dough into balls. Place each chunk of dough on a floured surface, and pass gently from hand to hand, turning, stretching and repeating a few times before bringing the ball together. At no point is Pat's labour forced – it's all done with a very light hand. When I make it, I usually flour my work surface and add a very slight sprinkle of water, shape my hand like a claw or a crab over the dough ball, and move it around in a fast circular motion until you have a nice even shape.

10. Oil the pizza balls with a pastry brush before covering very lightly with cling film.

11. Give the dough about 10 minutes' rest and they are, as Pat says, 'ready to rock and roll' for pizza, bread rolls or French sticks. It's a tried-and-tested routine with excellent results.

*Pat's toppings are always minimal: Italian sausages from the local deli, pepperoni or anchovies, fresh basil. One staple topping is a little Macroom buffalo mozzarella, from a herd of over 200 Italian buffalo on a farm in County Cork. First introduced in 2009 specifically to produce mozzarella cheese, these days they also make a beautiful halloumi and a feta-style cheese. You also need a good sauce base (see opposite).*

# Andy's no-cook tomato sauce
Makes enough for 2 or 3 pizzas

Here's a good tomato sauce I learned from my great kitchen sidekick and another pizza king, Andy Byrne. I had the pleasure of working with him at a restaurant in south Dublin, where his pizzas were a big hit.

It is very important to pulse this sauce as opposed to liquidising it. A lumpy sauce has two advantages: the bigger pieces hold the heat better, thereby helping the cooking process along. Also, it won't run all over the place. Plum tomatoes are much sweeter, cook hotter, and react better to the basil and oregano. These are the little tips I love to hear from the experts like Andy, who is very particular about his sauce.

1 x 400g tin of plum tomatoes, chopped
A little pinch of oregano, fresh or dried
1 dollop of ketchup
1 bunch of basil, with trimmed stalks
Sea salt and ground white pepper

1. Place all the ingredients in a food processor and pulse a few times but do not blend.
2. Season to taste.

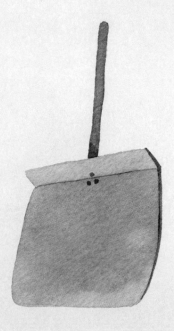

# Rocket pesto
Makes about 150g

Buy yourself a large pestle and mortar. Many believe that the pounding and crushing extracts much more from the oils in terms of the nutrients. You also have much more control on the consistency, it's far easier to clean than a food mixer, and you get a bonus workout for your biceps. You can of course use the mixer just as well.

2 cloves of garlic
Sea salt, to taste
1 tbsp pine nuts, toasted in a dry pan, or confit in a little olive oil, if desired
Mix of fresh herbs – a bunch of parsley, a bunch of basil and some tarragon leaves
1 bunch of peppery rocket
Extra virgin olive oil

1. Crush the garlic, sea salt and pine nuts with a pestle and mortar.
2. Add the herbs and crush.
3. Add clumps of rocket a bit at a time and crush.
4. Add the oil – it's worth getting the best olive oil you can afford. Bring to your preferred consistency. Some like it smooth, but I prefer a slightly rougher consistency.
5. Taste and adjust to your preference.
6. I dot this liberally over a hot pizza before bringing it to the table. It will keep in the fridge for a few days.

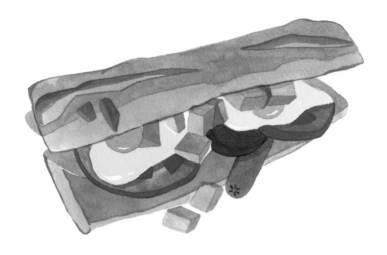

# THE JUMBO BREAKFAST ROLL

Waterford chef, food writer and TV host Paul Flynn came down to record a piece for his TV series *Irish Food Adventures*. He wanted to present a healthier version of Pat's infamous breakfast roll, celebrated in his number one hit single 'The Jumbo Breakfast Roll'. Two eggs, two rashers, two sausages, two puddings – one black and one white – all placed like a tower on top of each other, etc. It was sung the length and breadth of Ireland, and it nailed a daily scene at all Celtic Tiger truck stops as couriers rushed from their vans, builders emerged from dusty sites and travelling salespeople ran from their Jags to queue for a coffee and a leaking brown-paper-wrapped mass of a breakfast roll as their engines purred away in the forecourt.

Paul's idea was to spruce up the breakfast roll and produce a healthier option. I boiled twenty eggs for seven minutes exactly, sourced and chopped some quality chorizo sausage, rinsed some of Pat Coffey's organic rocket leaves, made fresh mayonnaise and had a box of soft Blaas delivered that morning. (A blaa is a somewhat protected species of fresh bread roll exclusive to Waterford, Wexford and Kilkenny, where it is mainly produced. It's a beautiful piece of baking.)

Myself and Pat were then instructed to go across to the deli to get the ugliest breakfast roll imaginable for the opening shots. Dorothy duly obliged, but when she presented the roll to Pat he said, 'Fill it again.' When she presented the second version, he said, 'Shur, fill it one more time for the *craic*.' The result would easily have fed a family of four grown adults, four children, a couple of the neighbours and the dog. The contents were bulging through the paper wrap, ready to explode. Blobs of tomato sauce, brown sauce and mayo came seeping through the cracks. By the time we returned to the crew my white jacket was a mess.

Paul tried hard to keep a straight face as he set about creating the alternative version with a constant running commentary from Mr Shortt. The chorizo was cooked lightly in the wok, cooled, the eggs were mashed in, followed by the mayo and a little seasoning. The blaa was lightly buttered, then liberally filled with the spread, topped off with a handful of Pat Coffey's fresh leaves. Each blaa was then quartered and distributed around to the audience. Paul went from table to table recording the reactions until he came to our manager Mikie John, who squirmed after the first bite; leaves were not really Mikie's thing at all.

'Well, what do you think? Is that not much healthier than the other one your man keeps singing about?'

'Jaysus, lad, I don't know. I can't see this thing catching on here at all.'

'CUT!' The entire room went into convulsions and the director moved swiftly on to another table. He eventually got Mikie to smile and say nice things about the new breakfast roll, but looking back at the footage, his expression never changed from that first take.

## THE END COMES TO US ALL

*Drivin' through the wind and rain,*
*Heading back home again.*
*All I want is to be with you,*
*And the closer I get to you*
*Gone are these lonesome blues.*
*All I need is to be with you.*
          – 'Cradled in Your Arms', *What You Know* (2002)

Donna always maintains that I got my mojo back while working with Pat. I certainly learned to laugh again, both at life and at myself. Laughter is indeed a tonic, and we had plenty of it at Shortt's. Pat and I are joined at the hip now, constantly in touch and all in support of each other's careers. What we created was a very special place to eat, drink and be merry. I would like to think we brought our own touch of sparkle to the beautiful village and villagers of Castlemartyr.

In 2013 it was time to leave it all behind and return to Dublin, as that adventure had run its course. I needed to be back at home and was offered a job to test recipes for a new restaurant due to open before Christmas. On my final night at Shortt's I bade a very sad farewell to the musicians, staff from the cookery school, Rory and the crew from Ballymaloe House, friends from Castlemartyr and Ballycotton and so many of the food producers who had helped me create and live a dream that was indeed a beautiful affair.

# CHAPTER 13

# ELEANOR SHANLEY

*At the station she boards a train,*
*All wet with tears and rain,*
*And a father holds a mother's empty hand.*
*She whispers as she goes*
*Of all the things you need to know,*
*What I have I hold forever in my heart.*
*– 'We Had It All', A Couple More Years with Eleanor and Ronnie (2002)*

## THE ISLAND OF THE WHITE COW

The beautiful island of Inishbofin is situated off the Connemara coast in County Galway. It is only accessible by boat or ferry from the mainland village of Cleggan. Inishbofin comes from Inis Bó Finne, meaning island of the white cow; popular explanations of the name include some mysticism about witches, and white cows turning to stone. The island has a rich history dating back to early Christian monks, who may have been its first inhabitants, followed by centuries of clan takeovers until the English came and used it as a fortress and prison. The population of the Island was decimated after the Famine, and dwindled further through the last century. It is still sparsely populated, with only about 200 permanent residents. Each year, a reclusive winter and reasonably quiet spring make way for the hustle and bustle of summer visitors, who arrive on its shore in their thousands to amble or cycle the narrow roads, or head out on the water before an evening of good food, beer and live music.

I was invited out to the island to perform with my friend and soulmate Eleanor Shanley, who's no stranger to Bofin. She finds her inner peace there, and on a stroll around the island with Eleanor you get a sense that you are in fact on her home soil, as she meets and greets the locals at every turn, stopping for little chats about all sorts of things well beyond the weather.

## COLLA VOCE

On the afternoon of our concert Eleanor invited me to lunch on her friend Pat Lavelle's boat in the harbour. Pat wanted to feed us all before the gig. I'd never refuse such hospitality, so I left the hotel to ramble my way down to the pier. As the corncrake signalled the end of my descent, I stood to listen for any familiar voices but instead caught this beautiful unmistakable waft of fish sizzling on a pan somewhere close. I followed the sound of rising laughter until I spotted Eleanor on the deck of a small fishing boat bobbing gently in its moorings. 'Come on,' says she. 'The party's already started. All the food will be gone if you don't hurry up!'

Our captain Pat Lavelle had retired from business in Sligo to sail, living through the summer months on this, his favourite patch of fishing ground. The channel between Inishbofin and Inishark is subjected to strong tides and heavy swells, and can only be fished in settled conditions. It offers the fisherman a great challenge and a wonderful bounty of pollack, coalfish, haddock, wrasse, turbot, ling, conger eel, squid, and of course tons of mackerel. His boat, a Vancouver 27, is named *Colla Voce*, which roughly translates to 'with the voice' or 'follow the voice'. How apt, I thought, considering that I had just followed the sound of laughter to find my way there.

Pat ushered me to a seat and the kettle took its spot beside the frying pan on a kerosene stove. On a narrow table sat an old china plate stacked high with layer upon layer of freshly sliced brown bread, a pound of butter, a bottle of red wine, some odd-sized glasses and an array of mugs. A roll of kitchen paper stood beside a bunch of knives and forks. The feast had already begun, as some of the guests mopped up the remnants of a haddock with liberally buttered brown bread. Pat offered me a plate and lobbed a golden fillet of turbot onto it, and pointed to the bread. So began an epic lunch. After each course – or rather, fish – the pan was cleaned and put back on the stove as Pat rooted around in a heavy-duty bag, holding another fish aloft.

'Now we have a bit of ling! Be careful with this one – it's very bony, but tastes lovely. I spotted a piece of cod in here somewhere . . . oh look, Mike. Have you ever tried pollack? Now that's a mighty fish to eat . . .'

It was non-stop service and chat as he cooked course after course of fresh fish. We were like children, eagerly waiting and watching to see what prize would be pulled from the magician's bag.

Pollack is indeed a great fish to work with, fleshy and full of flavour. I usually bake it very simply, with a light crust of ground fennel seeds and some sea salt. Serve with fries, roast wedges of potato or, at Pat's table, buttered brown bread and a mug of wine. 'Tis your only man.

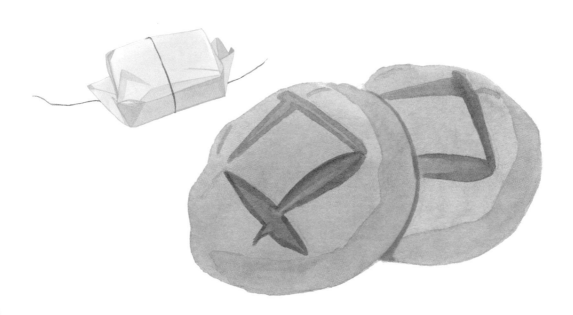

# Pollack with a fennel crust and wilted leeks
Serves 4

50g butter
Olive oil
8 baby leeks, washed and cleaned
A pinch of fresh thyme or marjoram
A pinch of saffron
250ml good veg or fish stock
1 tbsp fennel seeds
1 tsp flaky sea salt
4 fillets of pollack, about 250g each
Zest and juice of ½ a lime (reserve the rest)
50g Parmesan, finely grated (optional)
Sea salt and freshly ground black pepper
Potato wedges roasted with a little rosemary and oil, to serve
Fresh parsley, chopped, to garnish

1. Preheat the oven to 160°C/140°C fan/gas 2.
2. Heat the pan with the butter and a glug of oil, then add the leeks, thyme or marjoram and saffron. Gently coat the leeks, turning regularly.
3. Add the stock and a little salt and pepper.
4. Simmer gently for 20 minutes until the leeks are tender.
5. Meanwhile, toast the fennel seeds in a hot, dry pan – don't burn them – and crush them with the salt.
6. Massage the fish with the fennel and salt mix, and set aside.
7. Grease a casserole dish with olive oil. Put the fish into the dish, allowing a little space in between the fillets, and squeeze the zested half of the lime all over.
8. Bake for 15 minutes, then remove from the oven and scatter over the Parmesan.
9. Place the fish under the grill until the cheese is slightly toasted.
10. Put a portion of leeks at the centre of a warmed plate. Place the fish on top, and scatter a few potato wedges around with a sprinkle of parsley and the other half of lime. Drizzle any remaining juices onto the plate and serve with an old mug of good wine.

# STARFISH

The star of the day on the *Colla Voce* was without doubt the fresh mackerel. I have great childhood memories of our lodger Tom Greene returning from his home in North Clare laden down with a sack full of freshly caught mackerel, which he duly distributed to us and our neighbours. The whiff of frying mackerel lingered long in the evening heat as we played our games out on the St Michael's Villas green. I've tasted it many different ways, pan-fried, baked, soused, poached, smoked and in several versions of pâté. My vote is for the *Colla Voce* technique.

Years before I even thought of Ballymaloe, I was on tour with Ronnie Drew and he suggested we call in to say hello to his friend Darina Allen at the cookery school. We were ushered into her kitchen class, handed two aprons and positioned among the students to receive a cookery lesson from the lady herself. Pan-fried mackerel was the subject of that day. Darina cooked her fish just like my dad: a dusting of flour, a little melted butter and a hot pan, being sure to let it crisp and to hold it down with the spatula so it doesn't shrink. Little did I know that, in a few years' time, I would be standing at the very same spot as a full-time student, and later again hovering around as one of its teachers.

Simple as the method is, I'd like to insert some controversy. The general rule is to serve fish skin side up, which means that the skin is the first to hit the pan. Personally, I don't like the sight of crispy skin on top of a fancy mash or whatever it may be; I like to see my fish in all its glory. For the same reason, I prefer my sauce, if there is one, on the side, as I am always suspicious of a chef who feels the need to cover up a beautiful pan-fried fish. I am of the opinion that flesh side to a hot pan produces a much nicer flavour – I know, it's not very cheffy of me, but that's how it is in my kitchen.

If you would like something really sensational to serve up along with your mackerel, look no further.

# Mackerel with roasted rhubarb

Serves 6 as a starter

I was in a restaurant in the south of England before a show with Ronnie and Eleanor, and was treated to a mackerel with roasted rhubarb in honey and sherry vinegar, finished with crispy sage leaves. I could not wait to get home and try to recreate the flavourama. Years later it caused quite a stir as a starter special on Pat Shortt's bar menu.

6 large stalks of rhubarb, washed and cut into lengths, not discs
½ tsp mustard seeds
A few fresh sage leaves
1 tsp honey
A little water
A few cherry tomatoes
1 tbsp sherry vinegar
1 pan-fried or grilled fillet of mackerel per person, to serve
Lemon wedges, to serve

1. Preheat the oven to 160°C/140°C fan/gas 2.
2. Place the rhubarb, mustard seeds, sage leaves, honey and a little water on a roasting tray, separating the sage leaves to allow them to crisp up.
3. Roast for about 15 minutes, or until the rhubarb is tender to the touch. Put the sage leaves aside.
4. Heat a pan and add the rhubarb mix, cherry tomatoes, sherry vinegar and a little water. Heat for a minute, then tilt the pan slightly and spoon the liquid continuously over the rhubarb and tomatoes until they lightly burn and split.
5. Pour a ladle of the soft rhubarb on a plate, lay a fillet of mackerel by its side – flesh side up – add a few halved cherry tomatoes, and pour a little of the rhubarb juice all over. Crumble the sage leaves and scatter all around. Add a wedge of lemon.

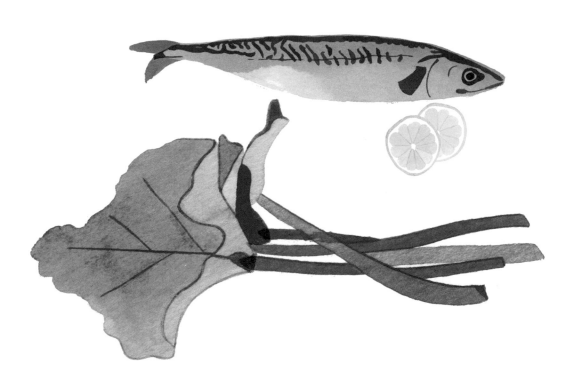

# A COUPLE MORE YEARS

Eleanor's professional career began in 1990, singing with De Dannan, from where she moved on to a very successful solo career, recording several albums and showcasing a diverse range of musical influences. In between constant touring, she gives much of her time to various charities, selfless and beneath the radar. She has a voice full of emotion, remarkable energy, and is always up for a challenge.

In 2000 Eleanor's then manager, Mattie Fox, called to suggest that she and Ronnie might be interested in a duet of a song called 'A Couple More Years', with me on guitar. Both the song and the vocal pairing had form: the song was written by Shel Silverman and first recorded by his band Dr Hook and His Medicine Show back in the 70s, and Eleanor and Ronnie had previously recorded 'Boots of Spanish Leather' together for the Dubliners' very successful *30 Years A-Greying* album.

We met at my house for our first rehearsal and sat at the kitchen table eating and talking music for a very long time before looking at the song. After a first run-through we knew instinctively that something special was in the air. You would be forgiven for thinking that the song was specifically written for the pair of them: an older man advising a much younger girl, possibly his daughter, urging her to be careful as she takes her first steps into adulthood, and to be mindful of the advice from those who have gone ahead of her, for one day soon, he says, she will find herself standing on the very same spot, giving similar advice to her own young son. Powerful lyrics and sentiments presented with Ronnie's low, rasping voice full of life and experience, against the angelic sound of innocence and respect from the younger Eleanor.

Over the following weeks we worked on a full set, adding a few more great duets. We played a few gigs, and in true whirlwind music business fashion found ourselves one afternoon very unprepared on the stage at Vicar Street, recording an album of twelve new songs. The show was also set for video. Our friend, guitarist Bill Shanley (no relation to Eleanor), was drafted in to help. We had very little rehearsal time and that is evident on some tracks, but there are some lovely songs, like their beautiful rendition of 'The Parting Glass' paired with Bob Dylan's 'Restless Farewell', a reprise of 'Boots of Spanish Leather', a version of my song 'We Had It All', and of course 'A Couple More Years', which was simply magic.

On the day of recording we had a slew of technical problems between the mobile recording unit, the video sync and house PA system. It was a nightmare of a session, and nerves were running high. Camera rehearsal time was given up to troubleshooting a litany of issues, and eventually we arrived on stage, frazzled but determined. The crowd turnout was also a disaster, with barely a hundred locals showing up for the free afternoon gig. This caused a major headache for the director, who had planned multiple audience participation shots, and it's funny now to look back and see the same faces appearing again and again from various different angles. We may as well have filmed the crowd scene in one of our neighbours' houses. Back in the studio we had to find some way to add a layer of ambient audience samples to enhance the live atmosphere, and I think we eventually settled on audio from a crowd at the Royal Albert Hall.

When the song was released, all those hiccups mattered nought. The vocal performances were so outstanding we had an instant hit on our hands. Several TV appearances and radio shows led to a nationwide sell-out theatre tour, and from there we went on to Holland and Germany. It was an exciting time, even though Ronnie and Mattie were often at loggerheads, but it mattered little in the end, as the duet flourished and indeed continued to do so right up to Ronnie's untimely death in 2008.

# EL AMOR DE MI VIDA

I was asked to produce Ronnie and Eleanor's second album, *El Amor de Mi Vida*, in 2006 at Sharon Shannon's studio in Killeeneen, County Galway. Prior to recording, the three of us locked ourselves away in a cottage in Kilkenny to find the songs and make a plan. It was their first studio album, and both wanted to make it special. We listened to so many songs, rehearsed every day for hours, and in the evenings cooked beautiful food and talked late into the night. I was delighted with the challenge of it, and we had a special time putting the album together with some great musicians when we got over to Galway. Sharon's lovely friend Catriona Cunniffe was our chef for the duration of our time there, and produced delicious food day after day. On our first morning, the menu for the week was posted on the wall with a note: 'Anything ye don't like, please let me know.' There was goat's cheese tart, smoked fish chowder, roast pork, lamb moussaka, and her Thai green curry. Lunch and dinner were family affairs, with all the news and gossip of the day. After a few days in the studio, we noticed Ronnie was missing a lot from the control room. Every spare moment, he was in the kitchen with Catriona, watching her at work and chatting about food – or so we thought. He was also drinking an unusual amount of coffee, way more than he'd normally have, but there was no sign of his favoured jug of pouring cream. Ronnie was a creature of habit, and went to extraordinary lengths to get his supply of pouring cream, but suddenly he was quite happy without. After a few days, we discovered he was substituting a bottle of Bailey's for the cream, and had poor Catriona sworn to secrecy. No wonder he was always in such high spirits in that kitchen.

I was delighted with the resulting album. Ronnie and Eleanor were at their best, as were our great musicians: James Delaney on keys and piano, Paul Moore on bass, Sharon, Robbie Casserly on drums, and guitarist Steve Flaherty from Ennis. We had guest appearances from Paul Brady, John Shanley, Winnie Horan, Martina Goggin and Tess Purcell. Leon O'Neill was my trusty lieutenant on engineering duties. What a crew. They sang Irish songs, as well as numbers from Nick Cave, Tom Waits and, believe it or not, one from my favourite band, the Eels, 'The Good Old Days'. The title track was written by Warren Zevon, and had Ronnie singing to Eleanor in his fluent Spanish. It was magic to watch each track slowly come together.

The three of us travelled many roads and laughed practically all the way. Ronnie's final gig was at Ballymaloe House and it was poignant that Eleanor was on stage with us, along with our good friend Frankie Lane.

Months after Ronnie passed, myself and Eleanor met to rehearse a gig and thought about singing 'A Couple More Years' in his honour. We couldn't get past the second line. It was never going to happen – we just looked at each other and knew that this was just a no-go area. Ronnie's presence was still with us, and it was a very eerie feeling. Ten years later we celebrated his life on Ray Darcy's radio show and managed to get through the song without a tear, but it was still eerie, even then.

## THE SHANLEY HOUSE

Eleanor was born and reared on a farm in the beautiful village of Keshcarrigan in Leitrim on the shores of the Shannon. They reared cows, cattle, pigs, chickens, turkeys and geese, and grew their own vegetables. Her mother Eileen tended to the farm and its inhabitants, milking the cows twice a day, cooking and baking and all the while rearing her family.

One of the national newspapers had Ronnie, the Dub, switch lives for a day with country girl Eleanor, and by all accounts he had a great day on the farm with Eileen and Eleanor's brother John, who also has a wonderful singing voice. Ronnie dressed for the mud and the sludge, donning a pair of wellington boots to milk a cow and feed silage to the cattle. In the evening, they retired to the village pub and sang the night away. On the flip side, Eleanor was selling apples and oranges at a stall on Dublin's famous Moore Street, and reports say she even mastered the Moore Street brogue.

## Mrs Shanley's boxty special

Boxty is a traditional Irish potato cake. Its name may derive from the Irish *arán bocht tí*, poorhouse bread, and it's not unlike my nan's griddle cake. Boxty is quintessentially under Leitrim control, much like the blaa is protected in Waterford. For years now, another Leitrim family have been the brains behind the very successful Gallagher's Boxty House restaurant in Dublin, where chef Padraig Gallagher has developed many recipes celebrating Boxty beneath their banner of 'the humble spud made beautiful'. There, it's presented as dumplings, in loaves, in all sorts of wraps and even as boxty chips. Here is a more traditional take on boxty from Mrs Shanley's kitchen.

500g potatoes, peeled
200g flour
½ tsp bicarbonate of soda
140ml milk
1 tsp sea salt
Fried egg (optional)

1. Preheat the oven to 170°C/150°C fan/gas 3.
2. Grate the potatoes and strain them through muslin or a colander until the moisture has drained off.
3. Mix the potatoes, flour, soda, milk and salt – and stir like hell!
4. Put the mixture into a loaf tin and bake in the oven for approximately 1 hour and 15 minutes, until cooked.
5. Leave to cool, preferably overnight. Slice, and fry in a pan until browned on both sides and heated through. Enjoy on its own, or preferably with a nice runny free-range fried egg.

# FOLK THE RECESSION

Some time around 2014, Eleanor invited me to join a group of her friends in a fun-time band called Folk the Recession. My first show was in the backyard at O'Donoghue's on Baggot Street for the ill-fated Arthur's Day, a festival created by Guinness to celebrate its great name by providing free music in most of Dublin's pubs. The line-up was Eleanor on vocals and guitar, Paul Kelly on fiddle and mandolin, Frankie Lane on guitar and vocals, Brendan Begley on various accordions and vocals, with myself on guitar and vocals.

Fortunately for the country, the recession was finally ending, but unfortunately for us, it proved difficult to justify the name as the economy recovered, so we only played a few more short tours before it finally fizzled out. Those journeys were the making of my friendship with Brendan. Each year with four friends, Brendan rowed a *naomhóg*, a handmade wooden-framed type of curragh, through many difficult waters with trips around the Irish coast, another to the Scottish isles and also across to Wales and on down to northern Spain to walk the final leg to Santiago de Compostela. The year I joined Folk the Recession, the crew were navigating their way around the coast of Ireland. I collected Brendan from a few very remote harbours, where they moored to allow him to fulfil the gig commitments. As myself and Brendan travelled the many miles, we talked much about the impending centenary celebrations for 1916. We both had a keen interest in our history, so we agreed to look at the prospects of a stage show focusing on the songs, poems and music of 1916. Little did we know at that time just how much we were to learn about that incredible period of our history. That show, *Dublin Burning*, proved a real success.

In June 2017 Brendan and his crew returned once more to row to Santiago de Compostela, but an unfortunate accident took the life of his great friend, Kerry poet and writer Danny Sheehy, as the *naomhóg* overturned while negotiating rough waters close to the Minho river estuary on the Spanish-Portuguese border. All the men managed to get to shore, but Danny took ill and died on the strand. Such a sad day for many. I met Danny on a few occasions when he came to support our shows. He always struck me as a kind and loving man.

# THESE DAYS

I still enjoy a few gigs with Eleanor and her voice continues to soar as she takes on some very interesting collaborations with Leitrim band, Garadice, the odd gig with the great Charlie McGettigan, poet Gerald Dawe, or a truly beautiful duo with classical guitarist John Feeley. We have great freedom in performance as we weave through the set without any rigid pattern, always free to go where the mood takes us. Dare I say, it's organic. I love sharing a stage with Eleanor; we're comfortable in each other's company, close friends, and I suppose we share a country mentality and heritage that binds us together.

# CHAPTER 14

# ARTISAN PARLOUR & GROCER

*Inside I'm dancing all by myself,*
*Inside I'm dancing by myself,*
*Kick off my shoes and dance this night away,*
*Inside I'm dancing by myself.*
– 'Inside I'm Dancing' (unrecorded, 2018)

# GULP

Club DJ and owner of the Dalkey Food Company Ivan Ivarian suggested I call Martin Thomas, who had just opened a new restaurant, the Artisan Parlour & Grocery, with his wife Venetia in Ringsend in Dublin. Ivan was one of the more flamboyant pupils I taught at Ballymaloe; his approach to food and its presentation bordered at times on the outrageous, but he always managed to create excitement among students and teachers alike. His final exam starter was something out of a Captain Nemo movie: mussels, langoustines, whelks, periwinkles, shrimps, oysters, clams and sea grass served on an oval bed of ice with a wasabi mayo, clam jus and an oyster emulsion. 'Stunning presentation,' someone remarked, 'but how in God's name are you ever going to make any money out of that?'

On his return to Dublin he set up the Dalkey Food Company to service shops and offices with his superb range of homemade soups. He must have adjusted to the realities of portion control, as the business grows from strength to strength, though his flair for the dramatic is still alive and well. Ivan is essentially a performer, in and out of the kitchen, and he has occasionally shared a stage with Newstalk science radio host Jonathan McCrea to present their unique food theatre show, *Gulp: The Science of Food and Cooking*, about the weird and wonderful aspects of how we cook, eat and taste our food.

# WELCOME HOME

Armed only with my introduction from Ivan, I walked through the front doors of the Artisan Parlour at 90 Fitzwilliam Street in Ringsend. I was overwhelmed by a sense of belonging. The atmosphere was buzzing, with people queueing at the counter, enjoying lunch at little tables and browsing the various odd-sized wooden shelves for artisan and organic produce.

I was transported back in time to an old grocer's shop, yet I was somehow very aware that I was in the now. There were olive and rapeseed oils; Chardonnay, cider, peach and raspberry vinegars; stacks of pasta, risotto and paella rice; jars of red and green pesto, piquillo peppers and pickled cucumbers. Next to that were natural skincare products. A glass-fronted service fridge was filled with colourful trifle bowls full of luscious quinoa, sparkling roasted rainbow beetroots, kale and green bean salads. Inside the main door, a free-standing metal shelf held a dozen or more sourdough, granary and yeast breads. Overhead, I read the chalkboard of daily specials: 'FRESH SOUP' was crossed out, with the word 'GONE' scribbled alongside. There was a fridge packed full of artisan butters, black and white puddings, blocks of Irish cheese, chorizo, cooked hams and pastramis. The coffee machine was in full flow, and behind that was an array of fresh leaf tea, from regular to goji berry to lavender. Brown AP&G stamped paper bags hung from a hook, and a laptop was belting out 'Common People' by Pulp. Above all the commotion, a mock black boar's head kept a watchful eye on proceedings. There was a lot going on in this small, quirky space – and I loved it.

## ALL-IN-ONE KITCHENETTE

The dining area, with its assortment of multi-coloured wooden chairs and oddly shaped tables, was full of chatting customers in a swirling buzz that echoed wall to wall. Down at the back I noticed a high counter, which I assumed led into the kitchen. It looked like a service area – until a chef's head appeared and presented the waiting staff with four plates of hot food. 'Oh my God, it is the kitchen,' I realised with a start. I walked down to say hello to a very busy chef and spotted a two-ring electric hob, a small TurboChef oven, a domestic fridge and a double sink. I sat down, slightly deflated, and surveyed the rest of the dining area. The walls were covered with art and posters: a beautiful Steven Mannion sketch of Joyce hung beside the million-dollar quartet of Elvis Presley, James Dean, Johnny Cash and Carl Perkins. There was a Paula Moen portrait of John Lennon and a gorgeous painting of a bright red Gretsch electric guitar. There were photographs of local Ringsend 80s rockers the Blades and rockabilly heroes the Mosquitos – but no sign of Bono anywhere. Ivan had sworn Martin was a huge fan.

In the corner beneath the kitchen pass stood an antique oak-framed glass sideboard, complete with crystal glasses. That piece of furniture alone captured the look of the Artisan Parlour – very retro – and it took me back. In our house, it's where Dad kept the whiskey that almost poisoned our annual Christmas visitors, it was home to my mum's treasured trifle bowl set, my nan's brandy tumblers, Nanna's fine bone china cups and saucers and my auntie Peggy's bottle of sherry. It was always out of bounds, home to all the fancy things in family life. Yet in the Parlour, it sat there in the middle of the very contemporary hustle and bustle, a little reminder of so many Irish homes in times gone by.

## JOHNNY ROTTEN'S DRESSING ROOM

I was ushered up the narrow wooden stairs into an 'office' that screamed CHAOS. Scattered across a Formica desk were suppliers' books, torn envelopes, invoices, bills, a tobacco pouch, a red-wine-stained crystal tumbler and an ashtray, full to the brim. In the corner, two bright red multi-drawer cabinets held row upon row of takeaway containers, a half-empty toolbox and a large yucca plant that stood uncomfortably by an open window that drew in the sound of the street as it exhaled puff clouds of tobacco smoke.

Somewhere in the clutter sat Martin Thomas, a gangly-looking character with a greying orange goatee and a mop of thinning curly brown hair, dressed in a floral shirt and the most amazing brown shopkeeper's coat with letters 'AP&G' proudly emblazoned above the breast pocket, with its obligatory blue biro. He looked up and gave me an infectious smile, as if urging me to ignore the surroundings.

'This could be Johnny Rotten's dressing room,' I quipped.

'Howya, Mike. Nice to meet you! So, you're looking for a job, eh? Don't know if we can afford you, though. You're probably far too expensive for the likes of us down here in Ringsend . . . Ballymaloe and all that,' he winked. 'I remember Stockton's Wing. Jaysus, ye were a great band.' He started to speak passionately of his vision for the Artisan, and he was on a roll: 'We're only using the best natural Irish products, local suppliers, wonderful beef from our butcher's in Sandymount, pork from County Louth, real vegetables, quinoas, lentils, beans, pastas, stuff like that, natural juices for all the early morning-joggers and the healthy feckers from Google. We have a lot of Irish producers really interested in what we are doing, as well as an excellent Spanish food supplier who has awesome chorizo, really amazing. In the kitchen, Gena cooks brilliant food: keeping it simple, but using the best ingredients. We also want to cater for the kids. We have three young kids ourselves, so we want to create a space for families to come in, hang out and eat good food, none of that frozen shite that you get in so many places these days. We could really do with someone from Ballymaloe, because I love Darina and her food philosophy, I'm a real fan.' He barely paused for breath.

'We hope to extend the hours to get the extra bobs in, but the kitchen is tiny, so that'll restrict us somewhat, but I think slow-cooked beef cheeks or stews, a bit of charcuterie with cheese and wine will do well. None of that Michelin shite now, mind you – that stuff gives me the pip, with one . . . feckin' . . . pea floating in a puddle of reduction, and all sorts of squiggly shite and designs filling up a plate that costs a fortune. No, we don't want that. We want people to come in, eat some cool food, have a drink, a chat, listen to some good music and hang out with all the beautiful people . . . people like you and me, Mike,' he winked again.

'Myself and Venetia had an idea of an old grocer's shop like the ones back in the 50s but with much better music, without the pictures of the Pope or the Blessed Virgin or De Valera – although if I got a nice one of Michael Collins, I might make an exception. Both of us help Gena with the menu, but she is the star cook. Unfortunately, she can only work certain days of the week, so we need someone with experience to take over for the rest of the time, especially at the weekends for brunch.'

There was no sign of Martin coming up for air any time soon. 'This will be the first of many, we hope. We have plans to expand, but we need to get this one up and running. We're waiting for some more really cool art from our friend Stephen Mannion – do you know Stephen's work? Incredible. We might have a few book launches, possibly a few gigs – ya might even play yourself, Mike,' he grins cheekily. 'What? I'm serious! We can stick you up there in the corner with your guitar to sing a few songs – that one, what's it called? "Strange Affair", I love that one. You could sing that after feeding everyone a nice bowl of stew? What do ya think, eh? How cool would that be?'

He went on to talk about Facebook and Twitter and hoping to attract a few reviewers in to put Ringsend on the food map. 'By the way,' he added, as he finally drew breath, 'what's a rock star like you doing in a feckin' kitchen anyway? Are you mad or what?'

I assured him I was indeed a bit mad, and asked when he needed me to start. 'Sure, no time like the present. Why not come in tomorrow morning? Alvaro our Spanish chef will show you around and take it from there. The kitchen is quite small, but we hope to extend. I'm not a great cook, but we both love our grub and that Ballymaloe stuff is so beautiful. I'm sure you have lots of great ideas to bring to the table. If the food is good, then I'll sell it, that's my gig. See you then, and welcome to the Artisan Parlour, hope you enjoy it. Oh, and by the way, I hope you like U2.'

## MY OFFICE

And so, it began. The kitchen was tiny, with barely enough room for two bodies to pass by. Alvaro, the very experienced and organised Spanish chef who had come for the initial set-up but stayed much longer than planned, devised a system. The kitchen was divided into hot and cold sections, with each chef working their section to a definite prep list. It was strictly one dish at a time from start to finish. As soon as that was completed, you cleaned down, washed and dried, and

INDIAN SUMMER ME HOOP

only then moved on to the second dish. There were no deviations and certainly no pile-up of dishes – not that we had that many in any case. When all the hot lunch dishes were cooking on the stove or in the oven, we came together as a team to fill the deli with an array of salads, sandwiches and other cold options. We had four sandwiches of meat, chicken, veggie and seafood; the only movable options were salads, as they depended on ingredients delivered. Every day was busy as we rushed to get everything up for lunch, but Alvaro's greatest talent was keeping a cool head – that, and a wicked sense of humour.

Unfortunately, the place was never designed for commercial food production, so we played catch-up from the outset. Each week as our customer base grew, pressure and demands increased on this extremely limited space. We moved from one crisis to the next, and at one point I thought we might have to employ a dedicated lawyer to deal with the civil servants who traipsed through our doors with ever-growing lists of regulations and adjustments. It was never-ending: Article 2 of this European directive states that . . . and regulation 154 requires you to do such and such. The industry certainly requires regulation, but some of the laws most certainly cripple a small start-up before they even get to turn the first screw. It's not a level playing field by any stretch of the imagination, and in that regard, I felt for Martin as he grappled with the regulatory side of the business. Our health and safety officer was very fair, though, and understanding; she knew we had a good system in place, even if we were lacking essential equipment, but she helped us through so many issues. We eventually did get our extractor fan, so at least we weren't smoking out the customers any more, although one day a local pigeon somehow got through the outside vent and cooed her way through lunch and afternoon tea before we managed to set her free.

## GOLD-PLATED QUINOA

About a week into my job, I went through the order sheets and was alarmed at the level of stock and related costs. It was clear that the purchasing system needed attention. I pinpointed some items that were clogging the upstairs storage room, among which was a particular coloured quinoa that was coming in with a very hefty price tag. I called Martin aside and said we needed to stop buying that gold-plated quinoa.

'What do you mean gold-plated? It's not, surely!'

'Exactly,' I said, 'so we don't need to be buying fancy-coloured quinoa when regular will do the exact same job.'

'Fair enough. Gold-plated quinoa me hoop . . .'

Martin offered me the job of kitchen manager, thereby allowing Gena to concentrate on the menu. I wrote a full suppliers list, compared costs, pinpointed some savings and suggested we meet with everyone, including the small-time producers. I then introduced a working HACCP system for health and safety, and called a general meeting.

## SUPPLIERS

After a great meeting with the staff, it was time to introduce myself to some of the larger suppliers – Mr Quinoa in particular. In some kitchens, suppliers are treated like the enemy, but I never liked that approach. Like the rest of us, they're professional people whose careers rely on results. Since moving back to Dublin, I'm acutely aware of just how spoilt I was in East Cork, where the suppliers were also friends. It took me a little while to adjust to the pace and attitude of the Big Smoke, where 'MARGINS' is written in capital letters.

My first call received the following classic reply: 'No problem. So, is the party over then, Mike? Ah sure, it was good while it lasted. No bother. I'll be in tomorrow.'

Turned out Mr Quinoa was an ex head chef, and I got to like him quite a lot. Many of our suppliers were small start-ups trying to promote their new products or ranges, and their passion and total dedication was infectious – hence our overstocked storeroom. I got to know and taste some amazing Irish products, vinegars, oils, breads, butters, ice creams, cheeses and all sorts of healthy drinks, which we incorporated into our menus – albeit in slightly more sustainable amounts.

## GENA

Gena Walker is a superb cook with so much natural talent for flavour and matching ingredients. Essentially, she was a domestic cook with a very keen interest in the art of food and its presentation. We shared a devotion to spices of all kinds, which we used daily to put sparkle into our salad counter. Her recipes were always seasonal, some tried-and-tested and others created on the day. When she left, I assumed the role of 'head chef', but she left me with a wonderful recipe base along with a very high standard to maintain. She had an immense influence on my cooking.

Sandwiches were a necessarily big feature of our food, it being a busy lunch spot. Our offerings were sometimes very left of centre, and always creative. In food parlance we deconstructed regular sandwiches and presented them Artisan Parlour style. It was a creative feature of our kitchen, and I maintained that approach when Gena moved on.

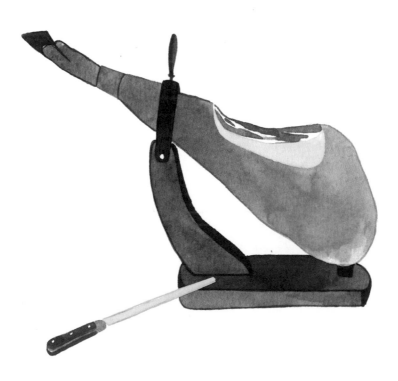

# Ham hock crock

It all began with an idea from Venetia about the croque monsieur; before long, we had our ham hock crock. So, a few pointers, as there's a bit of prep time involved. You need to pre-boil the ham hocks with some caraway seeds and peppercorns for 2 to 3 hours. Allow to cool. You will get at least four if not five good sandwiches from each hock, so for this recipe I am only cooking two hocks. There are plenty of uses for the leftover meat. There are three recipes in one here: ham hocks, a Mornay sauce and a sandwich.

2 slow-cooked smoked ham hocks
50g butter
50g plain or gluten-free flour
1 tbsp mustard seeds
1 litre milk
1 tbsp smooth Dijon mustard (or you can substitute these last two with wholegrain mustard)
200g strong Irish Cheddar (I love Hegarty's Cheddar), grated
4 doorstep slices of fresh yeast bread, white or brown, lightly toasted
Tomato and green salad, to serve

1. Take all the meat from the hock bone, making sure to include some of the fat. Set aside.
2. In a wide frying pan, melt the butter gently and add the flour. Stir to make a roux – the base of a white sauce. Gently cook for a minute, but do not brown. If it browns, just start again.
3. Add the mustard seeds to the roux, then add the milk one third at a time, stirring constantly with each addition until you reach a smooth consistency.
4. Add the Dijon, then slowly stir in the grated cheese little by little until you reach a smooth consistency, and set aside. You can keep this in the fridge for a few days.
5. To assemble, spread a thick layer of the sauce over a slice of lightly toasted bread, and add copious amounts of smoked hock. Place under a grill to sizzle.
6. Meanwhile, spread the sauce on the other slice of bread, place on the sizzling hock, sauce side up, and watch it bubble and crisp slightly under the grill. Cut and serve with a nice fresh tomato and green salad.

# CHRISTMAS BELLS

Christmas was special at the Parlour, a real community hub of laughter, carols and so much fun for everyone, especially the kids, who were given a wall to paint and draw on at will. Martin and Venetia drove the Christmas spirit with all sorts of special offers and hampers, as advertised on the blackboard: 'Hampers, smelly and savoury'. Venetia urged us to create Christmas menus and we came up with some beautiful dishes.

## Mulled lamb

Serves 6

This dish has to be prepared the day before.

**For the spice mix**
1 tsp fenugreek seeds
1 tsp ground coriander
1 tsp fennel seeds
1 tsp black peppercorns
½ tsp cardamom seeds
½ tsp dried chilli flakes
½ tsp cumin seeds

**For the lamb**
2 tbsp spice mix (see above)
1 kg diced lamb, neck or shoulder
2 tbsp rapeseed oil
1 onion, peeled and diced
1 clove of garlic, crushed
2 carrots, diced
2 celery sticks, peeled and sliced
1 tbsp plain or gluten-free flour
1 medium glass of good port
250ml stock, preferably lamb
1 star anise or stick of cinnamon
Fresh mint leaves

Sea salt and freshly ground black pepper
Mash or red cabbage, to serve

1. To make the spice mix, heat a dry pan, and add all the spices except the chilli flakes and cumin seeds. Toast for a few minutes.
2. Add the chilli flakes and cumin seeds, then remove from the heat and allow to cool.
3. Grind using a spice grinder – my coffee grinder is a designated spice grinder, but alternatively use the pestle and mortar. Store in a jar until required. You will find several uses for this mix.
4. Rub the spice mix into the lamb pieces, add a little salt, then cover and store in the fridge for a few hours or ideally overnight. Take it out about an hour before use.
5. If you are going to cook the lamb in the oven, preheat it to 150°C/130°C fan/gas 2.
6. Heat the oil in an ovenproof pan and brown the lamb pieces on a medium heat. Remove the meat from the pan and set aside.
7. Add the onions, and cook until soft. Add the garlic, carrots and celery, and cook for 1 minute.
8. Return the lamb to the pan and add the flour. Coat everything and cook for about 1 minute, then add the port and let it reduce for a few minutes. Add the stock, star anise or cinnamon. Taste for seasoning.
9. Cook on the stove or in the oven for 1 hour or until the lamb is soft and succulent.
10. Serve on mash of your choice: parsley and potato; champ; celeriac and potato; or just plain. I have served it with a side of red cabbage and apple for a wonderful feast.

# Artisan snowballs
Makes about 30

When a fresh batch of these was ready, the blackboard outside would read,
'Try Mike's snowballs'.

125g plain flour
125g self-raising flour
75g caster sugar
1 tsp ground cinnamon
A pinch of sea salt
75g cold butter, diced
1 egg and 1 egg yolk, whisked
150g icing sugar
200g desiccated coconut

1. Preheat the oven to 200°C/180°C fan/gas 6.
2. Mix the flours, sugar, cinnamon and salt in a bowl, then rub in the butter until it looks like breadcrumbs.
3. Mix in the egg and bring it all together to form a dough. You may need to add a tiny drop of water if it's too dry. Knead for a few minutes, then cut and form into little balls. Place them on a parchment-lined or non-stick baking tray.
4. Bake for 12 minutes, until golden. Transfer to a wire rack and leave to cool.
5. Put the icing sugar into a bowl and slowly mix in a little water to form a thin paste.
6. Scatter the coconut over a lined tray. Dip each cooled biscuit into the icing, then roll in the coconut and set aside in the fridge for about 2 to 3 minutes, or until the icing dries out.

# BRUNCH

Without doubt, the highlight of my week was brunch, as customers arrived in their droves. I had so much fun creating new recipes with my two amazing commis chefs, Jorge and Gareth. There were no limits, as long as breakfast was hearty, tasty and very Artisan. Brunch was our domain and we made it our own: eggs Benedict became Mex Benedict, we had our own authentic tortilla, huevos rancheros, a very tasty Artisan hash brown, our healthy mac and cheese, with lots of goodness for the children. We tried breakfast cakes, sausage and squash bakes, and pork blaas with a kick.

# The Mex Benedict
Serves 4

I created this dish from a few different versions of a Mexican favourite of mine that kept me going on many long days touring America. Chipotles are difficult to locate, but the chipotle sauce that is now regularly available is OK to use too. We have a couple of great Mexican shops in Dublin, and sometimes the Mexican shelf in bigger supermarkets can surprise you. I use slow-cooked shoulder of pork, but if you want to fast forward, use bacon or cooked ham or just go veggie. The pork recipe can be used for a variety of dishes.

1 shoulder of pork
1 dsp mix of caraway and fennel seeds and 1 tsp of chopped fresh ginger, crushed together in a pestle and mortar
1 orange, sliced
2 onions, peeled and halved
1 small butternut squash, washed, deseeded and sliced (optional)
1 stick of cinnamon
1 carrot, peeled and sliced
2 celery sticks, roughly chopped
1 tbsp soft brown sugar
1 tsp mustard seeds, or mustard powder
1 chipotle (smoked jalapeño) chilli, chopped
500ml cider
500ml chicken stock
Sea salt and freshly ground black pepper

**To serve**
Chipotle hollandaise (see opposite)
4 slices of sourdough, toasted
Iceberg lettuce, shredded (optional)
8 poached eggs
Coriander leaves
Salsa (see opposite)
Lime wedges

1. Preheat the oven, if using, to 140°C/120°C fan/gas 1.
2. Massage the pork with the spices, salt and pepper and place in a slow cooker or casserole.
3. Add the rest of the ingredients and cook on a low heat, or in the oven, for 3 hours until the meat is really tender.
4. Strain the veg, hold onto the liquid and put the veg onto the compost heap. Return the liquid to the pan and reduce to a thick sauce. Store in the fridge until required.
5. Shred the meat when cooled and store in the fridge until required.
6. When ready to serve, reheat the pork in a pan with the sauce reduction.
7. Spoon a dollop of chipotle hollandaise on each slice of toast. Add some shredded crispy lettuce, a little of the pork, a couple of poached eggs, and spoon another dollop of the hollandaise on top. Sprinkle with coriander leaves and serve with the salsa and a wedge of lime.

## Chipotle hollandaise

4 egg yolks
Juice of 1 lime
240g melted butter, unsalted if you have it
2 dried chipotle chillies, heated gently in a little water, then removed and blended using some of the water to thin the mix
Sea salt

1. In a small bowl, whisk the egg yolks with the lime juice and some salt.
2. Slowly whisk the butter into the egg mix until the sauce thickens.
3. Add the blended chipotle and mix. Store in a warm place.

## Salsa

2 tomatoes, chopped
1 red onion, peeled and finely diced
1 tbsp fresh coriander leaves
1 lime, zested and juiced
1 tbsp fresh parsley, chopped
Sea salt and freshly ground black pepper

1. Mix all the ingredients in a bowl.
2. Season to taste.

# VENETIA

Venetia is a radio and TV presenter and a newspaper columnist. She met Martin in 1996 at a fashion show at the Pod nightclub. Martin was the new kid on the nightclub scene, enjoying the recent success of his much-vaunted Strictly Fish club. His innovative approach to Dublin clubland, taking dreary venues and turning them into glitz and glamour, was gaining him many friends, and he went from strength to strength until it all came crashing down after the 2007 fall. Many of our entertainment businesses were destroyed during that period, as staying in became the new going out.

In 2014 Venetia was invited to partake in a new RTÉ-sponsored TV documentary series called *Connected*. The show featured six women from different backgrounds and ages, each capturing a time in their lives on hand-held cameras. Some were single, some married, some students, and others were working mothers like Venetia, with three young children and helping her unemployed husband Martin in his quest to open up a food business. They spent many weeks searching for a suitable venue to open the Artisan Parlour, and as the series progressed, the camera probed deeper and deeper into their lives. Martin being Martin soon began to hog the camera a little and then quite a lot. Venetia christened him Martina, the seventh woman of the series, and he became something of a Twitter sensation, attracting as much troll abuse as loving reviews for the duration of the run.

While Martin was the frantic passionate energy that raced through the Parlour, Venetia was its beating heart. Her affinity with customers, staff and suppliers gently drove the Parlour on its daily path, and her measured approach to problems was invaluable to me in all kitchen matters.

Venetia loved my ketchup recipes, and always hoped one day, to produce an Artisan range. I would have loved that!

# AP&G apple and tomato ketchup

Makes about 1 litre

If you make this once, I doubt you will ever buy ketchup again from the shelf. It freezes well. You will need a piece of muslin and a jam pan or a large heavy-based saucepan.

1 tbsp olive oil
5 red onions, peeled and roughly chopped
1kg apples
2.5kg ripe tomatoes
400g caster sugar
500ml cider vinegar
10 cloves
2 star anise or 1 stick of cinnamon
3 fresh bay leaves
12 juniper berries
Sea salt and freshly ground black pepper

1. If you have a jam pan, use that, but if not, place a large heavy-based saucepan on a medium heat. Add the olive oil, and when it's warm add the onions and sweat for 5 minutes, or until soft and translucent.
2. While the onions are sweating, core and roughly chop the apples and tomatoes. Add to the pan, and stir in the sugar and vinegar.
3. Tie the spices and juniper berries in muslin, as this makes them much easier to remove once the ketchup is cooked. Add to the pan and stir well to combine.
4. Turn the heat to low and cook gently for 1½ hours, stirring occasionally to ensure that the ketchup doesn't stick.
5. The ketchup is ready when the sauce is cooked right down and is all glossy and homogeneous. Add a really good pinch of salt and a few grindings of pepper.
6. Turn off the heat and allow to cool before spooning into sterilised jars. It will keep for a few weeks in the fridge. If I do lots, I tend to store it in freezer bags and use it for our summer barbecues.

# EVENING SERVICE

We received great reviews for our daily and evening service and tried everything to attract more customers. On one Friday the 13th, Martin's blackboard read: 'Friday 13th – Lucky for some. All dishes 13 euro'. We had TV and radio slots, magazine articles, you name it, but our location was just not conducive to evening dining, so we struggled to get them in at dinner time.

We created some amazing recipes, though. Local chef Vicky O'Sullivan arrived home from America to work in the kitchen, and we immediately clicked. She is a talented chef, no-nonsense in service, full of passion and creative ideas. She spent weeks working on this veggie burger, which is stunning, but be warned – it's all in the prep. It is by far the best veggie burger I have ever eaten. It deserves a light, slim, soft bun – not too doughy. Best results are from frozen, but it works well after a short set in the fridge.

# Vicky's veggie burger
Makes about 8 burgers

This burger was always a hit at the Artisan Parlour. The recipe is forgiving, and can vary depending on what's in the fridge.

180g quinoa
300ml veg stock
1 pinch turmeric
1 celery stick, peeled and diced
1 carrot, peeled and diced
1 garlic clove, crushed
1 x 400g tin of chickpeas, almost drained, but keep about a tbsp of liquid
300g cooked edamame beans
200g frozen garden peas
1 x 150g tin sweetcorn, drained
1 tsp thyme
Sea salt and freshly ground black pepper
150g breadcrumbs
1 egg, whisked
2 tsp rapeseed oil
Salad, to serve
Apple and tomato ketchup (page 291), to serve

1. Preheat your oven to 180°C/160°C fan/gas 4.
2. Cook the quinoa in the veg stock and turmeric according to packet instructions.
3. Meanwhile, gently sauté the onions, carrots and celery until soft.
4. Add the garlic, chickpeas, edamame, thyme and a pinch of salt and pepper. Cook for three minutes. Allow to cool.
5. Transfer to a blender, pulse and then fold in the garden peas and sweetcorn. Taste for seasoning and adjust.
6. Add the egg and breadcrumbs, if using, and bind the mixture together. If it's too wet, add more crumbs.
7. Shape your burgers by hand, or use a scone cutter to ensure even sizes. Freeze for a few hours.
8. Heat a pan with a little oil and cook the burgers 5 minutes per side. Transfer to the preheated oven for 10 minutes.
9. Serve with a mixed salad and apple and tomato ketchup (see page 291).

# FISH IN A BAG

Martin arrived at the kitchen one morning, hands juggling the air. 'I was thinking last night about our evening menu. The pan-fried fish on a plate is boring, Mike. We need more excitement, something different.' I suggested a fish en papillote: 'It's retro, but could sit in with the vibe you are looking for, a nice piece of lemon sole with some tarragon, lemon, wine . . .'

He gave me that wink. 'Yeah, I like it. I like it a lot, but let's not call it that poncy uppity papi whatever shite. Call it a bag of fish – no, better still, call it 'fish in a bag'. Can you imagine the customer when the dish arrives at the table? Theatre, Mike, it will be pure theatre.'

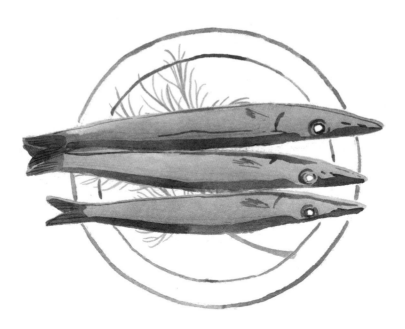

# Fish in a bag

This is a recipe for one parcel; each parcel serves one. The secret is to seal tightly, and slightly undercook, as it continues to steam on its way to the table.

1 tsp chopped fresh tarragon and parsley
¼ of a fennel bulb, shaved very thinly
1 shallot, peeled and thinly sliced in the round
A handful of mangetout, washed
A small handful of French beans, cooked in salted water for 4 minutes and
    cooled in a bowl of iced water
A shot glass of Sauvignon Blanc
1 lemon, ½ juiced, ½ thinly sliced
A little softened butter, and extra to grease
A little sea salt and freshly ground black pepper
1 medium fillet of lemon sole, lightly seasoned, rolled up like a cigar and
    set aside
Herbs, edible flowers and rocket, to garnish (optional)
New potatoes and salad, to serve (optional)

1. Preheat the oven to 180°C/160°C fan/gas 4.
2. Mix all the ingredients in a bowl, except the fish and the sliced lemon, and set aside for 15 minutes but no longer.
3. Cut a heart shape from a 30cm square sheet of baking parchment. Butter one side.
4. Strain the veg mix, retaining the liquid, and place the mix on the left side of the heart, leaving room at the edge for folding.
5. Place the rolled fish fillet on top. Sprinkle on some of the reserved veg liquid and finish with a layer of very thin lemon slices. Fold over the right side of the heart. Beginning at one end, tightly fold the edge all the way around – then do it again to form a tight seal. It will help if you press the edges with a palette knife or the flat of a dinner knife as you go.
6. Place on a baking tray and cook in the oven for 10 minutes.
7. Carefully remove the parcel. Drain any excess liquid, and transfer to a warm plate. Drizzle some herbs, edible flowers and rocket around the bag. Serve at the table and cut an X in the parcel using your kitchen scissors. Serve with new potatoes and a nice, sharp green salad on the side. Let the show begin.

# Beef blade
Serves 6

I got this recipe from Pat Lalor, whom I first met while working at the
Merrion Inn in Dublin. I was drawn to Pat's affinity for ingredients, in
addition to his being an inclusive and encouraging head chef. There was
always room for laughter in Pat's kitchens, regardless of the docket count
or busy traffic at the pass. He has been, without doubt, one of my greatest
influences. I have learned much from this very talented man. I've used this
dish every which way. Although the blade requires slow cooking, it does
pack a punch on the dinner table.

1 beef blade
1 large onion, peeled and sliced
2 celery sticks, chopped
2 carrots, chopped
1 tsp fennel seeds
½ tsp ground cinnamon
1 tsp coriander seeds
2 cloves of garlic, sliced
A glass of good red wine
1 tbsp red wine vinegar
500ml beef stock
Sea salt and freshly ground black pepper
Celeriac and potato mash, roasted kale crisps and gravy, to serve (optional)

1. Marinate the beef with all the remaining ingredients overnight.
2. Simmer the meat in the marinade on the stovetop or in a slow cooker for
   4 hours, until the beef is tender. Drain the meat, reserving the marinade
   and discarding the veg. When cool, trim all the outer fat from the beef
   blade and wrap the meat well in tin foil, tightly forming a barrel shape.
   Leave overnight in the fridge.
3. To serve, reduce the marinade liquid to a thick gravy consistency.
4. Slice the beef into 2.5cm thick steaks, and fry each side for a minute on a
   high heat. Serve on a bed of celeriac and potato mash, with roasted kale
   crisps and lots of gravy.

# FINAL DAYS

Hindsight is futile at the best of times. It would probably tell us that the business had been doomed to failure from the outset. Yet hindsight should have no say, influence, hand, act or part in this particular story. There are times in life when you have to follow your instinct, and if needs be, sail into the swell and keep sailing regardless of the warning bells. Sometimes, to mix metaphors, it's simply worth all the gold in them there hills to throw caution to the wind in the hope that your star might shine. I have been doing that my entire life. During Martin's brief stint as a reality TV star, they captured the moment when he heard he had the keys to the building for the Artisan; his dream was coming true. 'Fuck it, that's it then. We have the keys. Hope it works, 'cause I've no plan B. Mmm . . . All my eggs are in one basket.' Scratching his goatee, he stared right into camera with his divil-may-care optimism. 'But! They're free-range! And Irish, of course. Fuck it,' he grinned, as he pressed the off button.

However, despite all our superb reviews in the national broadsheets, countless features in glossy magazines, the high-profile social media presence and positive customer feedback, being the talk of the town was not enough to deal with the harsh realities of a fledgling business in an economy reeling from a crash. The mitigating factors were the lack of decent footfall, serious investment and parking, which all together affected our ability to extend into evening service, but the most frustrating of all was that our location was only a few hundred metres from the edge of all the action.

Martin and Venetia were acutely aware of the situation as they tried everything in their power to save the business. Venetia in particular showed a courage so powerful and inspirational that all the remaining staff just responded with support and kindness, gutted though they were; walls crumbled but humanity stood firm. I was with both of them on the last day, when the room itself ached as we packed away the remnants from those quirky wooden shelves, and a sadness filled the air of a once vibrant, exciting, happy space.

I found friendship at the Parlour and discovered much about the cook inside of me, I laughed a lot with staff, suppliers and most of all those amazing customers who made every early-morning cycle ride worth the effort. For almost two years everyone associated with the somewhat disordered Parlour dream left a little of their magic in the Ringsend air. Between its walls were an assortment of somehow mutually related oddities, and therein I suppose lies the paradox and charm of the Artisan Parlour at 90 Fitzwilliam Street, Ringsend.

*There comes a time when you look around,*
*And you see the ocean rise before your eyes*
*Showing no surprise.*
*So you make your way down to the shore*
*And you climb aboard, and give yourself a smile,*
*It makes you feel alive.*

– 'Beautiful Affair', *Light in the Western Sky,* (1982)

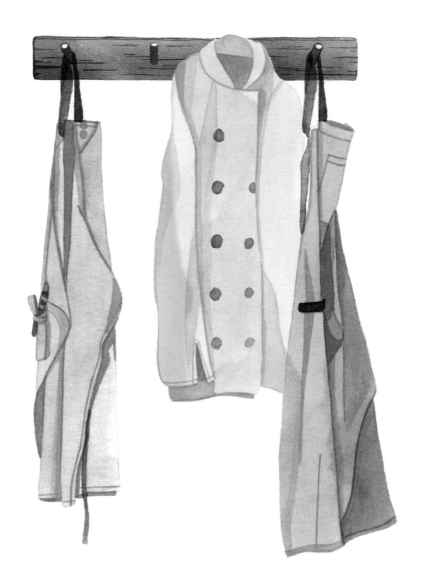

# CHAPTER 15

## ENCORE

# SO, WHAT HAVE WE GOT FOR THE ENCORE?

At the first ever Lisdoonvarna Folk Festival in 1978, the great piper and music collector Séamus Ennis finished a blistering set with one of our greatest reels, 'The Bucks of Oranmore'. He walked off the stage to thunderous applause. Within seconds, he strolled back out, leaned into the microphone and announced, 'Thank you, ladies and gentlemen, thank you very much – but I'm afraid you just can't follow "The Bucks of Oranmore". Good evening.' And with that, he ambled off into the darkness. I've never forgotten it – genius.

Ronnie Drew also knew when it was time to close the show, as he'd sit back in the dressing room, listening to the fading applause. 'Let's leave it at that, Mikie. They might come back for more tomorrow.'

In my last kitchen, Farm Hill in Goatstown, I was a line chef given very little room to be inventive. I started playing more gigs, and as the pendulum swung once again, I felt I'd reached a natural conclusion to my culinary journey. I never came into food to simply clock in and cook by numbers, but those creative impulses were being satisfied by music once again.

The decision to hang up my whites finally came after reading a very good review from *Irish Times* journalist and food critic Catherine Cleary, who wrote of my lunch special, 'A pork belly salad that sounds modest but is several great things on a plate.' The pork slices, she said, were 'cooked slowly in their own fat until they're fudgy on the inside, crisp outside. To cut through all that luscious pig there's a spanking fresh salad of mustardy mizuna leaves, a lip-tingling horseradish mayonnaise, blobs of excellent fennel and tomato chutney . . . [a] truly lovely salad is finished off with pomegranate seeds that tasted like they were just freed from the white flesh of a fresh fruit.'

Catherine's visit came during a particularly exciting few weeks for myself and my buddy Andy Byrne, as our head chef was away on annual leave, so we took full advantage. It was the perfect proverbial 'Cats Away' moment, as we played with our unused creative skills for lunch and evening specials, smuggled new ingredients into the kitchen, and set up a pizza night to showcase Andy's amazing talent (see page 252). We made the best of it, knowing full well that we would soon return to the cooking-by-numbers game.

I finally felt that I had contributed something good to Farmhill, and the great review itself had a profound effect on my waning confidence. It was a timely reminder that I had a natural flair that needed a revival and renewed expression. Ronnie's words rang true: 'Let's leave it at that, Mikie.'

# LESSONS

Food has always been a personal journey of knowledge, creative opportunities, understanding and expression, not unlike music. Although both can be very challenging, therein lies the excitement, and in my ten years cooking, I certainly discovered the essence of kitchen culture.

In recent times there has been a proliferation of cookery shows, 'reality' TV, books and documentaries that tend to centre on kitchen stress, anger, humiliation and thankfully, regular bouts of genius. It's all true; it's all part of the mix. I was quite old to begin with when I started my career as a professional cook, but because of my age and music background, I had a great deal of experience dealing with people. While I found the aggression difficult to accept, I tended to meet it head on, and very early. As a result, most chefs accepted me on to the line.

One major difference between a kitchen team and a band is that while some chefs have difficulty giving junior staff opportunities to shine, good bands are typically more collaborative and less hierarchical. While every group needs a leader, it's so much easier to produce something wonderful from a solid team that works to everyone's strengths. A kitchen, though hectic, can be a place of fun, laughter and friendship – much like the stage with a good team of fellow musicians.

# THE CROSSING

Maybe the pork salad was my 'Bucks of Oranmore' moment, I'm not sure, but it was another turning point, another crossing. These days I feel like the prodigal son, back at home, but being back gigging again has a much deeper meaning to me now. Gone is the desire to take over the world, replaced with a real sense of privilege every time I step out onto that stage, be it with Stockton's Wing, Leslie Dowdall, Eleanor Shanley or a rare and wonderful show with my brother Kieran.

Each gig is a social occasion; from the moment we meet there's chatter and laughter, there's always food, and then the pre-gig huddle that sends us out to tell the audience who we are. Later on, in the quiet of my hotel room, I sometimes dream of hosting a great big dinner party down by Doolin Pier to say thanks to the many friends who helped me on my way. I can see Maura O'Connell shucking oysters, Ronnie Drew prepping garlic, Eleanor on spud duty, and Darina Allen showing Leslie Dowdall how to bake a cake. The Wing are by a white Merc bus buried deep in sand, pushing for all their worth, and Sharon Shannon is scooping vegan ice cream onto a tray of crushed ice. Tommy McGann's pickup shuttles guests in, while Pat Shortt directs traffic to the water's edge, dressed in that brown shopkeeper's coat. My mum and dad dance a half set to the Micho Russell Céilí band. Security is tight: his name is Finbar Furey. Suddenly there's a crack of fireworks, and everyone looks to the heavens to view the spectacle of light rising from the grounds of the Doolin Hilton Hotel as it marks the opening of the annual gap year Festival of Cultures. As the final flame abates, a hush descends and PJ Curtis calls out, 'A Nobel call for Mícheál Roche.' My uncle steadies himself, and I hear those words I first heard as the holy water splashed over my tiny forehead.

*Friendship brought us all together.*
*Friendship makes our hearts unite.*
*And friendship leads a life of pleasure.*
*'Twas friendship brought us here tonight.*

# ACKNOWLEDGEMENTS

This book is dedicated to Donna Barnes, my friend, partner, wife, confidante and constant presence at every crossing. Without you there would be a lot less to me.

To the memory of my wonderful father Jackie Hanrahan; to my beautiful mother Mary Kelleher, thank you.

To the memory of Stan Barnes, my lovely father-in-law; to Ettie, Karen and Stan Jr. Thank you for the warmth and joy of a second family.

To Louise Dobbin, who initially read some of my scribbles and suggested I go knock on a few doors. To Publishing Director Eoin McHugh, who read a full chapter of those scribbles, encouraged me to believe, and then turned my dream into reality. To my seriously talented, patient and hard-working editor, Nora Mahony, who connected with my scribbles and straightened out a good few of them. I am truly thankful we met along this journey.

Thanks also to the exceptional sales and publicity crew at HarperCollins in Ireland: Tony Purdue, Patricia McVeigh, Ciara Swift and Jacq Murphy; to the production team in London, Sarah Hammond, James Empringham, Fiona Greenway, Alan Cracknell and Monica Green; and to the audiobook team, especially Fionnuala Barrett and Gavin Glass at Orphan Recording Studios.

To copy editor Annie Lee for her patience and good humour; proofreader Jane Donovan; to the artistry of illustrator Charlotte O'Reilly Smith; to photographers Mick Barry, Charlie Collins, John Cook, Brian Hand, Manuela Kohns and MJ Smyth.

For wonderful moments shared with musicians, singers, producers, engineers, drivers, roadies, agents, managers, record companies, publishers, fellow songwriters and fans. For endless hours of adrenalin and creative pleasure with chefs, cooks, kitchen crews, floor staff, managers, teachers, producers, suppliers, critics and customers.

To those who helped me to remember: Uncle Haulie Kelleher; Uncle Chris Hanrahan; Cousin Marie Kelleher; Theresa McGann; PJ Curtis; Brian Hand; Tom O'Brien; Steve Cooney; Tim McGee; TV Honan; Barbara Galavan; Adrian Gaffney; Gill Bell; Venetia Quick; Pat Shortt; Paddy McCormack; Cliodhna Drew; Rory Allen; to two wonderful inspirational sisters of the kitchen, Sorcha Moynihan and Camilla Stoddart; and very special thanks to the precious box of treasures I found hidden in my attic.

To Kieran, Tommy, Maurice, Paul and Mick, my first band of brothers.

To my song 'Beautiful Affair' itself; don't know where you came from, but you have brought me far and wide.

To Mother Nature, for her incredible gifts. May we take much better care of her. Finally, much love to my family of eight black sheep. Ger, Joe, Kieran, Gabriella, Adrian, John and Jean. I was the odd one out.

*Take it easy, Mike*

Ennis, Easter Monday 2019